touching eternity

the enduring outcomes of teaching

touching eternity

the enduring outcomes of teaching

TOM BARONE

FOREWORD BY DAVID C. BERLINER

TEACHERS
COLLEGE
PRESS

Teachers College, Columbia University
New York and London

Published by Teachers College Press, 1234 Amsterdam Avenue, New York, NY 10027

"Things of Use and Things of Beauty: The Swain County High School Arts Program," reprinted by permission of *Daedalus,* Journal of the American Academy of Arts and Sciences, from the issue entitled, "The Arts and Humanities in America's Schools," Summer 1983, Vol. 112, No. 3.

"why // do the." Copyright © 1958, 1986, 1991 by the Trustees for the E. E. Cummings Trust, from COMPLETE POEMS: 1904–1962 by E. E. Cummings, edited by George J. Firmage. Used by permission of Liveright Publishing Corporation.

Certain sections of Part II were originally printed in:

"The Enduring Consequences of Teaching: Some Findings from a Narrative Study," *Curriculum and Teaching Dialogue 2*(1), pp. 47–53. Copyright © 2000 by American Association for Teaching and Curriculum.

"Among the Chosen: A Collaborative Educational (Auto)biography," *Qualitative Inquiry 3*(2), pp. 222–236. Copyright © 1997 by Sage Publications, Inc.

Library of Congress Cataloging-in-Publication Data

Barone, Tom.
    Touching eternity : the enduring outcomes of teaching / Tom Barone ; foreword by David C. Berliner.
      p. cm.
    Includes bibliographical references and index.
    ISBN 0-8077-4112-4 (cloth : alk. paper) — ISBN 0-8077-4111-6 (pbk. : alk. paper)
    1. Forrister, Donald. 2. Teachers—North Carolina—Biography. 3. Teacher-student relationships. I. Title.

    LA2317.F663 B37 2001
    371.1'0092—dc21

                                                                                    00-069092

ISBN 0-8077-4111-6 (paper)
ISBN 0-8077-4112-4 (cloth)

Printed on acid-free paper
Manufactured in the United States of America
08 07 06 05 04 03 02 01   8 7 6 5 4 3 2 1

CONTENTS

FOREWORD

Teachers are the most faithful members of society. They take as a primary article of faith that they can profoundly influence their students. They believe fiercely and deeply that they can imbue their students with proclivities, tastes, sensibilities, styles of thinking, attitudes, and values, and by doing this, deny the determinism lurking within genes or families. Testimony that one special teacher did in fact influence his students in precisely these ways, like the attestations of a miracle performed by a person soon to be granted sainthood, allows the propagation of the faith for decades and decades to come. This book provides the kind of testimony that propagates such faith in teachers, but the story told is not an uncritical one. This could have been a simple devotional text, but it is not. Perhaps by challenging our beliefs about teaching and methods for studying teaching, Barone is reminding us that faith that confronts and resolves its doubts will be even more robust.

Almost alone in the history of educational research, these rich and sensitively written narratives of how students were affected by a particular teacher provide for every other teacher the opportunity to regenerate their individual faith. These narratives allow an entire profession to strengthen their own beliefs about the value of their mission and their worth to society. But the writer, Tom Barone, is a perverse scholar in a number of ways. He certainly does retell the stories of witnesses and participants, so we can come to know the miracle of worthy and influential teaching. And in so doing he advances the case for this teacher's beatification. But simultaneously Barone takes on the role of devil's advocate, forcing us to question whether the methods used to record the miracles are valid and whether this teacher's accomplishments really justify our continued faith in teaching as the most useful way to touch eternity.

But first let me assure readers that in the pages that follow they will meet a real teacher-hero, one whose accomplishments I envy and whose presence in our profession renews my faith in my calling. I believe that Donald Forrister, the teacher, etched deeply on the souls of his students. They knew that he cared for them, that he expended emotional labor at rates well beyond what anyone else in their rural and conservative school and community was giving them. They sensed that he was both an exotic and one of them, a person who saw beauty in at least three things: He saw beauty in the high culture of the outside world, beauty in the Appalachian environment he loved, and beauty in the youngsters put in his charge. He was a kind of wizard who could transmute base objects into gold, which is what he did with the found and "borrowed" objects needed for his arts classes and what he did to and for some of his students. The ones he chose to be close with understood that he required them to make their next project—a photograph, a sculpture, a job, or a personal relationship—better than their last project. Don Forrister wrote the book on high expectations!

Perhaps because of his dreams for them, many students gave Forrister their permission and their imaginations so that he could mold their lives. In particular, students who were a bit different knew that they received from Forrister permission to be themselves. Forrister taught these children tacitly, by example, that they could be their own persons. In the beautiful imagery of Barone, "Forrister . . . recruited [these students] into his [art] program to equip them with additional resources for maintaining an internal aesthetic playground, for guarding the silence of their secret spaces against the noisy distractions of the larger culture."

The stories of Forrister's influence on his students' lives are ahead for the reader, and I suspect most readers will feel as I do, renewed in their faith. But two problems remain. One is how we keep our faith, in light of some possibly disturbing "facts" about this book. The other is a reevaluation of Forrister's influence from a more critical perspective. Let us look first at what a renewed faith might be based on.

These accounts of Forrister's influence were filtered, distilled, and often made more interesting and insightful than they may have been in their original form. There is no raw data appendix accompanying this report. The respondents' commentary on Forrister is filtered through their original teenage perceptions and then distorted by their memories over the years. After Barone called these respondents and said he was following up on an apparently "good" teacher, we can expect the influence of powerful halo effects to be operating. Thus they can be expected to say one nice thing after another about "old Mr. Forrister." And on top of all this, we have the artistic writing of these "highly suspect" accounts by the "novelist," Tom Barone, who makes no attempt to cast this study as an ex post facto, social science, qualitative, survey, or panel design. He even urges his readers to be suspicious of him as the writer; acknowledges the "gaps," exaggerations, distortions, and inconsistencies in the data; reminds us that some of what is written is, in a certain sense, fictional; and eschews being thought of as author because of its link to the concept of authority. So on what kind of evidence are we renewing our faith?

I was forced to ask myself if, when viewed from a social scientific standpoint, any of these flaws in the design of the study detracted from my reading of it? They did not. Then I asked myself if the documentation of Forrister's worth and influence was actually enhanced by situating this study outside the bounds of traditional social science? It was. I think my general faith about a teacher's ability to influence students and my particular faith in the evidence of Forrister's long-lasting positive influence are actually stronger because of this rendering of the story than had the "evidence" been presented any other way. The writer-artist Tom Barone has told the story of the visual artist Don Forrister. That is proper; it has harmony. It allows justice to be done to this tale of remarkable achievements. Forrister, his students, and Barone, the researcher, jointly make up a database assembled by Barone, the writer, that has the qualities of plausibility, credibility, and fidelity to a reality that we always perceive through a veil, regardless of the method used. Could, or should, this tale have been told more objectively, more scientifically? I do not think so.

So what lessons does this teach us about the validity of claims coming from the scientific methods, or from any other methods? I think the lessons to be learned are that the warrant underlying a claim is the most important concern we should have, and that strong warrants are not tied to a single method of inquiry. While warrants can be strong without being scientific, they can never be strong if the scholar isn't careful, critical, and reflective—a problem that exists in equal measure for the quantitative, qualitative, and humanistic scholar.

In the case of Don Forrister, the warrant for admiration, if not beatification, is strong. But the case is assuredly not perfect and may not even be convincing to everyone because Barone's nature is to turn his object of study around, like a prism, and inspect Forrister's light-emitting qualities from different angles. Barone raises two concerns of great importance if we are to judge Forrister's, or any other teacher's, influence in its fullness. First, we must question what Forrister actually accomplished in his arts program if most of his students did not choose to pursue art in their lives. This is the question of transfer: what does anything our students learn from us in school have to do with their later learning or living? But Barone properly forces us to wonder if it is ever possible to capture, objectify, and analyze the kinds of human transactions that Forrister engaged in with his students. From these complex and ambiguous interactions long-term transfer can easily be inferred, based on the consistency of the stories told by Forrister's students. Exactly what was transferred is still inexplicable, but it certainly wasn't just the doing of art.

Second, we must ask whether Forrister's influence on individuals was as dramatic as his influence could have been, had he been concerned about broader structural issues in society. The second question is similar to the question raised about the saintliness of Mother Teresa. Of course she did wonderful things for individuals, but did she have any effect on the structural conditions causing poverty in India? Would she have had a greater impact if her goal had been grander than taking care of individuals? Each reader of this account of the lasting effects of Don Forrister on his students will have to answer both of these questions as they judge him. And as they judge themselves.

Barone played his multiple roles well. I have come to greatly admire Forrister and his impact on his students. But I am also left to wonder about his (and my) total impact on my students and my world. Readers are likely to be left a little more perplexed than they thought they would be as they read about this admirable teacher. And readers will wonder about the power and validity of literary nonfiction or fictionalized stories of teaching. A lingering perplexity is precisely what Barone wanted his readers' response to be to this elegantly written, intellectually stimulating, and methodologically perverse book.

David C. Berliner
Sedona, AZ
September 2000

ACKNOWLEDGMENTS

This book has been years in the making. Along the way, I have received assistance, encouragement, and support from many people. In the beginning was the essay that is reprinted as Part I of this book. This essay was produced under the auspices of the Rockefeller Brothers Fund in the early 1980s. I especially want to acknowledge the help of Lonna Jones, Director of the RBF Awards for Excellence in Arts Education Program at that time.

I also want to thank the administrators, teachers, and students of Swain County High School who were, in the 1980s and 1990s, willing to grant me access to the school and to spend time in the research process. This includes the many students and former students of Don Forrister who agreed to be interviewed, especially the approximately two dozen Swain alumni who met with me in the late 1990s to provide their perspectives of the impact of their former art teacher on their lives. Those who collaborated further with me, sometimes returning one draft after another until I got their story right, deserve special recognition. Most of all, I thank Don Forrister for his patience, generosity, understanding, and (with Jean Ellen Forrister) hospitality during my several years of research and writing.

Others have contributed in other ways. Research assistant Marsha Harrison accompanied me on one trip from Phoenix to North Carolina. Margaret Carr and Paula Wolfe transcribed an enormous number of taped interviews. Nick Appleton generously provided released time from teaching at a crucial point in the writing process. Many doctoral students read and critiqued various parts of the manuscript in my graduate courses on qualitative and narrative forms of research. So did colleagues and participants in several Winter Institutes on Arts-Based Approaches to Educational Inquiry sponsored by the American Educational Research Association.

The encouragement and support of my friends and colleagues David Berliner, Ursula Casanova, and Karen Anijar were truly appreciated. And the huge debt of gratitude that I owe to Elliot Eisner, friend and mentor since my Stanford years, who guided me down the path toward arts-based and narrative forms of research, can never be fully repaid.

I am also grateful to several people at Teachers College Press. Executive Acquisitions Editor Brian Ellerbeck was willing to support a book based on a case study that sometimes deviated from most texts written for professional educators, in tone, writing style, formatting, and research approach. Development Editor Wendy Schwartz helped me to understand, among other things, the assistance many readers need in approaching the unconventional features of this kind of text. And Amy Rosenberg was always available to answer my questions.

Finally, I have been blessed with the love of family members, especially my wife Margaret. Without her constant encouragement, her sage advice, and her understanding as, over the years, I would disappear into my upstairs office, this book could not have been written.

INTRODUCTION

"A teacher affects eternity," said Henry Adams. "He can never tell where his influence stops."

That comment by Adams expresses a hope felt by many of us who are, have been, or aspire to be school teachers. We want to believe that we can make a significant difference in the world through our work. But that remark also raises questions about the real power of teachers. What important things can be taught and learned in school that will indeed endure? Are only certain sorts of teachers able to influence students over the long run? What kinds of teachers are those? What if a teacher's lessons run counter to those taught by other significant figures in the lives of students and by powerful forces in the larger culture? To what extent can a teacher heroically, single-handedly, teach against that grain and still touch eternity?

Many of us—teachers, teachers-to-be, professors of education, educational researchers and evaluators, parents of students, members of the general public—may have never asked ourselves these questions. Others may have presumed certain answers that have foreclosed a serious engagement with them. Indeed, this book was born out of a discontentment with the general confusion surrounding the desirable and actual outcomes of teaching and schooling. As an educator, I wanted to satisfy my own curiosity about the enduring consequences that can flow from the experiences provided for students by their teachers. I suspect that that curiosity is widespread. So this book was written for everyone who wonders about whether and how teachers can indeed make lasting differences, and about what those differences might be.

But researching and writing this book did not answer those questions for me with finality. Readers may likewise come to accept the likelihood that the answers can never be known with unqualified certainty. This is because of the enormously complex, wide-ranging, highly ambiguous, profoundly personal, unquestionably social, intrinsically political, and inevitably subjective nature of the outcomes of teaching and learning. Nevertheless, the process of searching for these answers may offer the pleasantly unexpected: the appearance of additional questions quite numerous and splendid.

Those additional questions may arise out of this book about the long-term influences of one high school teacher on some of his former students. The researching and writing of this book was not fueled by a curiosity about the immediate and the ephemeral, whether it be academic content temporarily held or skills gained and soon lost. I sought out, instead, the constant and the significant, evidences of deep etchings by a teacher on teenage souls, impresses of all sorts that had somehow lasted for a significant part of a lifetime. But I also wondered about the ultimate value of these etchings and about what had *not* been taught and learned. And I explored the nature and sources of alternative influences on the lives of these students.

The shape of this book has, itself, been influenced by recent developments in the fields of human inquiry. These include the turn toward what has been called *narrative research*. The book investigates the meaning of teacher-student encounters within the life narratives of those who lived them and through an assessment of the significance of those encounters from my own vantage point as an educational researcher.

Moreover, certain sections of the book reflect a literary turn in human studies. The life stories of the teacher and former students upon which the book is based generally exhibit characteristics of imaginative literature, including expressive, evocative language and an aesthetic form. The book may, therefore, be considered a work of *arts-based research*.

Additionally, the book reflects certain elements of *postmodernism* in its approach. For example, rather than offering a seamless, unified text throughout, the book exhibits a variety of formats, styles of writing, and discursive forms. Indeed, it may be seen as an experimental, postmodern piece of literature, a variegated text that includes life stories, edited interview transcripts, and critical or evaluative essays. Many voices are heard in the text; several points of view related to the underlying educational themes are presented. Indeed, to read this book is to journey into the lives of one teacher and his students, to see facets of their selves from a host of perspectives, none of which is granted a privileged status. And ultimately this book is meant as an entree into the worlds of schoolpeople other than those directly portrayed in its pages, as its events and characters become analogues of teachers, students, and former students who reside within the reader's own experiential neighborhood.

Because the voices heard within are often conflicting, this is a book that is meant to disturb and puzzle. It is designed, in both content and style, to challenge the reader, to raise important questions about educational issues—indeed, it aims to provoke the reader into asking questions about the nature of truth itself. If I have achieved my goal, one's beliefs about the fundamental purposes of education, and a teacher's ability to achieve them, will seem more tenuous than before reading this book. Habitual ways of thinking about them may be disturbed and challenged. One's reaction to that observation by Henry Adams may be less confident and certain. And questions long buried under answers may be unearthed.

AN OVERVIEW OF THE BOOK

This book is divided into five parts. The first four comprise the Swain Report, a longitudinal case study based on the life narratives of a teacher and a cohort of Swain County High School students-turned-alumni. The final part is devoted to an exploration of epistemological and methodological issues arising out of the writing, researching, and reading of the Swain Report that are generally relevant to studies based on life narratives. Here, in somewhat greater detail, is what awaits readers of this book.

Part I introduces the cast of characters and the educational program they shared. In the early 1980s, as part of my involvement with the Rockefeller Brothers Fund's Awards for Excellence in Arts Education Program, I researched and composed a case study of a high school arts program in Swain County, North Carolina, designed and presided over by a teacher named Donald Forrister (real name). Forrister's one-man arts program had been chosen in 1982 by the Fund as one of ten outstanding public school arts programs in America. I accepted a request to write an evaluative essay about the program. The study described the program and discussed the quality of Forrister's teaching and his relationships with his students (fictitious names). Although my research was undertaken after the awards had been announced, I was given absolute autonomy over the contents of my critique. But upon becoming well acquainted with Forrister and his program, I came, independently, to view him as a remarkable teacher and person, indeed, as a hero of sorts, someone who had almost single-handedly developed an outstanding high school arts program. That judgment is reflected in my 1983 essay.

A slightly abbreviated version of the essay is reprinted here as Part I. Entitled "Things of Use and Things of Beauty: The Swain County

High School Arts Program," it is meant to provide a loose equivalent of what quantitative researchers call *baseline data*. It serves to introduce readers to the world of Don Forrister and his students at the time of its writing, and presages some of the themes that emerge in their subsequent life stories. The opening essay—more than the rest of the text— is angled toward issues of arts education. But this book is ultimately about qualities in teacher-student relationships and educational outcomes that are not specific to subject matters or content areas.

Part II provides glimpses into the lives of several alumni who were students of Forrister in the early 1980s, when the original essay was researched and published. This section contains edited interviews with former students of Forrister and lengthy biographical and autobiographical narratives that trace themes in the lives of individuals, pairs, and groups of former Swain students before, during, and following their experiences with Forrister. A picture emerges of a vast array of educational outcomes that have been identified as significant by the protagonists, attributed to Forrister's influence, and nestled within the complex web of ongoing life stories.

And all perched precipitously on the rusty ledges of memory and perspective. Indeed, the subjective, ambiguous, and fragmented character of the Swain Report is evident in the occasionally contradictory descriptions of the same educational event by different participants, who experienced it years earlier. Nevertheless, what is perhaps most remarkable (and perhaps, for some readers, most disturbing) is the level of consistency in their depictions of Forrister as a teacher-hero, because of what they view as his positive impress on their lives. Indeed, Part II is ultimately about the reconstruction of the teacher and person who is Don Forrister through the prisms of the life stories of his former students. Adopting their perspectives, the reader may surmise that Forrister may indeed have managed, after a fashion, to touch eternity.

Part III consists of a biographical essay of Forrister that I composed after extensive interviews with him. It provides details of Forrister's life different from (although not necessarily, in any final sense, more "truthful" than) those available to his students. This story suggests how, from his perspective, the course of his life was altered through his relationships with many of those students. Indeed, the entire Swain Report may be viewed as an experimental, postmodernist biography of the teacher and person who is Donald Forrister. And while not employing gender theory, the book may be seen as addressing the serious deficit in our knowledge and understanding noted by Casey (1995–1996): a "dearth of [narrative forms of] research on male schoolteachers' experiences and interpretations" (p. 240).

In Part IV, I offer my own analysis of the efforts of Forrister, and the other educational phenomena on display, much as I did as commentator in the original 1983 essay. I reach into the thickets of particulars in previous sections to locate and draw forth themes and issues that might otherwise remain invisible, nestled inconspicuously within the plots of the life stories. Observed from my more distanced and analytical perspective and placed within a theoretical envelope, the life stories are thereby transformed into life histories.

Taken together, Parts I and IV serve as analytical "bookends," providing scholarly, interpretive frameworks for the heartfelt narratives of former students and teacher. But Part IV was written nearly 2 decades after the original essay and therefore, in a certain sense, by a different person than the Tom Barone of 1983. Postmodernist thinking emphasizes the discontinuities, disruptions, contradictions, and inconsistencies in the formation of identity, and I (much like the characters of these life stories) have indeed changed—matured? regressed?—since I first entered the doors of Swain County High School. Some theoretical frameworks have shifted, at least a few experiential lenses have been traded in for others, as I have, over the years, reached deeper into the educational literature for scholarly sustenance. And when I later reentered the world of Swain County and listened more intently to its maturing cast of characters, my original visions of pedagogical heroism—and my hopes for talented students, superbly taught, blossoming into magnificently self-actualized adults—became subject to greater scrutiny.

The first three sections of this book do indeed paint a quite positive educational picture, one that makes plausible the facilitation of enduring educational experiences by a singular teacher for his students. Educational experiences were, for John Dewey (1938/1963), life-affirming events that yielded mastery over future experiences. The opening essay and the life stories of the former students are studded with examples of those kinds of educational encounters, and the reader will quickly sense that the teacher at the center of this study is remarkable in many ways. I do not apologize for the revelation— and celebration—of those personal and professional attributes found in Don Forrister. Indeed, I second the concern of Sarah Lawrence-Lightfoot (1997) that educational researchers have unfortunately tended to be "much more vigilant in documenting failure than they have been in describing examples of success" (p. 8).

Nevertheless, in Part IV, I add a layer of ambiguity to the text, offering readers a pair of analytical lenses for viewing the phenomena confronted in the earlier parts of the book. One choice is to accept the earlier portraits of Forrister as talented and dedicated, an individual teacher struggling alone against formidable and debilitating societal and institutional forces. A teacher who successfully transmits enduring messages about autonomy, character, and living life with a disposition toward bold, judicious acts of self–re-creation.

The other analytical lens provides a more skeptical interpretation of the nature and endurance of Forrister's influences. Within this critical perspective individual heroics are seen as cutting against the achievement of real educational reform through collective effort. For Don Forrister is pictured here as apparently more adept at enlisting allies among members of the Swain County arts community than in joining forces with colleagues in his school. Choosing to focus directly on the development of his students' private aesthetic awareness, he denies a view of education as primarily a political act. From this standpoint, Forrister's ultimate influences on his students may be severely limited by certain conservative forces in the culture, the powerful nature of which are not clearly comprehended by the "good" teacher or his grateful students. Those forces *may* be the ultimate winners, no matter how determined the efforts of an individual pedagogue.

The conflicting analyses provided in Part IV are designed—especially when placed against the backdrop of the earlier text—to disturb the reader into asking important questions about the nature of the teaching act and the meaning and purposes of education. For the reader is coaxed into seeing issues that arise within the context of the Swain Report as pertinent to other places and times, including proximate ones.

And the scholarly, but still accessible, style of the text in Part IV is meant to serve as a kind of bridge between preceding and subsequent sections of the book. Parts II and III are composed in a language that is vernacular in character and in a variegated format. Its narrative and storylike features include the use of everyday language rather than narrowly technical speech. Part IV addresses the specific interests of educators and educationists as well as broader ones of laypeople in a manner that is "friendly" to both audiences.

Part V is, however, more technical in form and content, exploring topics of interest primarily to specialists in educational research methodology. It presents (as postmodernists would have it) the "inside" story of the writer who researched and composed the study; a discussion of issues related to the informants' revelations of their life narratives in the interview process; and a consideration of the phases, and appropriate attitudes, involved in reading the text.

Issues of power, authority, generalizability, definitions of the self, modes of representation, and so on—issues arising out of the writing, researching, and reading of the Swain text—are addressed in terms of the fundamental purpose of the study. That purpose is a formative and heuristic one, and is, I claim, best furthered by an experimental, postmodern text than by a traditional work of social science that aims for certainty rather than ambiguity. And indeed, this book aims to promote a conversation between the author of a work, the various characters that inhabit it, and the story's readers. As each brings a distinct perspective to the conversation, the likelihood of a singularly privileged, final, impartial, objective outlook is subverted.

Nothing would satisfy me more than if this book led to richer discussions about the ultimate purposes and meaning of education, of what can and should be accomplished in schools that might make a positive difference in the future lives of youngsters, and of how that might be done. The book is an attempt to raise my own voice, not in a declarative fashion, but in one that entices readers into such discussions. For I believe that observing closely what and how a single Appalachian teacher has taught, listening carefully to what his exstudents purport to have retained and appreciated over the decades, and thinking deeply about the significance of these testimonials and about what they fail to include, can give us much to discuss. In the process, profound questions may be raised about whether and how eternity might be touched in schools throughout North America.

PART I

INTRODUCING A TEACHER AND HIS STUDENTS

*Things of Use and Things of Beauty:
The Swain County High School Arts Program*

THE ESSAY BELOW introduces the world of Donald Forrister, a high school teacher in North Carolina, and his students. I wrote it in 1983 at the request of the Rockefeller Brothers Fund, which had just awarded Forrister an Outstanding Teacher prize. I visited the classroom, the school, and the surrounding community for one week, observing, interviewing, and, in general, comporting myself like a qualitative educational researcher.

The result is a description and analysis of three important educational commonplaces: the teacher, the students, and the milieu in which teacher and students shared educational experiences. A fourth commonplace is subject matter content—here, the arts. The opening essay emphasizes this dimension more than do subsequent parts of this book, even though only a few of the long-term consequences of the experiences shared by Forrister and his students were content-related. Ultimately, this book as a whole may be viewed as a story that raises questions about the potential impact of teachers on students in all subject matter areas and, indeed, at all grade levels.

As with all stories, the beginning is crucial to the development of the plot. But inevitably there is change. Complications intrude and initial impressions shift. Later parts will reveal growth in characters (including the author) over time and offer alternative interpretations of the meanings of events previously encountered.

But first let us encounter those events in the early 1980s in a school in the Appalachian highlands and wonder about how they might have permanently altered the lives of the participants.

AN INTRODUCTION TO THE PROGRAM

It is clear that children should be instructed in some useful things . . . [but] to be always seeking after the useful does not become free and exalted souls.
—Aristotle, *Poetics*
Weaving, hit's the prettiest work I ever done. It's asettin' and trampin' the treadles and watchin' the pretty blossoms come out and smile at ye in the kiverlet.
—"Aunt Sal" Creech of Pine Mountain, Kentucky

The Appalachian mountains of western North Carolina are aging gracefully. Millions of years ago (geologists tell us) they possessed the kind of brittle, angular, energetic majesty of the Rockies. But with an infinite patience, Nature has rounded their formerly pointed peaks into gentle curves and cushioned them with a lush green canopy. Underneath this blanket of vegetation, one can observe the aging process up close, as streams etch wrinkles into the face of the earth. The centuries of erosion have worn down these mountains, but strength and dignity clearly remain: Even at their age, they are still able to lift themselves into the grandeur of the clouds.

Somewhere within these ancient hills lives a young man named Donald Forrister. Every weekday morning around half past seven he leaves his wooden-frame house, climbs into his pickup, and heads north. Down a narrow dirt road to the highway he rambles, to the town of Bryson City, and then into the parking lot of Swain County High School.

Forrister is an art teacher—the only art teacher—at the school, and the old Smoky Mountains provide an apt metaphor for what he has accomplished here. Slowly, carefully, patiently, Forrister has succeeded in shaping formless adolescent talents into aesthetic sensibilities of impressive maturity. Almost single-handedly he has created a high school arts program that is not only outstanding, but—perhaps even more remarkable—cherished by both the school and county communities. Any such embrace is, we know, quite rare in an era in which the arts are often treated, in Jerome Hausman's (1970, p. 14) phrase, like "unwelcome boarders in a burgeoning household." So even though the story of the Swain County High School Arts Program is, in many respects, a singular one, I believe we might learn from its telling much that is pertinent to the survival and flourishing of the arts in our schools.

MOVING INSIDE

It was a spring morning in 1982 when I first met the central characters in the Swain story: the students. That morning, as usual, they flowed down from the mountains like individual drops of dew that coalesced into a stream. Along the way they were joined by Don Forrister, members of the Swain administration and staff, and me. Together we poured through the school doors.

The mountains looming above the school provide a sense of locale, but move inside, and where are you? Many places you have been before: the more or less standard Modern American School Plant, circa 1978. The building's right-angled innards seem familiar: the variously sized cubicles of space that stare blankly at the newcomer, the pro-longed rectangular corridors that invite without a hint of destination. I am surprised to find here in rural North Carolina a school building similar to those where I live, in the Cincinnati suburbs, partly because of my preconceptions about the level of financial support for education in a county so rural and with so small an economic base. But there it is: the same charmless modernity, the refreshing lightness of the glass and brick, the airiness of the pleasingly massive open chamber that domi-nates the heart of the building and serves primarily as a reading area and media center.

But a startling difference, so crucial to our story, becomes vividly apparent: From the boldly executed abstract expressionist painting hanging on the brick wall near the lobby for the administrative offices to the cloth wall-hangings (stuffed tubes intertwined playfully into serpentine knots) dangling above the stairwells, to a remarkable set of drawings near a side entrance (one, a carefully composed and bril-liantly colored still life of red and green apples), there is art. To be sure, there is room for many more pieces, but the presence of any student artwork of such quality adorning the inside of a high school is unusual and exciting, and serves to whet one's appetite for learning more about these students and their arts program.

The student body of Swain County High School averages about 500, of which 80 usually elect to take art. During their freshman or sophomore year (in Art I class), students are introduced to the founda-tions of aesthetic awareness: line, form, design, and color. These con-cepts are explored not only through examination of the works of major artists but also through individual projects completed under the criti-cal eye of the teacher. The forms of arts and crafts offered in Forrister's program include macramé, pottery, fibers, weaving, drawing, photog-raphy, silk-screening, papermaking, batik, stitchery, quilting, lettering, and airbrushing. According to Forrister and his students, it is from this exposure to a smorgasbord of possibilities that a student will sense pro-clivity toward one or more areas, in which he or she then selects a set of major projects for Art II and III. It seems probable that the range of activities enhances the overall success of the program.

The emphasis in this program is on the visual arts; the development of musical talent is under the aegis of the school band, literature and theater in the English Department. That many of the visual art forms, including all forms of painting, are missing is owing to the program's primary financial source: Supplies, equipment, and the services of Don

Forrister are paid for largely by federal vocational funds. Hence, the emphasis on the commercial arts and crafts (although not a totally ex-clusive one) provides the program with a strong, local Appalachian flavor. To paraphrase Oscar Hammerstein, the hills are alive in the Swain County High School Arts Program, which accounts for some measure of the program's success as well as its local support. To docu-ment this link with the community, we move outside into the hills.

COMMUNITY CONTEXT:
NATURAL RICHNESS, ECONOMIC POVERTY

Most of Swain County, North Carolina, is a park—over half of the county is situated in the Great Smoky Mountains National Park, and over half of the Park is in Swain County. About one half of the Chero-kee Indian Reservation, including the town of Cherokee, is also within the county lines, but, like the park to the north, outside the county's governmental jurisdiction. Because the federal government controls 82 percent of Swain, only 18 is left for local taxation.

In the lower third of the county sits Bryson City, the county seat by default, and hardly a city at all; it is a town of 1,500 people, and, except for Cherokee, the county's only municipality. The texture of life in Bryson City is of course influenced by its locale, but in other ways seems typical of small-town America. One observes the same qualities that Sinclair Lewis's Carol Kennicut found so dismaying in turn-of-the-century Gopher Prairie: a self-satisfied provincialism in values and mores, perhaps; a cultural bleakness that even rules out most forms of public entertainment (save a games arcade and one "last picture show"), certainly.

Rebutting this notion, a local newspaper asserts: "Bryson City ain't very fancy, but it's real." If that sounds like a cliché, it also has the ring of truth. I observed among the populace a genuinely courteous and friendly demeanor, with no hint of pretense. And though much of the town's commercial property is incessantly drab, many of its houses exude a homemade charm lacking in the dour architecture of Gopher Prairie.

And unlike the folks of *Main Street*, one can detect a curious am-bivalence among some of Bryson City's natives concerning its small-town status. The local press may insist, "If you're looking for a place with a lot [of] neon, fast-food restaurants and crowds of people, don't come to Bryson City"—and rightly so, for Bryson City has indeed man-aged to escape some of the cultural blight of the twentieth century. But there is a note of false bravado, perhaps even thinly disguised desperation, in that quote. For one thing, there is an unmistakable feeling of pride among the locals in their newly opened Hardee's, the first national fast-food chain to locate a franchise in Bryson City. But, more important, the quote comes from the *Smoky Mountain Tourist News* (1982, p. 2), so its seeming disdain of crowds is in reality an open plea for carloads of tourists and a suggestion that in coming to Bryson City they will somehow manage to escape from one another. No doubt there are those in Bryson City who would love to see it swell to the size of Gatlinburg, Tennessee, the overwhelmingly commercialized tourist mecca over across the Park, no matter that Bryson City's major selling points are the very virtues (the peaceful isolation, the wilderness sanctuary, the small-town charm) that Gatlinburg has chosen to prostitute. But since the Bryson City area is on the edge of the tourist belt, miles from the nearest interstate highway, it must be carefully sought out by vacationers for the attractions it offers: hiking, picnicking, white-water rafting, and above all, the natural splendors of the mountains.

I was not really surprised to hear Don Forrister speak one night of the spirituality he perceives in these mountains, for in them I too experienced a rare communion with nature. Sitting on the porch of Forrister's mountain home after a twilight thunderstorm, I watched the fireflies painting in watercolor on a gigantic canvas, their speckled phosphorescent moments of light diffused and softened by the mist. I recalled a poem by William Cullen Bryant, "Thanatopsis," that I had been forced to memorize in high school long ago, but which was much later helping me to see and hear "the voice of gladness, the smile, the eloquence of beauty, the mild and healing sympathy" that is the lavish gift of Nature.

This natural richness must surely suffuse the lives of the inhabitants of these mountains and compensate somewhat for the economic poverty that pervades the county. The average per capita income in 1979 was $5,705, compared with the national average of $8,773 (Center for Improving Mountain Living, 1981). In April 1982, when the national unemployment rate was 9.2 percent, Swain County's was a staggering 26.2 (*Asheville Citizen*, 1982). But poverty in Swain County has a long history, which may be why, as one Bryson City inhabitant insisted to me, "folks here is poor, but they don't feel poor." Another suggested that, because of a tradition of self-sufficiency, including vegetable gardening, canning, building one's own furniture and often one's own home, hard times in these hills are less painful than in the city or suburbs. Perhaps. It is a sociological truism that the poor have less to lose to a depression. But many from the middle class are also out of work in Swain County, and the testimony in a local newspaper article of several of the jobless, concerning their emotional shock and alienation, sounds like an echo from far-off Detroit or Akron.

Of the 4,000 in Swain County's labor force who *are* employed nearly half are either tradesmen or workers in furniture and clothing factories. (A blue-jeans factory closed in early 1982.) Most of the others work at some level of government or in service-related businesses—the motels, gas stations, cafes, and gift shops that cater to the tourist dollar. The tourist business is seasonal, of course, but still important to the Swain County economy.

THE CRAFT HERITAGE: AESTHETICS AND FUNCTIONALITY

Tourists are lured by the wilderness of the mountains, and once there, attempt to preserve their memories by purchasing souvenirs of the mountain culture. The countryside is speckled with craft and gift shops: the River Wood Craft Shop, the One Feather Craft Shop, and (within a stone's throw of the pink-and-white Teddy Bear Motel) Miller's Groceries and Crafts. The shops contain tons of mass-produced bric-a-brac, but items handcrafted by the Cherokees and White mountaineers also abound—baskets, pottery, quilts, rugs. The genuine handiworks are a fundamental part of the Southern Appalachian heritage. Popularized in the series of *Foxfire* books, the crafts of the White Southern Appalachian Highlanders have evolved for generations since the arrival of the first pioneers in the late 1790s and early 1800s. By considering their cultural artifacts, it is possible, I believe, to discern several qualities of life among these people. I will suggest only three.

Perhaps the most obvious one has already been mentioned. It is an almost totally *self-sufficient lifestyle*, demanded of a people kept apart from the rest of civilization by distance and even isolated from neighbors by a rudely intervening mountaintop. Once, in these hills, everything was handmade: cabin, furniture, clothing, utensils. Second, one senses the enormous *care* invested in these artifacts. It is surely a patient people who were (and are) willing to wash and straighten animal and vegetable fibers, to stretch, twist, and spin them, to dye and weave the yarn into cloth. Only someone inspired to create a thing of beauty and excellence could produce from that hard-earned cloth the intricately patterned Appalachian "Sunday" quilts. And that inspiration must surely have come, as did Bryant's, from the "various language" spoken by their natural surroundings. One senses a link between the aesthetic pleasure that must have pervaded the creation of these artifacts and the satisfaction derived from the beauty in these hills.

But ultimately, there is *pragmatism*—indeed, the traditional pragmatism of the American frontier. These early mountaineers were not artists in any full-blown technical sense; they were craftspeople. In their work, aesthetics was clearly subordinate to function. The generally harsh circumstances of their lives strongly suggested a utilitarian channel for release of any artistic tendencies: "Direct your need for the creation of beauty toward the things of survival." Thus their pride in a cabinet built or a basket woven must surely have sprung not only from an appealing form, a pleasing design, an interesting texture, but also, and perhaps primarily, from the work's practical attributes—its strength, its durability, its general usefulness.

THE OFFICIAL VOCATIONAL ORIENTATION

One escape route from poverty in Swain County nowadays is through the production and sale of arts and crafts. The people of Swain County are aware of this fact, and a rationale for an arts program that rested on it would, it seems, be viewed quite sympathetically, for it would be the latest manifestation of the pragmatism that has informed this region (indeed, this country) for decades. The Swain County Arts Program is in fact strongly vocational. The program is funded by the federal government and administered by the North Carolina Vocational Education Department. Its official raison d'être, therefore, is to equip students with the knowledge and skills needed to become commercial artists, artisans, and craftspeople.

Within the school, the thrust of the program is also seen as primarily vocational—Mr. Frizell, the school principal, for example, spoke of it strongly in those terms—and written documents support this notion. For example, in *Art*, the Swain County High School Arts Program booklet prepared for a school accreditation process, it is stated unequivocally that "Crafts as a Vocation is an individualized program concerned with occupations in the crafts industry. (Crafts as a Vocation is taken as an Art II and Art III elective by graduates of Art I.) The greatest portion of time is spent in laboratory activities while increased emphasis is placed on developing skills for local crafts industries" (Forrister & McKinney, n. d., p. 2).

Again in the booklet's description of the commercial arts courses, one reads: "At least 50 percent of the allocated time for this class will be used in the lab or shop for hands-on experience, *illustrating their relevance to the work world* [italics added]." And why are the "basics"—color and line, design and layout, balance and proportion—taught in that course? "In order for the student to develop competencies relative to the occupation" (p. 7). Likewise, two of the major objectives of the photography course (taken as Art III) are "to prepare individuals for gainful employment in occupations relating to photography" and "to become aware of sales potential and prepare and practice selling photographs" (p. 11). And so it goes. One cannot escape an awareness of the program's official orientation.

History was not on the side of the development of this arts and crafts–based vocational program. The last half of the nineteenth century was the heyday of the vocational rationale for the teaching of drawing and the crafts in the public school. But ironically, after John Dewey and the progressive education movement finally provided a rationale for the fine arts as an activity central to the educational process, both the justifications for, and the methods in, courses of the fine arts and the practical (or industrial) arts grew more disparate. They remain so today. Indeed, in Swain County, according to Frizell, "it was not easy to get the crafts and commercial art into the vocational program" back in 1973. But the school administration decided to make the attempt when the state-funded arts teacher–counselor retired. The intercession of the Superintendent of Public Instruction was required, but the Swain County Commercial Arts and Crafts program was finally accepted by the state Vocational Education Department.

The Swain program must be resubmitted every year, with projections of courses to be taught and numbers of students, along with follow-up studies of program graduates. This last process is crucial, for the survival of the program depends in large measure on the percentages of Art III graduates who choose to pursue arts and/or crafts as a vocation or as a major in a technical school or 4-year college. The required percentage fluctuates, but according to Alice Lance, the school's vocational guidance counselor, it usually hovers around 50%. "It is totally up to the Vocational Education Department," she said. "They go by the numbers. . . . What's saving the program is that the students have been using [their arts and crafts training] . . . but it's scary."

This number seems astonishingly high, especially considering the traditional disinclination of the region's people toward higher education, and it stands as testimony to Forrister's profound influence on the career choices of his students. So, despite its slightly tenuous future status, the program has indeed proved successful in terms of its official mandate. And while that accomplishment itself is interesting, there are, I believe, even more compelling achievements in the Swain County High School Arts Program. To consider those, we must look closer at the program in action.

NONVOCATIONAL OUTCOMES OF THE ARTS PROGRAM

Three arts and crafts rooms are presided over by Forrister. The main classroom is located, fittingly, in the school's vocational wing, while reaching the other two (the photography darkroom and the weaving room) requires considerable transit through those right-angled corridors. Forrister's classroom is L-shaped (the lap of the L is an adjoining arts material storeroom), its angularity somewhat softened by the layers of student crafts and artwork that cover the horizontal surfaces and cushion the walls. Entering this room is like exiting from the building: One leaves the nowhere-land of the school plant and slips back into Appalachian hill country. The sense of place returns, thanks largely to the local flavor of objects like the baskets woven of birch twigs, the large, intricately designed "Sunday" quilt, and the drawings of hill country still lifes. Many of these exhibit the same blend of the aesthetic and the functional seen in the artifacts of the Southern Highlands pioneers.

And the longer one remains, the stronger wafts the aroma of the hills, not only in the distinctive accents of the students, but also in their open and friendly demeanor, a reflection of their elders on the sidewalks of Bryson City. And certainly, the perseverance and care of the students as they tussle with their materials are the qualities one can see fossilized in the artifacts of the mountain pioneers. Does the same fuel that fired the engines of the mountain craftspeople move these students in Don Forrister's classroom? Is it indeed a struggle for economic survival that motivates them? Are the scarlet threads woven into that rug merely to supply a tangential beauty, placed there primarily to catch the eye and only secondarily to please it, not as an end in itself, but as a means of ringing the cash register?

Just what does motivate these teenagers? It is an important question because the answer can provide a clue to the *educational* significance of the program's outcomes, the character of its impact on the lives of these students. Having spent only 4 days in the school, I will avoid pronouncements and instead share my reasons for some strong suspicions. They are based on observations of student comportment, on their informal comments, on mass, whole-class discussions over which I presided, and on interviews with individual students.

An Eclecticism of Purpose

First, many different motives coexist here; as in most human endeavors, there are a variety of prevailing causes and reasons for actions. The career/economic/commercial incentive is present, although the amount seems small, given the program's stated intentions and sources of funding. Consider the case of Robert, the senior voted Most Talented in Art by the graduating class, an adolescent whose sensitive and technically accomplished drawings are an emphatic testimony to that talent and whose family (according to Forrister) is of extremely modest means. Quite moved by one of Robert's drawings, I expressed interest in acquiring it, but his refusal to sell was absolute: "I keep all of my drawings." Don Forrister assured me that this disinclination to part with their work for money is quite common among his students—and their parents. Only a few of them (including the craftspeople) will merchandise their handiworks. More often, the creations will either adorn their homes or become gifts, providing lasting pleasure to themselves, their kin, and friends.

Regarding plans for future employment, the current crop of upperclassmen appears to fit the pattern of the past: Of the 14 I surveyed, 8 expressed an intention to work at an arts- or crafts-related job. For some, following in the paths of former students like John Herrin, a truck driver who "moonlights" in macramé, crafts may provide a supplementary income. But for the majority of Forrister's students, different motives seem to dominate. Their interest in arts and crafts is not based primarily on the acquisition of a salable skill. Here is the question I posed to an assembly of 16 Arts II and III students: "Suppose it were impossible to use what you have learned in this class in terms of a job. Would you still have taken this class, and would you still enjoy it as much?" A show of hands indicated a nearly unanimous affirmative response.

So while the image among much of the Swain County public, members of the school administration and faculty, and the distant bureaucrats in Raleigh and Washington who administer and fund the program, may be of students learning to draw and weave for the primary intention of acquiring future economic self-sufficiency, reality begs to differ. Economics and the practicality of their ancestors are, for most of these students, clearly subordinate to motives more compelling. What are they?

A Personal Pride

One motive concerns a personal pride in their accomplishments. Facets to this pride include a degree of vanity from the attention their talents attract. Occasionally, a sense of self-importance could be detected among Forrister's senior students, an awareness of a privileged status usually associated with talented athletes or a self-importance found among high school thespians backstage before the senior play. This status, as far as I could tell, was not flaunted—and might partly be explained by the fact that many of the upperclassmen were already members of the school's "power clique" (Cusick, 1973). But this status also resulted from an acquisition of many awards and honors. The students readily welcomed this recognition. The elixir of victory is heady stuff; the scent from a drop or two can apparently provide the momentum for many a painstaking project. This attention and excitement may be particularly impressive to the large percentage of Forrister's students who are, according to Lance, less than academically able in other subjects. Can we imagine the impact on the psyche of an 11th grader who, after years of frustration, boredom, and perhaps even humiliation in math and English classes, is suddenly flown to New York to receive a national award for his drawings?

Nevertheless, many junior and senior students insisted to me that visions of plane trips to exotic locations, or even the regional trophies and blue ribbons, did not lure them into Art I. As freshmen or sophomores, they could not imagine that they might possess such talent. Just a few years later, however, the pride in creating, in their words, "things of excellence," or more accurately, the accolades received from those creations, does seem to explain partially the students' reluctance to sell them.

An "Expression of Their Art"

But many students are unwilling to part with their lesser works as well. Might this indicate a more intrinsic satisfaction in their creation? A closer inspection of *Art* reveals this beguiling passage:

> A great many people work at crafts as a hobby or avocation and a growing number are . . . producing crafts as a vocation. For some, craftwork is an "alternative" vocation . . . preferred above the nine-to-five job. For others, it is their sub-occupation and expression of their art for which the benefits can seldom be calculated in dollars and cents. (Forrister & McKinney, n.d., p. 1)

A priceless "expression of their art"? Is there really a nonvocational incentive producing outcomes infinitely more valuable when measured with the kind of economic yardstick implied in the program rationale? The phrase suggests a purpose more concerned with the needs and development of the individual, as opposed to an exploitation of the needs of the marketplace. There are, of course, many rationales for aesthetic education that pertain to the personal well-being of the individual, such as the development of artistic talent, aesthetic appreciation, and the therapeutic value of the artistic process. However, "expression of their art," in the present context, inspires two thoughts: First, it is reminiscent of the aesthetic pleasure that was an important by-product of the time-honored process of crafts making in these hills; second, it is a phrase that evokes a particular branch of art theory, expressivism. The theorists of expressivism see art as an embodiment of the artist's inward feelings and images into an objective, outward "expressive" form. They often speak of a subjective inner life— "the life of feeling," as Susanne Langer (1957) puts it—and the aim of art, in their view, is to promote insight into and understanding of this inner realm. As Wordsworth saw it, art is emotion recollected in tranquillity. But according to the expressivists, recollection is also a publication: A work of art is a transmutation of personal feelings and imagery into a unique sensible form—an objectification of the subjective. Objects of art, said Langer, articulate and present "ideas of feelings" for our contemplation.

But are we not placing an overwhelming burden on the shoulders of a single phrase in a single paragraph in a single program booklet? Is the development of the students' creative self-expression really a significant feature of the daily activities in Forrister's classes? The evidence, it appears, leans strongly toward the affirmative, especially for the more advanced students.

According to Forrister, Art I students are more interested in making or decorating functional items, such as the silk screen designs for their tee shirts. With maturity, however, expressing oneself through the creative process also becomes important: In my private conversations with senior students, several described how they inform their materials with "a part of" themselves. One telling discussion was with an articulate son of a Baptist minister. Jim, an Art III student, was pursuing the art of papermaking, a process of sifting pulp through a wire screen, painting it with colors, often including other materials such as straw and newspaper photos, for a collage effect. In one sensitive piece, a photo of a pensive old woman in a rocking chair sits among brooding clouds of purple, green, and yellow-gray.

Tom: Why do you like papermaking?
Jim: I like to be able to . . . it's not so defined. I like the freedom of it more than anything.
Tom: What do you mean by "it's not so defined?" That you can make abstract sorts of things?

Jim: Yeah, like lots of times you'll make something that you're not sure why you're doing it, but when it gets finished, you really like it.

Tom: When you do your papermaking, do you ever think, "Well, that has a certain feeling to it," . . . like it's expressing an emotion?

Jim: Oh yeah, it depends on when I come into class, what kind of mood I'm in. That comes out in some of my work.

Tom: Like, for example, the one that you're doing now of the old woman. What kind of feelings does that express?

Jim: Kind of a lost feeling. You see, I graduate in about a week . . . and I feel kinda worried about it. I guess that's coming out in it. At least I think so.

Tom: You probably wouldn't have done that one . . .

Jim: Earlier on? No, I wouldn't have . . .

Tom: When was the first time you realized [you were expressing yourself through your art]?

Jim: Probably sometime last year when I was a junior.

Tom: But in Art I, it . . . was just techniques?

Jim: Yeah.

Tom: Do you think other art students . . . also express themselves like that?

Jim: Oh yeah, a lot of them . . . 'cause basically you [are allowed in Forrister's class] to do what you want to.

By the freedom "to do what you want," Jim did not mean the license to scratch and scrawl angrily on a drawing pad or, in high spirits, splash paint randomly on a canvas. Such behavior is only primitively "expressive"; it is not artistic expression. In Forrister's class, the individual student is preeminent, but the "individualism" has a distinctly Deweyan cast to it. In lieu of a mindless outpouring of unbridled emotion, there is a considered channeling of impulses into purposeful actions. The student's artistic activity is in fact comprised of careful negotiations with the materials, ardent attempts to create forms that communicate ideas and images. Degrees of success vary, of course, but in this process, qualitative forms of intelligence can clearly develop.

Working Hard at Self-Expression

Several students described the process of self-expression as "fulfilling" and "enjoyable," but also insisted that it was "hard work." No question that I asked of Forrister's class was greeted with more chuckles of affirmation than this one: "Is art as hard a subject as the others you take?"

Some admitted to electing art with hopes of coasting through with minimal effort. They apparently harbored a notion quite common in our society, the one that associates crafts like basket weaving with extremely low rates of mental taxation. To their astonishment, these students soon found Art I, in their own words, "harder than other subjects," because they had not anticipated a "striving for perfection." Who, after all, would have expected this newfound desire to "make your next project better than your last?"

But in Forrister's class the nature of the "work" is different from the Calvinistic notion of work implied in Weber's famous critique of the Protestant ethic, the conception that has prevailed in America's schools for centuries and that remains the image of educational virtue held by parents, schoolteachers, and administrators (including many at Swain), and much of the general public. Such "work" demands a deferment of present interests and needs for a vision of future rewards, the imposition of self-discipline to withstand the tedium of, in today's educational lingo, the "time on task." The result is said to be the development of certain personal attributes, as noted in this description of the weaving process of the mountaineers by Frances Goodrich, an early-twentieth-century preservationist of the hill country artifacts:

> In the younger women who were learning to weave and keeping at it, I would see the growth of character. A slack, twisted person cannot make a success as a weaver of coverlets. Patience and perseverance are of the first necessity, and the exercise of these strengthens the fibers of the soul. (quoted in Dykeman & Stokely, 1978, p. 107)

Patience and perseverance are indeed personal qualities helpful in overcoming the monotony of the production phase of the weaving process (or the boredom of the assembly line), for further implied in this notion of work is the mindless replication of a prototype—and thus a personal distancing, an alienation from the process. Indeed, any intellectual engagement with one's materials could be harmful to the faithful reproduction of the prototype. What is needed, instead, is skill in copying precisely—and in the arts and crafts, a training of the mind and eye might provide such skill.

It is not surprising that during the late 1800s—the period of maximum coziness between art education and industry—this image of work was most clearly reflected in the methodology of art instruction. The methods originated in Great Britain. The British "Cole System" was transported to the United States, and its aim was, indeed, to train students manually in copying. Soon art instruction in American schools was pervaded by alienating exercises of meticulous reproduction of master designs.

The activities in Forrister's class, however, provide a stark contrast with the Cole System. Technique is indeed mastered there, but as a means to a greater goal rather than as an end in itself. And the students do seem to be "working," but in a sense different from that implied in the Protestant ethic. Patience is certainly present, but it often seems less imposed than arising from a more immediate gratification. The effort appears to be generated from within the activities themselves and directed toward an original transformation of the ideas and experiences of the individual student.

One can observe in this process a dialogue between the student and the materials being shaped, a qualitative problem-solving process in which the student-worker-artist struggles with possibilities, tentatively moves on the material, encounters resistance, and manipulates the component parts. For example, at one point in "working" on his paper collage, Jim incorporated some torn pieces of white paper above the head of the woman in the rocking chair, hoping to achieve a daydreaming effect. The "product," however, spoke back to him: "Perhaps too bright, distracting the eye from the central figure." Jim listened, reconsidered, added a more yellowish cast that reflected the woman's sallow facial tones, and that skirmish ended successfully.

Thus was the aesthetic tension between creator and creation resolved, as Jim used his "freedom" to "work hard" at portraying his own distinctive ideas, feelings, values, and ends-in-view. Aestheticians are prone to words like *authenticity, self-actualizing, liberating,* and *emancipating* in describing the effects of this creative process. It is a process that celebrates individual growth, as the student wrestles with the materials in order to create meaning, to make sense of his or her life.

Expressiveness in Crafts

The result of this process—a result Maxine Greene (1970) has called the "recovery of the self"—is a far cry from what one might expect in a vocationally oriented arts program. Nevertheless, this kind of personal unfolding occurs not only in the more obviously artistic endeavors of Forrister's students, but sometimes in their crafts making as well. There are many similarities in the processes: the same attitude of caring, the personal attachment to their products, the pleasure in their creation. In craft production, of course, the intended function or use of the object

imposes limitations on shape and form. Some aestheticians would disqualify most crafts from membership in the realm of fine arts on this
basis: They are not "virtual objects," objects whose only function is to
"create a sheer vision, a datum that is nothing but pure perceptual
form" (Langer, 1957, p. 41).

Yet it is clear that crafts making can involve aesthetic judgments, as
argued by Edward Mattil (1971), who in this passage could have been
speaking of the early Southern Highlanders:

> [T]he earliest tools and utensils of man were restricted to considerations
> of utility. As their efficiency improved, there was a steady evolution of
> form. In any situation where people were first required to produce the
> necessities of life by hand, the useful concern was of prime importance
> and as long as impoverished or stringent conditions continued, the art
> quality of the object rarely exceeded the functional design of the object.
> However, as soon as time and skill permitted, the craftsman was fairly sure
> to elaborate or decorate his objects and it was at this point in mass devel-
> opment where the matter of choice entered into the picture. For example,
> when man became able to create a variety of clay bowls, each good for
> holding grain or water, he found himself engaged in the process of mak-
> ing judgments—practical *and* aesthetic—in determining form and decora-
> tion. (p. 3)

Today's Swain County High School students also often create
meaning in their crafts, arranging elements of color, form, and texture
into imaginative relationships that communicate feelings. Indeed, they
told me so: When I asked the assemblage of advanced students to
divide into two groups—art students to the right, craftspeople to the
left—no one moved. There was near unanimous insistence that any
arts/crafts dichotomy would be an unimportant one. The students
whom I had observed "working" at crafts like weaving, quilting, and
batik making clearly perceived themselves as "doing art." Indeed, dis-
tressed by their inability to respond effectively to the question in a
group setting, two students sought me out later for private discussions,
and insisted that there is "art in crafts" because they were able to express their emotions in the design phase of their weaving. (I was able
to extract an admission that, in the production phase, some "work" was
required, as Frances Goodrich has assured us—but even that process
was said to be filled with the excitement of seeing one's design "come
to life" with personal qualities.)

Interestingly, the Arts Program booklet (Forrister & McKinney,
n.d.) suggests that it is those once tangential, individually produced

aesthetic qualities that today provide the craft products with their functional value:

> In our age of mass production where a certain "sameness" marks most products, there is a growth market for goods that are unique and distinctive. Craftsmen who . . . design and produce articles with [personal] aesthetic value . . . have access to a market with which mass production cannot compete. (p. 1)

Thus the "functional" value of today's craft objects may be defined less by their utility than by their ability to persuade a prospective purchaser visually. The mountain folk of yore could have survived the winter under an ugly quilt, but today's Appalachian craftspeople must beware the frigidity of the uninterested consumer.

Recall, however, that Forrister's students are generally not interested in selling their wares and can therefore give freer range to their own personal aesthetic values in the construction of their objects. Individual self-expression thus seems central not only to the activities of Forrister's future artists but to the crafts making as well, and that is surely one of the sources of a profound satisfaction that attracts them to Forrister's classes.

Here, then, is what we have learned thus far about the Swain program: It exhibits major nonvocational features, including motivational factors such as a thirst for self-esteem and a need for self-expression; and these incentives result in program outcomes that are officially unsanctioned and therefore officially ancillary, but of central importance to a preponderance of the students.

These findings are especially intriguing when viewed in light of a certain ongoing dialogue among some educationists. Radical critics of schooling have long portrayed schools as extensions of the modern technocratic state, as agencies ideologically committed to the corporate social order. Through both the overt and hidden curriculum, it is said, the institution of the school transmits the dominant cultural system. Schooling thus promotes a subversion of individuality in favor of attitudes and a worldview that further the mechanistic purposes of business and industry. In the rather pessimistic critique of some of the radical determinists, any piecemeal reform of this monolithic apparatus of control is extremely problematical. Teachers, in particular, are seen as ineffective change agents, enmeshed as they are in the technocratic superstructure of the school.

The official vocational rationale of the Swain program would seem to pay homage to this point of view, but the program in action suggests the possibility of a more complex and attractive model. Here, classroom events and activities that reflected the divergent values of an individual teacher seemed to produce liberating rather than stultifying experiences. To elucidate this further, we turn to the history of the program and the role of its architect.

AN APPALACHIAN ARTIST DESIGNS AN ARTS PROGRAM

Donald Forrister knows these hills and their people, for he is one of them. Now a tall, slim, 33-year-old, he was born and raised in Appalachia and attended college at Western Carolina University, and certain features of a traditional Appalachian culture are clearly visible in Forrister's personality. There is, for example, his strong self-reliance and independence of thought and action. These manifest themselves in a variety of ways, including personal appearance. The beard and long hair of a couple of years ago were perhaps for some less "traditional" teachers an unwanted reminder of the stereotypical mountaineer and helped to solidify Forrister's image as (according to some students) a "weirdo." The beard, neatly trimmed, remains today, but Forrister's consistent casualness of dress and his general lifestyle and values are reminiscent of the "back-to-nature" movement among middle-class youth in the late 1960s and early 1970s. (The difference may simply be that Forrister never left.)

But his independence also manifests itself in other ways. He refuses to gossip and is intentionally uninformed about the politics within the faculty and administration. Though Forrister does not seem disliked by other faculty members, some may mistake his aloofness for disdain. For example, he often lunches in the cafeteria with students rather than with his peers—only a slight breach of the etiquette of collegiality, but surely a habit (again, according to students) deemed irregular by some teachers. These qualities of independence and a loose definition of his role status are greatly admired by some of Forrister's students and seem instrumental in gaining their trust and respect.

Hardworking is the trait cited most often by Swain teachers and administrators, and a large measure of his success is owing to his enormous investment of time and energy in the program. In class he is a blur of movement from student to student for seven class periods a day, and even, during some periods, from classroom to weaving room to darkroom. On closer inspection, the blur becomes a mosaic made up of individual exchanges between Forrister and students, such as a mini-critique of a choice of subjects, a quick nod of affirmation concerning a color mixture, or a one-on-one demonstration of a new technique. An arts course consists of an untold number of such interactions, each a piece of an emerging pattern. And Forrister's dedication extends well beyond the school grounds and class time. He can be found on weekends escorting groups of students to an art exhibit in Asheville, consulting with individuals on a photographic project, and so on.

The students prefer the word *caring* to describe this "hard work." But the latter, it seems to me, is simply a manifestation of the former, just as the perseverance of the early spinners and weavers followed on their desire for beautiful coverlets and quilts. That Forrister does indeed care very deeply about his program was obvious. One anecdote in particular highlights this. In attendance at a ceremony honoring the Arts Program was the mother of a former Swain student, who had won a $10,000 scholarship to a prestigious art institute, thanks, she said, to "that man. . . . And when we telephoned him to tell him the news, do you know what he did?" she asked. "He cried."

Forrister admits to "getting emotional" whenever a student creates an especially beautiful work. That emotionality is touching, of course, but it is important mainly insofar as it illuminates what lies at the heart of the Swain County success story: the simple but intense mission of a single teacher to enhance the lives of his students through art. And it is a cause that was achieved not only through the unswerving dedication of that one man, but by his shrewd intelligence as well.

Which brings us to our final commonality between the character of the Appalachian people generally and Don Forrister in particular: a deep-seated pragmatism. We saw that pragmatism in the hill folks' ingenious combinations of the useful and the beautiful in the utensils of everyday living. Forrister's work of art is his program, and his methods for assuring not only its survival but also its success in his own terms are also pragmatic.

Part of what Forrister did was to make the program famous. This high visibility was achieved through active participation in a wide variety of arts and crafts contests. Of course, the students' talents won the awards, and the incentive produced by recognition was developed in the classroom through the teaching process I have already described. But Forrister also played a leading role in the selection of student work for entrance in competitions, a tactic that often resulted in a legitimation of his expertise. One senior described the growth of his respect for Forrister's judgment:

I would want to enter one of my drawings in a contest, and [he] would say, "Why don't we try this other one. . . ." He would tell me why he liked it more, and I would say, "Well, OK." And. . . .when *he* chose the ones to enter, I would win [an award], and when *I* chose, I wouldn't. . . . So I figured he must really know what he's doing.

Forrister's primary aim in emphasizing competitions, I am convinced, was to heighten student interest in art, not to increase the visibility of the program. Furthermore, I believe him when he insists that his students' career decisions are of secondary importance to him. Nevertheless, a significant side effect was spawned by these two measures of success. Both the vocational influence and the contest results impressed many parents and the school's administrators. The regional and national recognition stirred local pride and, according to Lance, has even been noticed in Raleigh. As a result, Forrister has acquired a little of the aura of a winning football coach. His job certainly seems secure: Frizell has stated that, even if the vocational funds were slashed, "we would find the money to keep Forrister here."

Such a change in funding sources would probably increase Forrister's autonomy, and a few changes might ensue (such as the inclusion of "nonvocational" art forms like painting). But these should be minimal, since Forrister already possesses the freedom to pursue his own aspirations under existing arrangements, freedom that seems less a result of forethought than of fortune. Here is how it came about.

During the 1970s, according to Forrister, a regional representative from the State Vocational Education Department would visit his classes to monitor the orientation of his pedagogical methods and choice of curricular content. "For 1 or 2 years I wouldn't hear anything . . . then a new person would take over [in the regional office], and complain about my emphasis, and I would have to concentrate on commercial art, and lead them more into the crafts."

In the last 3 or 4 years, however, Forrister says that he has acquired greater latitude in his choice of content and methods, with more emphasis on generating intrinsic interest and less on vocational. This is because a decrease in the staffing of the regional office has forced the Vocational Department to rely on a less direct, more quantitative, and less informative program evaluation approach. I have only Forrister's word for this shift in emphasis, but the irony in such an occurrence would be rich indeed. Is there any other example of a budget cut resulting in the enhancement of artistic self-expression in students? I know of none.

Thus have the seeds sown by Forrister sprouted in the cracks of a concrete technocracy. The success of his efforts belies any notion that schools are necessarily the kinds of "total institutions" posited by some of the radical critics. Indeed, as institutions become more complex and cumbersome, their management and the monitoring of official mandates tend to become more problematical. Corporate hegemony tends to diminish, while individual prerogative is enhanced. So while Forrister's actions may in some respects resemble the kind of "resistance" in educational institutions described by Jean Anyon (1982) and others—that is, an individual agent's direct contestation of the systematic imposition of the technocratic will—a metaphor less antagonistic in tone seems more appropriate, one that suggests an accommodation of aims from a variety of sources. Direct contestation is not necessary in an organizational arrangement whose unwieldiness allows for a peaceful coexistence between formally sanctioned aspirations and those held by individuals charged with conduct of the program.

Note that in the Swain County program official criteria are indeed being met. The development of individual self-expression has not been accomplished at the expense of the mandated vocational outcomes. But neither has Forrister allowed the vocational imperatives to overwhelm his curricular decision making and pedagogy—even though compromises (already documented) were sometimes necessary. Even early in the program's history, Forrister certainly never resorted to any methods even vaguely resembling the anesthetic Cole System of training students. He has shown us that preparing students for an occupation in the arts and crafts does not today require an alienating, spiritually exhausting regimen of mindless exercises. Indeed, evidence suggests that the personal rewards flowing from creative activities often encourage a lasting devotion to the artistic process and therefore an inclination toward an artistic or crafts-related career. And it seems fitting to learn this from a native of the Southern Highlands, where functionality and aesthetic pleasure have traditionally cohabited within the arts and crafts.

But Forrister has also taught us that, regardless of a program's stated objectives, once it is in place, the successful attainment of the truly fundamental aim of art education—the intellectual and emotional growth of the individual—will occur only through the hard work, the dedication, the caring, the talent, and the intelligence of those in charge. Don Forrister has exhibited these qualities in fashioning a program that, although undergirded by a utilitarian rationale, nevertheless results in the flourishing of that fundamental aesthetic purpose.

The discovery of this possibility of coexistence between aesthetics and utility has been, for me, both instructive and inspirational. Indeed, I will remember that discovery—as I will the artifacts of the pioneers of the Southern Highlands and those of their descendants, the students of Swain County High School—as, itself, a thing of general usefulness and of a simultaneously singular beauty.

WHAT DO FORMER STUDENTS BELIEVE THEY LEARNED?

Traces of a Teacher in the Life Stories of His Former Students

NOW WE FLASH forward to hear the adult voices of nine Swain High School alumni who were students in Forrister's classroom during my initial research. Part II consists of their life stories and edited interview transcripts collected and composed during the late 1990s. In these stories alumni offer evidence of how their lives were altered as a result of their time with Forrister.

According to these former students, Forrister's influence covered a vast experiential landscape. For some, it included vocational skills and academic content that were successfully applied after graduation. For others, it reached into what may initially seem trivial, mundane activities outside of school, but which may have ultimately contained the most profound pedagogy of all.

In these tales Forrister is often portrayed as a hero. But have these storytellers romanticized? Have they, in fits of nostalgia, painted overly rosy pictures of their time with their teacher? Can the outcomes of their experiences be understood in ways that are less optimistic? Those questions must wait until Part IV to be directly addressed, and then, alas, with no final answers.

Meanwhile, the reader should be aware that these stories are literary constructions. The raw material was the information elicited within interviews, itself dependent upon a variety of research contingencies. Evidence of authorial construction is less obvious in some places than others. For example, in Keith Robinson's monologue, the interviewee's message is conveyed through minimal editing of interview transcripts. Other life stories appear more biographical than autobiographical, each theme identified by an interviewee woven by me into a story employing literary license. This involved my experimenting with textual formatting, language style, narrative tone, emplotment strategies, and other discursive features.

These literary design elements avoid gimmickry insofar as they yield a discursive form that embodies, or in Dewey's (1934/1958) term, *expresses* meaning indirectly rather than simply stating it. For example, the romantic tone of some stories, reflected in florid language and overheated metaphors, is meant to tacitly evoke the feelings of awe, affection, and gratitude held by former students for Forrister, feelings less effectively conveyed through other writing strategies.

This literary approach also means that the lasting influences of Forrister perceived by his students, although sometimes directly stated, are generally nestled unobtrusively within the storied texts. As with all literature, readers must remain alert for subtle clues to meaning. Only later, in Part IV of this book, is there explicit identification and analysis of the learning outcomes attributed to Forrister by former students. And for a more fully developed rationale for the construction devices used in writing these stories, see Part V.

Finally, a word about story titles: They identify the occupations of protagonists at the time of writing.

THE COLLEGE TEACHER

The life story of former student, now college teacher, Carolyn Wilson (pseudonym) represents a joint effort. The story is crafted primarily out of the information that I gathered in conversations with Carolyn and autobiographical materials previously written by her. In fashioning the life story, I have employed a particular literary conceit in order to avoid a relatively seamless chronological story form. The events internal to the life story of the protagonist are placed within the more immediate, external tale of her reconstruction of that life story over the course of one afternoon.

I chose to obey my strong suspicions that the complex process of re-storying one's life rarely evidences a perfectly rounded, seamless structure. Instead, there are erratic meanderings, jarring interruptions, and chronological juxtapositionings. This text is designed, on the one hand, to evoke those structural qualities in the acts of autobiographical reflection without, on the other hand, alienating or confusing the reader.

The veracity of the first, "inside" story (in italics in the text)—what Grumet (1988) might call its fidelity—is vouched for by Carolyn. It is an honest version of the meaning she has extracted from certain life experiences. To ensure that fidelity, she reacted to, and corrected, my drafts of the "inside" story. Because the story (like all stories) is told from a particular perspective, it is necessarily partial and incomplete. The incidents selected for inclusion were identified by Carolyn as representing, in retrospect, the most significant of her interactions with Forrister.

The second, "external" story represents a blend of details of my visit to Carolyn's home with fragments from my own imagination which suggest what could have happened after I departed from the research scene. As explained further in Part V of this book, this literary license is warranted only when employed in service of a legitimate research purpose: the generation of a conversation about important educational questions.

An Invitation to Re-story

The man was saying thanks again as he drove away in his white rental car. Under different circumstances her eyes might have followed him— Tom was his name—as he disappeared down the road, past the Baptist church with its unusual Russian dome, cruising back to somewhere else. Later she might indulge herself in memories of her own "elsewheres." But now her eyes were fixed on the movements of her 3-year-old, whooshing toward the road as if pulled into a vacuum left by the Chrysler LeBaron.

"No, Alice, let's go inside and Mommy will read to you."

Alice felt a motherly hold on her wrist and resumed the whining she had indulged in throughout the interview. Carolyn had been annoyed then, expecting Alice to be a tad more cooperative. Here she, Carolyn, was, confronting the difficult task of fashioning swatches from her life story into a meaningful pattern for this stranger from Arizona, designing something that would, most importantly, do honor to Don. And what was Alice doing? Interrupting the grown-ups, causing the tape to be stopped yet one more time.

But as distracting as Alice had been, Carolyn knew that the disturbance she felt flowed from a source much broader and deeper. It was, she thought, those "Sabbath Day blues," that Sunday malaise Walker Percy had identified for her in *The Moviegoer*, but emerging now to darken this once rather yellow Thursday. The malaise was a mysterious condition caused by a sense of something akilter, a part of a story demanding to be rewritten.

Aware of the sun's glare, she moved her child inside, into the small bedroom, to negotiate the choice of a storybook. It was, thankfully, nap time for Alice, and soon Carolyn was free to sprawl out on the living room couch and shape her thoughts.

She recalled Tom's introductory letter and their initial phone conversation. He had written an essay in conjunction with Don's award from the Rockefeller Foundation in the eighties. Now he wanted, years later, to see how lives had been changed because of Don. A study of characters whose narrow lives Don had widened, people whom he had taken from one particular place and brought to somewhere else. She was one of those people. But now, face to face with him, she had understood more clearly what Tom was asking. That she tell Don's story through her own. A notion at once appealing and disturbing: *Her* life would also be on display.

It wasn't that she minded the spotlight. But an honest account called for arduous effort, for reweaving the fabric of her memory in order to express precisely what Don had accomplished through her, for her. Of course, she was hardly thoughtless about the confluence of their lives. Actually, she had, in preparation for Tom's visit, been reconsidering an essay about teaching first found in the library at Columbia. She had located it among her piles of reading material and had presented it to Tom early in their meeting.

"This is interesting," she had told him. "It's from W. H. Auden. You can read it out loud if you want to." She would, in fact, be pleased to hear someone else speak it in her presence.

"Starting where? Here?"

" 'A teacher soon discovers . . . .' Do you see it?"

"OK. 'A teacher soon discovers that there are only a few pupils whom he can help, many for whom he can do nothing except teach a few examination tricks and a few to whom he can do nothing but harm. Children who interested me were either the backward—that is, those who had not yet discovered their real nature—the bright, with similar interests to my own, or those who, like myself at their age, were school-hating anarchists. To these last I tried, while encouraging their rebellion, to teach a technique of camouflage, of how to avoid martyrdom for the political.'"

She knew that Don was indeed selective. Impossible, anyway, to be really interested in *all* your students. Maybe he used the same yardstick as Auden in determining whose lives to touch? Did he choose her because she was among the backward, the bright, and the rebellious?

She hardly resembled some people's false stereotype of a "backward" Appalachian. It was clear to anyone from her presence, from the generic nineties blouse and jeans to the accent that recalled nowhere in particular, that she had been places other than this hilltop. Still, as with everyone everywhere, the past lived inside her. It had been hidden in the very first murmurs she ever sensed, sounds from her beloved Great-Aunt Edna, her first teacher. Aunt Edna who read stories to her from the time she could listen. She might as well begin her story with Edna.

A Person Unto Herself

Aunt Edna was from North Carolina, that was for certain, and her life was its own story. Slept alone with a Smith and Wesson revolver under her pillow, unfiltered Camels next to a stack of books by her bed. Loved to tell bawdy jokes. Never a bride, but Carolyn had heard the rumor of a miscarriage. Wild red hair grieved into gray. She stopped bathing, cleaning the house, and instead played solitaire, read her books, and learned to recite the monarchs of England in order of succession. Carolyn somehow knew that Aunt Edna had peeked at other worlds through her books, but she was assuredly from within these Appalachian highlands, not somewhere else. Aunt Edna, a story lover, had the blood of Carolyn's father, and so her own blood. "I'm still a member of the family, Edna," Carolyn once wrote in a poem to her, probably composed on a Sunday. Still a member of the family "after all these years."

Carolyn's first family—her Mom, Dad, and finally a total of five kids—lived in a trailer her Dad had brought up from Florida after a good year for construction workers down there. Tiny and cramped, but later enlarged, thanks to her father's talent with fieldstones from the 17 acres he owned above the Nantahala Gorge. Rocks and mortar to make the arches he loved, arched bookshelves sandwiching the fireplace, two arches on the front porch to suggest a castle, arches that would start here and move gracefully out there and then come home again.

The land was also a part of her family. The green mountains had nourished her as a child and subtly shaped the culture into which she had been born. She loved the land ferociously, like a member of the family, loved romanticizing the Little Tennessee River Road, still dirt at the end of the concrete millennium. She had written about driving down that road at dawn, windows down, cool mist rising off the river, alive as she would ever be, hoping to spot a black bear, a sign that nature was trying to reassert itself.

Aunt Edna, her family, the highlands, were, all of them, isolated and removed, but far more complex than outsiders could ever know.

And thanks to Don, she had grown in complexity, even if part of her would not abandon earlier things. Such as the blanket over the bed she shared with her sister Regina, an all-cotton blanket, peachy brown, beautiful Indian pattern. Warm, sturdy, double blanket, later dragged into her marriage, then her college dorm, the blanket that would have returned home again if its holes had not finally grown larger than the material of which it was made. But her love for the natural was in good repair, still with her wherever she went. She knew that she would always be a child of these hills, and was proud of it.

Well, that was part of the picture anyway. A chapter in the story, for sure. But there was much more to her than that.

She had been gazing out onto the green field, but now focused on the furniture about which she had apologized to Tom. Why had she done that?

Her mind returned to those arches, but now in a different light, to the secondary purpose they had been forced to serve. She shuddered as she recalled her father's attempts to impress potential clients, guiding them through the small house toward his handiwork. The objects of his meticulous craftsmanship had seemed so overworked in the context of the modest trailer, so incongruous in a chaotic household tended to by a mother who was simultaneously trying to grow a garden, raise five kids, milk a cow, maintain a marriage, and occasionally drift away with Ellery Queen.

Her need for order amidst the daily chaos was only part of a vague discontentment with things that didn't seem to bother others. But for so long the source of these feelings was a mystery, lying asleep beneath the surface of her understanding. Later she had recognized that they arose from her need for recognition as a person unto herself. She resented her existence as a diffuse glow in the larger familial blur. Hence the discomfort with an even larger blur, the fervid religiosity of her parents, the easy donation of their selves to their charismatic church. In her teen years, those seeds of discomfort had grown into a full-fledged crisis of identity, wham! radical down to the roots, wondering then not about which religious sect was closest to the truth, but about the very existence of God.

This pointed questioning had soon become diffuse itself, ignoring all ideational boundaries, but still serving to grant her distance from all that had held her too near. And the questioning, her rebelliousness, had been fed by a sense that she was indeed distinct from, and somehow (she now felt ashamed to admit) better than most of the people she knew. She was bright, she now knew, had said it out loud a moment ago.

But for a long time "bright" was what her sister was: honor roll, advanced classes, able to remember things verbatim. She saw now that it was this misreading of her own capacities, her lack of awareness of her giftedness, and not her allegiances to these ancient hills, that made her, in a strict reading of Auden, "backward." Which is not to say that, in the early 1980s, she, member of the Wilson clan, student at Swain County High School, never suspected the presence of unnamed talents.

The Man with the Necklaces

The telephone startled Carolyn back to the present. Wrong number: no one with an inkling of her precious thoughts. Meanwhile, Alice, oblivious, turned on her side, still clutching her favorite blanket. Carolyn smiled at her child.

Generations, she thought. Things passed on from then to now.

Alice's blanket sent Carolyn reeling back to her not-quite-double bed in that trailer room, roll-out window above, long horizontal panels sometimes letting in the fragrances of moss and decaying leaves, and the sounds of crickets and frogs, and other times the scary thunder that rolled down the mountain. And the closet doors, two feet from the end of the bed. She recalled the hours spent staring at the wood grain on the veneer, creating patterns from the moonlight that danced upon it. Sometimes she would see angels, sometimes demons, depending on her mood. Mostly she saw demons. Dark side, light side to all of us.

Carl Jung—she would later make the connection. She had always focused on the dark.

She thought of another occasion when her eyes had strained to interpret what she was seeing. A month or two before becoming a student of Don's, she had spied a man in the middle of town, tall, bearded, neatly dressed, rooting through the dumpster behind the five-and-dime, plucking out shiny things from among the used pizza boxes and dirty tin cans. . . . They were . . . cheap, plastic beaded necklaces. What had this man wanted with these trivial remains of a tawdry culture? Rescuing baubles from a future in the incinerator or landfill. She hadn't looked into his eyes as she moved on. Incident filed away.

She was not entirely surprised when she saw those beads again. By that time it had made sense. Don was always bringing all sorts of objects to his classes, cheap little items picked up from here and there, on a very tight budget in the arts. Had to be resourceful when it came to beauty, searching out and collecting its raw materials in the unlikeliest of places. His gift was the ability to imagine the future of those shiny little trinkets, rescuing them from a fate others would say they deserved, transporting them to alternate contexts, and so with great care and deliberateness, transforming them from nothing to something.

She thought of how in all the years she had known Don she had never heard him harshly criticize anyone, although he must have resented working in a high school where very little was allotted to the arts. Lots of money for football and other things they find important. But Don, never nasty or cynical, concentrated on the positive, especially on the potential in his students—as during one moment that stood apart from most others.

She had taken 3 years worth of Don's classes, all of them wonderful and nurturing. She thought of his small, quick glances, his movements toward this student or that, the nods of affirmation, the laughs at students' self-deprecating remarks, the clear-headed and not unkind criticism, the busyness of it all, but a busyness never devoid of compassion and joy. This particular incident had occurred during her first year with him, sophomore year, age of 15. Late afternoon. The class had been working on drawing still lifes. Hers had been a penciled rendition of a gnarled old tree on the River Road, a tree she loved for its natural dignity. After seventh period, everyone else had gone. She felt his presence. He had been looking at her drawing as she packed to go, and said to her at that moment, "You could be a good drawer."

Not "you are," not "if you worked hard," not the old cliché, "you have potential." Just "you could be a good drawer." Not gratuitous. Not meaning to flatter. Just stating a positive fact.

To this very day she remembered how flushed she had felt, in a glow, delighted that he had noticed her work, noticed her, intimating that her presence in his class was valued, at least to him, to one who knew so much about things like what makes for good drawings. She recalled that it had taken her years to realize that it had not been a compliment, but actually much better than that. Always on the lookout for beautiful things, since life's budget is so tight, why would he not announce that a gift had been spotted? Why would he not imply, since he truly believed it, that there was something special in her, something that could become far better than what was presently there?

From that point on she had considered herself among the chosen. Don was supportive of all his students, but she thought again about how he consciously selected some for deep interest. Some of these he would recruit into his art classes; others, like her, would be "anointed" after they were already there. But almost all who stayed with him into their senior year would become objects of intense, almost familial, caring, would have their lives opened up to unreckoned possibilities, find themselves becoming in specific ways far better than they thought they could be.

She had been one among the select, a small cohort of special friends, diamonds in the rough whose later lives would each confound the expectations of their respective Aunt Ednas, some lapsed charismatics and Methodists, others perpetual observers, bright young minds overflowing with outrageous questions, accepting little at face value, and solemnly excommunicated from the school's social elite for refusing to worship the football team. Instead of attending the games they had gone for walks, caught a movie, shared their copies of Rolling Stone *and* Vogue.

They had indeed reveled in the latest that the outside popular culture had to offer. For the bright and the restless, life was larger than Swain County. Their parents had instilled wonderful values in them, assured them that they could achieve anything they desired, but had not moved beyond the River Road themselves. Now it was time for their children to see where the river flowed, to see what the rest of the world could offer hill country kids with pockets full of questions.

Don knew what was out there.

Don could see things in these mountains that others could not. Because he looked with such care, observed from an unconventional angle. He could see textures in the ferns, colors in the stones, patterns in the moonlight invisible to the ordinary souls who had lived within these hills for all their lives. But he had also roamed the region beyond, into the universities, theaters, galleries, ethnic restaurants, places graced by dance troupes, sculptors, orchestras, famous authors, connoisseurs of life's exotica. More important, he had sometimes taken his students with him. Carolyn recalled the mess of wide-eyed 17-year-olds, off with their pedagogue for 4 days to the American Dance Festival at Duke University. Pilobolus, Martha Graham, Katherine Dunham. Life was being opened up for them. A time to savor and never forget.

Impossible to forget a man of such charisma, with his combination of steel-

like authenticity and otherworldliness, his unparalleled integrity so attractive to her and the others. Don had led her outward, yes, but also taught her to look inward, to nurture her untended singularity, to be true to herself, as the cliché went. Honor the essentials—he had taught this through his actions. Distrust conventions, ignore the tired and narrow-minded who would in ignorance or in vengeance deny you the life lost to them.

A flashback to a small but special moment of higher learning from Don. He was to take her to a showing of another artist's work at Western Carolina University and then to dinner at the Wellhouse Restaurant. They had emerged from the classroom and approached his car, an old, banged-up Maverick, Ford Maverick. Reaching the car, she had peered through the window and noticed the conditions of its interior. Strewn about were pencils and beads and bags of discarded dime store plastic jewelry, almost every inch of surface covered. Papers everywhere, many apparently memos from the school administration, memos that maybe he had read and maybe he had not. And dog hair, for this was before his beloved Cavalry died, Cavalry who traveled with him nearly everywhere. Tufts of smelly gray Weimaraner hair throughout. Don had opened her door and, making space for her to sit, shoveled onto the back seat some of the papers and books, along with the cans containing the Antonioni film shown in class the day before.

An observation had shot to her lips, but an opportune moment for actually speaking it did not arise until, following dinner, she had walked with her teacher through the swarms of fireflies competing for attention in the thick moonlight, and had reboarded the Maverick. By then she had felt a bit giddy and asked what she considered to be a humorous question.

"This car is disgusting; don't you ever clean it?"

She did not have to wait long for a response.

"I refuse to apologize for the state of my car."

"What?"

"I refuse to apologize for the state of my car."

The words now ricocheted through time, from that evening with Don to her childhood in that glorified trailer, back to the present moment. Old words performing new magic, still illuminating her world, telling her while not telling her that the creation of false images in honor of conventionality or status need not be among the highest priorities in life. As it had not been for her parents— or was it that their attempts at image enhancement had been botched? She knew that she herself occasionally lusted after material objects (or at least beautiful things), but that more important, thanks largely to Don, she refused to pay the stiff price the outside world demanded for them.

Her eyes moved to the fake-wood paneling in what, giving directions to Tom, she had described as a "wanna-be chalet."

Now she smiled to herself about herself. "I refuse to apologize for the state of my wanna-be chalet, my ersatz ski lodge in the middle of a cow pasture."

But more than in his disdain for fancy things, it was in his deeply private life that Don had most evidenced his disregard for silly social conventions. Carolyn recalled how curious she and her friends had been about that private life. How they had known full well that he slept places other than at his school desk. Had known, for example, about Sarah, his girlfriend. Or was she his wife? They weren't sure then whether he was married. Carolyn recalled how they had composed and rehearsed the questions about Sarah, and how he had deftly avoided the questions asked. It was his life and no one else's.

Of course they had all understood the need for discretion, his living in sin, as many in this county might have described it, living unmarried with a woman while teaching in that school. Dangerous, really, to be that particular kind of maverick. But she recalled that one day in class he had announced, great excitement in his voice, that some of Sarah's poetry had been read on public radio. Would you bring me a copy of her book, Carolyn had asked, and the very next day it had appeared. More like a chapbook, really, Poems of a Mountain Woman *was its title. In study hall, she vaguely recalled, or somewhere slightly secluded, a select, very privileged group had been allowed to read some of the poems out loud.*

So Don had never overtly encouraged rebelliousness. Rebellion meant to her a reaction to society's codes and mores. Don Forrister reacted to nothing, simply acted, simply was. Let society react to him, if it cared to. He was not an overtly political creature, so his long hair, jeans, and sandals, like the mess in his car, were never meant as a political statement. He had never camouflaged who he was, never compromised his authenticity for respectability, but neither was he self-destructive, it seemed to her, never eager for martyrdom, never flaunting the controversial elements of his personal life to make a point. He revealed his quiet, hidden verses rarely, and only then to teach others the importance of such private poetry.

Moving To and Fro

These thoughts about the muted tensions between Don and the local culture led her to reexamine her own, rather spotty record of rebelliousness against that culture. For example, by graduation day—member of the Swain County High School Class of 1981—her arch should have been ready to transport her to somewhere else. But she decided to postpone its completion, having fallen in love with a man from Charleston who had come on a scholarship and remained to teach kayaking. At the age of 18 she had married him.

A sense of shame returned now at the thought of disappointing Don. He had expected more of her, she knew, more than a day care center at minimum wage and an early marriage. He had expected college. Never flatly stated such, of course, but she had no doubt. He would call once or twice a year. To recommend a book. Had she read White Hotel, *by D. M. Thomas? Or did she know that the Alvin Ailey Dance Company was at the university? Would she like to go with him and Sarah? And she had usually said no and had heard the disappointment in the silence on the phone, a silence saying I thought I might have been a kind of bridge for you, an arch to other places, but here you are still, why are you still here?*

Until finally there came her first cautious move outward to nearby Western Carolina University. That had worked out well, she realized in retrospect. Her talent for writing was finally shining through, although whenever . . .

The telephone again, and who should it be? Eric, of course—she was not surprised. Eric, her first and only lover, capable escort to all sorts of wilderness locations, her very reason for being here now, specifically *here*, in this house, in this familiar rural setting.

Eric, she remembered, had been the one really to introduce her to the outdoors. Even though she had grown up on the doorstep of the Great Smoky Mountains National Park, her parents never went there, not even to poach like so many of the other locals. But Eric had brought her backpacking, canoeing, had even tried to get her, the lifelong aquaphobic, into a kayak.

"I was just thinking about you," she told Eric truthfully. He asked about their child, wondered what he would cook for dinner since it was her night to teach. She would see him briefly, she said, before she left for work.

Carolyn then recalled the time when she, having finished with Western, had left Eric—she, with her slowly disintegrating security blanket, abandoning him for a scholarship to Warren Wilson, a private college in Nashville. For the first time she had moved out of the range of her extended family and her familiar backwoods haunts. Eric had professed an inability to live without his kayak. Inspired by Don, she had in turn confessed a desire to be in a place where she could become more than she then was. It took less than a year for her to regret what she had done, returning to the familiar embraces of her husband and the forest. But another move outward was inevitable, just one year later. This time with Eric, all the way out to the urban opposite of her soft green Appalachian birthplace. She had been awarded a fellowship to no less than Columbia University, on frenetic, harsh gray, distinctly unnatural Manhattan Island.

How had she gained both admittance and fellowship? Great GRE scores, good letters of recommendations from former professors, and from Don. But she was convinced that geography—the Appalachian element—was crucial. White trash quota, she thought. She had played to this strength by populating her application essay with the likes of an Uncle Bobby who hunted ginseng and a chain-smoking Aunt Edna. Her success at purveying the required image of her-self had provided her further evidence of her cleverness. The image had been this: backward and bright and obviously, since she hankered to flee from what those naives would surely envision as Dogpatch, U.S.A., rebellious. "Marvelous combination," she had imagined the comments of the Auden wanna-bes on the admissions committee, "from a big Appalachian family, married young, but very intelligent." When she had arrived for the fellowship interview, one person had told her he expected someone in overalls with a hayseed between her teeth. Just barely joking.

What did Don's imaginary voice, interrupting her thoughts, say it thought of her disingenuousness? She could hear him laugh.

Although she learned much at Columbia, the match was far from perfect and near the end of her program she decided not to pursue a doctorate. She had been repelled by what she perceived as the phoniness of the academy, the enormous amounts of energy spent in rococo-style arguments about postmodernism and authorial intent and the deconstructionist marginalia of deMan and Derrida. She was still her father's daughter, too generous and trusting, and Forrister's student, too authentic and genuine, to adopt the frivolous and crotchety viewpoint of the poststructuralist critics, with their pathological suspicions about authorial hegemony, thinking of a story not as a story but as an evil set of power relationships, thinking of poetry as original sin. No, her passion for literature—was it modernist and passé?—was born out of its marvelous capacity to delineate the contours of foreign landscapes, to reveal the lives of strangers, arose out of the power of its images to force an examination of things held dear so that one might learn how to live with ever greater authenticity and virtue.

Still, she would have loved to remain in New York City, with or without a Ph.D. She had relished its energy, its vitality, its galleries and theaters and intelligent films. But because she knew how much interest was accumulating on her debt to Eric, and knew that he was even more her passion,

still is, she murmured,

she had torn herself away from New York at the conclusion of her 10-month masters program. Just as Eric had, in an equally generous gesture, removed himself from the highlands to be with her for that time in that place. The two of them had thereby continued to move together to and fro, as in all good lovemaking, as in all good writing in which the artist arches out into the world and back inside herself in order to move out again onto the page.

The next move was to a place closer to Swain County. They had traveled down Highway 23 just over the Georgia line to a high school in Raymond Ridge where she had found work. She had decided to become a teacher. So with Don in her mind's eye and Eric beside her, she had set about honing her skills in her new craft and folding her being into her craftsmanship. Although the influence of a teacher on a student is dispersed like fog throughout her being, here was a solid example of how he was living on in her life: She tried to become to her students the kind of person and teacher that Don had been to her. Humane, concerned, compassionate, demanding, authentic. She had, for example, developed Forrister's habit of roaming out from her desk onto their classroom turf, thereby returning to the only recently abandoned territory of the adolescent. The habit of seeking out the backward, bright, and rebellious, using literature, as Don had used the visual arts, to entice them out of a circumscribed past into a boundless future. And as she had thanked Don Forrister, her students had thanked her, naming her, in her fourth and final term, Teacher of the Year. In her last year at Swain County High the yearbook had been dedicated to Don Forrister. In her last year at Raymond Ridge the yearbook had been dedicated to her.

Generations, she thought again, things passed on from then to now.

But another quality she owed partly to Don would paradoxically prevent her from continuing her teaching at a changing school. Raymond Ridge had been an institution in transition. She was hired into this private school with a national reputation for Appalachian authenticity, school of Wigginton and the Foxfire *books, teaching students to uncover and to save their highlands heritage. But after her first year there, the school had moved closer to the kind of school Auden had described in that essay she had shown to Tom.*

She picked up the book, still at her feet, and found the passage in which Auden had likened a private school to a political dictatorship with gossip campaigns and purges.

An extreme analogy, perhaps, but there had in fact been purges at Raymond. Senior faculty who had devoted their lives to the place, but whose degrees had been from the wrong institutions. Good and decent teachers, people with families, informed that their contracts would not be renewed, in April, too late to get a job at another private school. All because a new sort of student was desired—affluent, preppy Atlantans, drawl-free candidates for Brown and Yale, or at least for Duke. And any faculty member with a slightly countrified demeanor, dripping overly elongated vowels, alumnus of any nearby highlands college, was suddenly an unwanted embarrassment.

Of course, the administration were actually solicitous toward her. Why? Because she possessed the cultural capital that they craved, and could have easily survived by behaving badly, but in her mind remaining at Raymond would have been an act of complicity. And as usual, just like Don, she had found herself incapable of politics, at least as Auden had defined them.

She thumbed through the essay and read this paragraph slowly: "To be forced to be political is to be forced to lead a dual life." This was, she understood, Auden sounding like Don Forrister. "Perhaps this would not matter if one could consciously keep them apart and know which one was the real one. But to succeed at anything, one must believe in it, at least for the time being, and all too often the false public life absorbs and destroys the genuine private life."

So she had quit. Yes, quit! For, as she had come to realize that absorption of her self into that venal institution was completely out of the question, she chose to deny to those scoundrels that which they prized the most, a talented teacher with an Ivy League pedigree. She would not allow them to use for their outrageous purposes the paper from Columbia that certified what was for them an admirable ascension from Appalachia. Fact was, her feet had remained firmly planted in Appalachia, and she thought of the honorable submission of her resignation as proof of that fact. It was what her father would have done. Her mother, and her Aunt Edna. But was it really what Don would have done, the Donald Forrister who, more than anyone had taught her to understand the true nature of success? She believed that, yes, Don's sense of integrity would have demanded such a defiant act, and this was indeed part of his legacy to her. But Don was also more complex: A formidable work ethic and pragmatic streak would probably have meant finding another job before resigning.

She looked around now to see what that refusal to fail at being herself had meant in cold hard terms.

That refusal had meant a drastic change in lifestyle, a financial plummet from a rather comfortable existence in campus housing provided by Raymond Ridge, to no place to live and zilch for income. She remembered Eric's state of shock when she informed him, night beforehand, of her intention to resign. But they had adjusted, or more accurately, were now adjusting, righteous wounds being slowly healed by the sweet-smelling pines, the murmurs of brook water, and of course by mutual love. Add up the plusses and the minuses and she was content to stay, at least for now. Eric. Her family. Extended family is important to a child, she knew.

And there was her job at the college, teaching 2 nights a week, Introduction to American Literature. Best of all worlds, really, a job at home that kept her in touch with the realms of literature. Auden had written that a large percentage of the occupations open to people do them harm, but she felt blessed to be a teacher, like Don, in love with both her subject and her students, or better put, the people whom her students could become.

Among the Chosen

Alice was awake now, singing a nonsense song about bagpipes. Essie the cat, perched atop the copy of *Art News* on the coffee table, bounded to the door when she heard the familiar motor sound at the front of the house. Oh, thought Carolyn, is it really 4? She hurriedly gathered her materials and kissed Eric on the cheek as she blew past him out the front door.

"Late," she said. "See you after class."

Then, approaching the basic, dusty Volvo they had obtained by trading a canoe to her father-in-law, she noticed the conditions of the shotgun seat. Irritated, but smiling, she shoveled into the back Eric's paddling gear and masonry equipment to make space for her precious papers and books. Then pulling onto the road, driving, as had Tom, through the tunnel of trees, past the old white church on the right, she drew in a deep breath. She felt tired after the arduous exercise of reconstructing her life story. But she also felt like Thursday again: the malaise had disappeared and she was strangely exhilarated.

She thought: I am a person, who, thus far, has led a happy life.

It seemed that she had closed a chapter of her life story, or at least had completed an afternoon of work on exactly who she was in the world. Her poem about the past sufficiently polished, she was free to imagine her future.

She would persist at her writing and was applying to a Master of Fine Arts program. Meanwhile, Eric would work toward a B.F.A. in photography. And Alice would continue to grow ever more splendid, learning to tell her own stories. A paradoxically scary and hopeful picture flickered of an adolescent Alice, no longer chasing the automobiles of strangers, but driving off in her own. But this vision was quickly replaced by the recurring image of the day.

The arch again: one side of Carolyn planted in the past, a child of the South, like most of her students, permanently located in the land of her birth, poor, proud, parochial. But like some other Southern women she had come to know— Eudora Welty, Zora Neale Hurston—the other side of her wondered about distant realms. These were somewhere-elses not found on a map, but future spaces in the soul that would be made real through imagination and hard work. These spaces would not be furnished with beautiful things she wanted but couldn't buy, original art, travel to the driest of deserts and the greenest of rain forests, a house of her own, god knows she had her list. But filled by the rich and varied lives of those close to her, her family, her friends, and by the effects of her work: the lives of her backward, bright, rebellious students.

Her tacit knowledge guided the car left at the stoplight and onto campus.

She would collaborate with them in crafting those lives. She would show her students, show at least some of them, what was out there. She would show them how other people, through imagination and hard work, had created their own life spaces and furnished them. And tonight it would indeed be Eudora Welty, she who had written that the single subject of all of literature was life it-

self. In teaching them the subject of life, Carolyn would strive to be humane, concerned, compassionate, demanding, and authentic. In this manner she would enable some of them to become far better than they thought they could be. And by teaching them to become both true to themselves and responsible for others, she would prepare them not to submit to a base and unjust world, but to make that world far better than they thought it could be. For that is precisely what, she was thinking, the place she was from, the stories she loved, and Don Forrister, her own best teacher, had prepared her to do.

She opened the classroom door and moved out among her students. All of them were special to her, but she knew that some would become the chosen.

THE RESTAURANT MANAGER, THE PATROLMAN, AND THE COLLEGE STUDENT

On a Saturday afternoon in early October a few good men assembled in the living room of a house in a rural area near Sylva, North Carolina. The house belonged to Derek Robinson, one of three brothers who welcomed me for an interview about their experiences with their former high school arts teacher. The oldest was Roderick, manager of a fast-food outlet in Atlanta. A second brother, Derek, was a North Carolina State Highway Patrolman. The youngest was Marcus, a senior at Western Carolina University. A fourth brother, Keith, second oldest of the four, living in Atlanta, was unable to be present. I introduced myself, expressed my gratitude for their willingness to donate a brilliant weekend afternoon to a nosy educational researcher, and began the interview. Below are excerpts from the transcript.

Tom: When did each of you first meet Don Forrister?
Roderick: I was around 9 or 10 years old. Our father was the director of the Job Corps Center in North Carolina. We would go to the Center for extracurricular activities, and Don ran the arts and crafts shop there.
Derek: Yeah, the earliest I can remember Don Forrister was seeing him arrive at the Job Corps on his motorcycle. He had long hair and a beard, and I remember thinking that he looked like a picture of Jesus. Don ran the canteen with candy and drinks and stuff, which of course we liked. And his art class had ceramics. We would go in and paint and do ceramics and make pottery. He still works at the Center. I think Don has always worked about 15 hours a day.
Marcus: Yeah, we would go up there a couple of nights a week. There

were molds that you poured the clay in and then put them in kilns and bake them and then paint them.

Roderick: We made things for our mother and things for around the house. I didn't realize then that Don taught at the high school that we would eventually go to. I took art because I knew Don from the Job Corps, and I thought that art was an elective that seemed easy. I found out that it really wasn't.

Derek: Then Keith took Don's class, and it just became a family tradition. Each of us took his classes for 3 years.

Tom: Derek or Marcus, did you hear stories about Don from your older brothers?

Marcus: Only from Keith, really. Keith was the real artist of the family, always winning art shows and contests. At dinnertime he might be looking at a picture he had made and talking about how Don had influenced him. Keith was the one who did things like that.

Derek: Right, you need to talk with Keith. I wish he could have been here.

Tom: I'll see him soon in Atlanta. But tell me what Don's classes were like. What kinds of projects did you do?

Roderick: I remember making a table runner for my mother with lots of brown earth tones.

Derek: I took photography. I drew, did macramé, silk screen. We did some weaving and some crochet. I've got a crocheted pillow. And a wall hanging. I have the silk screen that we did in class. My wife and I still display it in our house.

Marcus: And we painted tiles, and I also liked clay cutting. This piece right here went to the Governor's office and stayed for several months. I didn't know it was that good, but Don encouraged me and we worked on it a lot, and it became a real good piece. This was in my senior year, my 3rd year with Don.

Tom: This piece is very handsome. How would you describe it?

Marcus: The cutting itself is a piece of clay tile, just plain and flat, gray in color, that represents the head of a man, not African in style but Aztec-ish, I think. But Don said, "Let's imprint it onto newspaper," and I was like "newspaper? OK." So I got some newspaper but he said, "No, do it on the comic section." So I said "Oh, OK." Then we decided to have two imprintings, one above the other, to give a comparison between the black and white and the different colors. We sent it in to a state contest and it won, and they kept it at the Governor's mansion in Raleigh. I finally got it back after graduation.

Roderick: That's interesting. You know, I can't remember any of your work or Derek's. By the time Derek got into Forrister's class, I was away at college. But my class didn't get to do some of the things that you did, because funds were limited before that Rockefeller grant. But I do remember making a soft sculpture piece. The background was sort of round with a man with braided hair, but I can't remember now what I was trying to convey. And I did batiks that hung in our room. And this huge monstrosity of a macramé wall hanging.

Tom: How would he help you with your projects?

Marcus: Mainly by making comments and suggestions. He would talk to everybody for the first 15 minutes or so, and then go around the room and help us individually, one-on-one. He would ask you, what are you trying to do or how, what kind of stroke, or what kind of shade are you going to use. Stuff like that.

Derek: Yeah, we'd each do different stuff for which we'd need help, and he'd come around to show how to do it.

Tom: So in his interactions with you can you think of any particular experiences that impressed you?

Marcus: Yeah, one day we were doing macramé, and it was amazing just to see him whip up the knots in the burlap string in the front of the class. He would come by your desk and show you the different knots and give you a suggestion of what kind you could be tying to make it look better. He was so well-rounded, knew all different areas of the arts. He could do all kinds of things simultaneously. Even after I was out of school and I wanted to do a silk screen logo for a tee shirt, he helped me with that also, even after I was out of school.

Tom: Let me ask each of you to respond to this difficult question. Suppose that you had not had Don Forrister in high school. How do you think your lives would be different now?

Marcus: I'm sure that art challenged me to view lots of things differently. I mean, just the other day I was building a stereo system for my car and realized as I drew it out to scale that I learned some basic skills of drawing from Forrister that I still use.

Derek: Yeah, I know what you mean because I have to draw scenes of wrecks—accident scenes—I mean, and I got those basic skills from his art class. Besides, Don just helped me to appreciate different types of art.

Marcus: Me, too. I probably wouldn't appreciate art if I hadn't taken that class. Now at Western every time there's a new exhibit in the University Center I always walk through just to see what's on display. I wouldn't go there or to other museums, wouldn't be able to appreciate what somebody else had done. Now I study what other people have done.

Roderick: I agree. I look at things differently now as a result of Don. I think Don's interest with my brother Keith made me take more of an interest in art. Before Don Forrister I would see a painting or sculpture, and I might say "nice painting, nice sculpture." But Don would make you wonder what you see in that piece, what in that work brings out the emotion within yourself. Although my wife pushes me, I can't say that I go to many artistic events, but I do see things in a different light because of my experiences in Don's classes.

Tom: Did he also teach you to look at people differently?

Roderick: He taught me to look at the world in a different way, and reinforced how my parents taught me to look at all people, including White people.

Tom: Could you explain what you mean?

Roderick: Well, in Washington we were always around other Black children, but in North Carolina there were none. Part of the reason that I went to the Job Corps Center so much was the other Black kids in the program. Just to interact with someone that looked like me, other than my brothers, was reassuring. Because I would go to school and come home and tell my mother that I wanted to be White. I felt like White people in general got all the breaks. It just seemed that way at that particular age, fourth or fifth grade.

Tom: Do you think that's unusual for a Black kid?

Roderick: No, but our parents were very good at reinforcing the idea that we were no different from anyone else, that we could do anything that we set our minds to. And so once I got to high school, if there was racism I didn't notice it, because I had no time to notice it. I was too into my own group of friends. My White friends treated me no differently, as a matter of fact. If anything, we led a pretty sheltered life, with the exception of a few episodes. I remember once we played ball in a town called Robbinsville, in Graham County, and there were no Black people there, and they made it a point to let you know that Black people weren't welcome. I remember going to a basketball game and walking in the door and the place just went silent. It was a real eerie feeling . . .

Derek: . . . because you knew you were the reason . . .

Roderick: . . . and there were threats that would come from these towns by word of mouth that if you come here with Rod Robinson, he's not going to leave this county. I can remember my junior year going to Robbinsville and 4-year-old children would line up when we were warming up, using the "N"-word. Hateful stuff. But we were never taught as a kid to—if you will allow me the expression—"know our place." For us, being raised by the parents we had, that didn't apply. Our parents instilled in us that we can be anything we wanted to be. Even though it was sometimes difficult. I was the only Black kid on the football team, and my dad told me a story about when we were in the play-offs. At the hotel where we were staying there was a conversation about the predominantly Black team we were playing in the play-offs. Some local folks mentioned that Swain County didn't stand a chance of winning because there was only one Black person on our team. We went out and beat them, about twenty-three to nothing. The prejudice was there, but we acted as if it wasn't. We saw those isolated incidents as one of those things. And you said you have to forgive those people because they don't know any better. You just moved on.

Tom: Did you ever talk to Don about racial issues?

Roderick: Well, because of the relationship built up over the years, I didn't look upon Don as a teacher, but as a friend. I didn't feel uncomfortable talking to Don about certain things like I did with other teachers. For example, there was a White girl that I wanted to go out with and she wanted to date me. But we were sneaking around, cautious because of her parents and the views of many people on interracial dating.

Tom: What did Don tell you?

Roderick: He told me to follow my heart. He told me to follow my heart. He told me to do what I felt was right. It was one of those situations where if I had gone to anyone else, they would have frowned upon it, but Don was open-minded. He said, "You have to follow your heart."

Tom: That taught you a lesson.

Roderick: He taught me about the world in general. I think that part of the high school experience helps you become a well-rounded adult. I know that, had it not been for Don Forrister, I would definitely not see things in the light that I see them now. In small Swain County High School there was no other place where I could express myself and not have anyone be judgmental about it. Don and my parents taught us how to be open-minded, to give people the benefit of the doubt, don't categorize one particular race of people based on what you hear. Find out what they're about before you become judgmental. If everyone took that approach, speaking from a Black man's perspective, then the world would be a totally different place. Unfortunately, that's not the way it is.

Tom: Do all of you still keep in touch with him?

Marcus: I kept in contact until 2 years ago. I used to go up to the school. But it's been hard for me to get up there.

Tom: When you would visit the school, would you also visit other teachers?

Marcus: Some. But I would spend the majority of my time with Don. I would sit in class and see what the kids were doing. Just sit there and watch. I did that every time I was on a break from Brevard.

Tom: Brevard?

Marcus: Brevard College, in Brevard, North Carolina. I got an associate degree there before I enrolled at Western Carolina, where I am now.

Roderick: Well, you know, even though I haven't seen Don since he got married, it seems like he is still a part of the family.

Tom: How so?

Roderick: Well, my father, my mother, my wife and son, we all went over to Keith's for dinner last weekend, and I was getting ready to throw a bottle cap away and Keith said, "Don't throw that away, we're saving it for Don." And so now I'm saving bottle caps at home.

Tom: And why are you saving them?

Roderick: I have no idea, other than it's for Don.

Derek: I'm sure Keith could tell you why.

Marcus: Yeah, you'll have to ask Keith that question.

THE WAITER

The following life story is an experimental blend of biography and autobiography. The story is crafted out of the memories of Barry Larson (pseudonym) and the results of his conversations with significant others in his life, as related in several interview sessions. It includes life incidents that are thematically relevant to what Barry identified as Forrister's lasting gifts to him (summarized in the last paragraph of the story). It moves beyond the interview text only in the spirit of Barry's theme.

This is primarily a work of nonfiction (in the usual sense of that term). I have, however, taken certain storytelling liberties, while always remaining faithful to Barry's sense of the essential impact of Forrister on his life. Barry agreed that the story presented here conveys that sense. Further discussion of the crafting of this story is found in Part V of this book.

The Poem

With the end of autumn hanging precariously in the cold air that morning, Barry could hardly wait to finish his drawing. Soon its subjects—the last few leaves on the trees outside the window—would cease their posing and fall forever from view. He briefly considered snapping a photo of the leaves, but knew that he was obliged to engage in the slow and tedious process that was his assignment. So his anxious eyes bobbed back and forth from subject to pad and back again, through the pane of glass that spared the animated classroom from the deadly chill outside.

But barely into his work Barry sensed that he was himself the object of someone's scrutiny, his attention caught by a familiar visage reflected in the window.

Mr. Forrister.

Barry wheeled around to see his art teacher staring at him from behind the messy mound of materials atop the teacher's desk. An index finger beckoned him near. As Barry arrived, the lanky man unexpectedly leaned forward and whispered what he called a poem, although it sounded to Barry more like a volley of questions:

"Why," asked Forrister, sotto voce, "do the fingers of the little once beautiful lady, sitting sewing at an open window this fine morning, fly instead of dancing? Are they possibly afraid that life is running away from them, I wonder, or isn't she aware that life, who never grows old, is always beautiful and that nobody beautiful ever hurries?"

"What?"

"I wrote that for you. Think about it."

Barry returned to his seat flummoxed, wondering about the meaning of the words he had heard and the reasons for the special attention. What had he done to be honored with a poem composed by a teacher? Why had Forrister called him "she?" Why did he say that the window was open when it clearly was not? Barry felt both flattered and puzzled. Until one afternoon nearly 2 months later.

On that occasion fate had demanded Barry's presence in the school library and there insisted that he thumb through some books for an English class assignment. An anthology entitled *A book of poems by E. E. Cummings* fell open to a page from which Barry read the following:

why

do the
fingers

of the lit
tle once beau
tiful la

dy (sitting sew
ing at an o
pen window this
fine morning) fly

instead of dancing
are they possibly afraid that life is
running away from
them (i wonder) or

isn't she a
ware that life (who
never grows old)
is always beau

tiful and
that nobod
y beauti

ful ev
er hur

ries

Feeling deceived, Barry would have immediately stormed up to Forrister's classroom to demand an explanation, had school rules allowed it. The next day, finally free to confront his teacher, Barry brandished a copy of the poem in front of Forrister and stammered: "You . . . you didn't write that. You did not write this poem. I found it . . . found it in the library."

But Forrister was unrepentant. Refusing an apology, he offered only a paradoxical combination of sly chuckle and innocent shrug. And a question.

"Have you thought about the words?" was what he wanted to know.

Barry, of course, had not. It would, in fact, take years before he would become a real student of Forrister's suggestion, for it ran counter to all that Barry ever was, at least since birth and maybe even before.

Life Before High School

According to Larson family lore, Barry had even been in a hurry to be born. Speculation abounded as to why this was so. One theory was that he wanted to spare both himself and his mother the pains and dangers of a prolonged delivery. But then again, how could he ever have imagined what might be lurking in the background at such a glorious occasion as the birth of an Appalachian child? How could word have reached him (deep in there) that at births in these remote hills, death could not be warded off by the metallic instruments of distant doctor-priests, but must be nervously shooed away by the local sorcery of granny-midwives? No, Barry was surely born naive, ignorant of the dangers that accompany any important movement out into the world. So a more likely reason for not tarrying was an eagerness for life. That must have been why Barry had emerged so hastily into the world, ensuring that his own grandmother would see her daughter Martha and her grandchild pass swiftly through a brief night of agony into a wondrous new day.

On his departure from the darkness, Barry could perceive the world only as an amazing swirl of sounds and colors and shapes. Still, some primitive wiring in his brain may have caused him to commence a process of selecting purposely from that sensual array. His emergence into the light was the first precious opportunity to begin a composition of meaning that would continue for a lifetime.

Barry's family included his father, mother, and older brother Steven. As an infant, he quickly grew to cherish their daytime commands and caresses, as well as their nocturnal scents and murmurs in the single bedroom of their shanty. As a young child, he learned to thank the stars for lighting his way on those urgent round trips between the communal warmth of the bedroom and the frigid privacy of the outhouse. He came to endure the baths in the kitchen sink with water imported from an outdoor well. Each bath signaled the inevitable closing of a weekly cycle of hard play with his brother in the yard that separated their house from the gravel road.

That road seemed both enticing and scary to Barry. In time he learned that it led to, among other places, school. As in the moments following his birth, Barry cried upon his arrival at that place. But before leaving him there, his mother provided the necessary reassurance, and interest overcame fear. First it was Head Start, a federal program to introduce kids of poverty to academic settings. But soon Barry was willing to move outward from the yellow bus, skipping down the long hallways of Almond Elementary School, past the lunch room on the right, toward his first-grade teacher's picture books, then his second-grade teacher's crayons and clay, and, in third grade, the strange smell of the perfume worn by Mrs. Taylor.

During the week his parents worked at a furniture factory. At school Barry imagined himself forward into the weekends, into the shelter of his home. Because he cherished the domesticity of those weekends, Barry was reluctant to accompany his father on his frequent hunting trips. He would forever detest the one time he had. The abrupt early morning arousal from a safe and cozy bed, the sting of cold air on his face, the spooky yelping of the bluetick hounds, the desperate sneer of the treed raccoon, the deafening blast from the rifle, the messy, nearly dead, red and brown cargo—to Barry every element of the miserable business seemed to occupy the wrong side of the coin of Appalachian existence.

Never again.

He didn't mind helping his father skin the critters, or at least holding the animal skins as they were nailed onto boards to be hung out to dry on the small porch. But everyone accepted the fact that for Barry the flip side of mountain life seemed infinitely more appealing: helping his mother with the delicate tasks of gathering and selecting the herbs needed to camouflage the sour flavor of wild rabbit, and sewing the pelts into furry coats and hats. What was to be made of these proclivities toward domestic chores? No one among the Larsons saw any reason why these offerings could not serve as his contributions to the fund of familial love.

During Barry's 10th year the Larson family began to gather materials for a new house. Barry developed a knack for selecting stones of precisely the shape and size needed by his father and grandfather. The larger house seemed a miracle to Barry: his own room with a bathroom adjacent. The house was completed in time for his mother to risk death again for the sake of life. Barry and Steven were given the joint honor of naming their baby brother Lucas Edward Larson.

On the Christmas after Lucas was born, Barry received an important present. The gift was a camera. Merely a cheap little "110," it was nevertheless a gift he would cherish. With its ability to record reality instantaneously, the camera was suited to assuage his ever-present need for speed. Soon his photo album bulged with pictures of the new-born Lucas, of the gentle, brown-haired Martha Larson, and of Steven. There were even reluctant poses of Barry's shy and quiet fly-fisherman father with the trout he caught in the solitude of a cold North Carolina stream. But no scowls or sneers would be captured for posterity; snap-shots of fears or frustrations were excluded. And because the shutter-bug had decided to frame only objects of tender regard, the camera was left at home during certain nocturnal trips into Bryson City.

Although Barry was a homebody, the house in that leafy thicket sometimes felt more confining than comforting, and so he tended to accept his mother's sporadic invitations to accompany her into town. The occasion was often a funeral for yet another deceased member of the congregation of Southern Baptists to which their family belonged. Together mother and child would slip into the night in the family's dusty white pickup, each serving tacitly as the other's lucky charm against imagined dangers lurking in the wide blackness divided by a string of road.

Near the end of the 25-minute journey the sounds of organ music would pierce the stillness. Disembarking from the truck in the parking lot, Barry and Martha grasped each other's hand. Then together they walked a too familiar gauntlet, up the steps of the funeral home, past clusters of people in seemingly perpetual sorrow, into a small, dimly lit chapel, directly to the casket of someone last seen alive, finally to greet the face of Death itself.

Inevitably overcome with sadness, Barry cried, even sobbed some-times, whether the deceased was an uncle, a close family friend, or a nameless acquaintance. Then, their ghastly dues paid, he and his mother withdrew separately to what each felt had been earned—she toward mutual consolation with other mourners, he into the vibrant night air where the mirthful squeals of his contemporaries served as distractions from the ominous humming of the organ. He often won-dered, but never asked, whether his pals were, like him, laughing so strenuously in order to drown out the eerie music and playing espe-cially fast and hard in order to forget—or maybe to defy?—the stark reality to which they had been subjected.

The odd residue of those evenings remained with Barry even under very different circumstances. Paradoxically, happy occasions seemed happier, set against that gloomy background. And the happy mo-ments outnumbered the sad. Barry was happy designing and building things—houseboat, go-cart—with his uncles and grandfather. Barry was happy attending softball games, recording on film the triumphs of his shortstop brother Steven. And beginning in fifth grade Barry was happy palling around with his new best friend, Nathaniel Carter.

Nat's relatively affluent parents had abandoned the bustle of the city for the tranquillity of the mountains. Owners of a campground in the Nantahala Gorge, the Carters were gregarious, curious about Nat's friends, and acutely aware of the limited cultural and entertainment opportunities for kids in such a rural environment. So they would generously collect Barry from his home and transport him and Nat to distant locations—the nearest movie house, 40 miles away, or the bowling alley in the town of Sylva. Other times the boys would be invited to gaze through Mr. Carter's enormous telescope, or allowed as members of a pack of preadolescents to spend the night partying and terrorizing the family campground.

With the Carters, Barry first encountered an outsider's perspective on hill folk. Transplanted Atlantans, they good-naturedly joked about "mountain people," even as they offered them their warmth and friendship. Here was a different kind of parent: curious and knowledgeable about the world, possessing what seemed like boundless resources, and harboring no guilt about attending church fewer than 3 times a week. Barry was like a fish noticing for the first time that it breathed water. Although he felt, metaphorically speaking, at home in the water, Barry nevertheless yearned to inhale the rarefied air that surrounded Nat and his family. But movement out into their kind of world seemed nigh impossible to Barry. It would require the cultural equivalent of lungs, and his inklings of how to grow them were as vague and insubstantial as the mists that hung between his home in the woods and Nat's house in the gorge.

Life During High School

After eighth grade Barry and Nat each took who they were at that point in their lives to Swain County High School. Of course, most of the other freshmen cared very little about who they were. It was easier to tag them as "Almonoids," the derogatory nickname reserved for alumni of the feeder school with the most special education students. "Almonoid Mongoloid!" went the stupid taunt. But soon Barry and Nat saw the potential value of the obnoxious label. They decided to convert their anger from the insult into the productive energy needed to excel in high school.

Barry, an average student overall, shone in two classes that dove-tailed with his interests and talents. The first was home economics. Over 4 years he would develop a flair for designing and sewing clothes, a deeper knowledge of culinary matters, and a fondness for his teacher, Mrs. Decker. Through her connections Barry the sophomore secured his first restaurant job, dishwasher at a small cafe in Cherokee. Although Barry was one of the few boys in home ec, Nat joined him for a year, the basketball jock drawn to the aroma of freshly baked cinnamon rolls and the scent of an easy A.

Second to cooking, Barry's greatest love was photography. But at SCHS photography was available only to junior and senior graduates of Art I. So Barry elected to take beginning art as a sophomore, primarily as an entree into photography class. But soon he discovered that other arts and crafts held their own fascinations, including the unusual man who taught the course.

Intimations of a teacher named Donald Forrister wafted through the air early in Barry's high school career. Tales of Forrister were heard everywhere, his student admirers legion. One was riding the school bus on a pale January afternoon. Barry was pleased to be invited to sit beside the familiar face of Carolyn Wilson, whose family were friends with the Carters. The talk turned to teachers.

"Are you planning to take art with Don Forrister next year?" she asked.

"The weird guy with the beard? I've seen him in the cafeteria."

"He's not that weird. He just looks a little strange 'cause he dresses and looks how he wants to."

"What kind of stuff do you do in his class?"

"Oh, all sorts of things, but I like drawing best. Wait, I'll show you what I'm working on now. A sketch of a quilt that a friend of mine just finished sewing together."

He politely studied the pencil work, and wondered about a certain redundancy of media. More interesting to make a quilt yourself than draw one made by someone else, he thought privately.

"Neat," he said out loud.

Then as Carolyn folded her artwork, Barry thought he heard her say this: "Anyway, if you take Forrister's class, you'll never be the same again. Just knowing him could change your life."

Barry recalled this startling comment after his own introduction to Forrister the following September. He relished his art classes from the outset, seeing them as an extension of those creative moments of helping his grandfather design a piece of furniture. Introduced to many media and materials, Barry flitted from one project to the next, from designing and screen printing an emblem onto a tee shirt to batiking with a picture of some ladies from the cover of the JLB rolling papers. From linoleum prints to the never fully successful attempts at drawing, practicing thin lines, thick lines, dark lines, light lines, thin lines, thick lines, dark lines, light lines. . . . From the fabulous hand painting and airbrushing of silk to weaving a baby blanket for a pregnant Mrs. Decker.

In art class Barry felt born again. There memories of the drab curriculum of his math and grammar classes exploded into a wild profusion of possible textures, shades, and shapes, all available for personal compositions. The only danger lay in a failure to hook up the array of available materials to his inner feelings. And a safety net provided by his peers reduced even those minor risks. The social atmosphere was different from other classes. Camaraderie grew as students worked on projects in a classroom filled with friendly banter. Barry could count on his new comrades for the support and encouragement needed to soften the blow of failure in any finished product. Within this second home the young artist felt safe enough to travel abroad, free to take the risks that, next go-round, might move him beyond mediocrity.

Meanwhile, Mr. Forrister, roaming the classroom, would observe his endeavors, and interject comments that were usually practical and relevant, occasionally befuddling and troubling. On the one hand, Forrister's presence could be a source of anxiety for Barry, with comments suggesting that he expected the extraordinary from him, urging him to stretch his imagination so that something special might issue forth. On the other hand, his calm, sage advice was enormously reassuring, enabling Barry to dare to reconfigure shapes and colors and textures in bold new ways.

Barry soon became aware that cultivating his students' artistic sensibilities was Forrister's life work. And Forrister's workplace was larger than the classroom, as Barry realized the day he asked about an old maple drawing table that had appeared in class.

"It's from an old supply store in Asheville," answered Forrister. "I'm going back there this weekend; would you like to come with me?"

On Saturday morning he climbed aboard Forrister's pickup truck, littered with junk and permeated with a canine stench, and off they went.

Barry soon discovered that if Forrister could become aesthetically aroused in a military supply store, so could he. Barry was like a giddy child in that salvage warehouse, flitting from one interesting item to another, from a white enamel medicine cabinet to parachutes hanging on the walls. Forrister fixed his stares on only a few. In the end, they purchased the affordable, a pile of 6-inch-square bandages, each with a muslin strap for tying around a huge wound. Beauty in military bandages? Barry later dyed several of them garish tones of yellow, purple, and green, and shaped them into a wall hanging. He was, as usual, intrigued by the idea of recycling things made to be used under dark conditions into artifacts that brightened the surroundings of the living.

Barry was often oblivious to his teacher's interest in his work, only to be startled by the intensity of his attentiveness. One day Barry the sophomore had plopped on his desk some snapshots from a family vacation at Myrtle Beach. They were spied by Forrister, who asked permission to keep the negatives for a while. Barry consented, but was disappointed to see them disappear onto the top of Forrister's groaning desk, a permanent contribution, he figured, to its sedimentary layers of student artifacts. In a couple of weeks, however, three of the photos reappeared on Barry's desk, enlarged and matted. Surprise covering his student's face, Forrister announced that the photos would be entered in the upcoming Southwestern College high school competition. Although, in the end, none won a prize, the incident had convinced Barry of the authenticity of Forrister's interest in him. So Barry, for a few intense moments, studied those photographs, comparing them with those *not* selected by Forrister, straining to appreciate qualities so readily apparent to the educated eyes of his teacher. But prolonged scrutinizing was difficult for the impulsive teenager, as Forrister had already begun to notice.

Barry still imagined that his real talent resided in the quickness of his camera trigger finger, although he could admit that in both art and home economics persistence and determination resulted in good work. This admission was momentarily reinforced when he won two awards for, not photos, but items of painstaking craftsmanship. The first was a Scholastic Arts Award for a hand-painted silk depicting the Great Smoky Mountains. For this project Barry toiled late after school, with Forrister nearby, giving guidance about technique, questioning judgments about color and form, and sometimes, when Barry missed the school bus, driving him to his grandmother's house.

The second award was for a weaving. Mother's Day was approaching, and a shawl with a blended pattern of orange and sea-foam green would make a lovely present. But the extraordinary beauty of the shawl meant that Martha Larson would have to wait for her gift. In Asheville it won first prize in its class for the southeastern United States. That sent it automatically to the Corcoran Gallery in Washington, D.C.

One early morning in the May of his senior year, Barry, Don Forrister, and two other seniors, climbed aboard a long and luxurious vehicle, perhaps even a Buick, which flashed the tags of the super-intendent of Swain County Schools. All day they drove, Barry giddy with expectation, and not only about the possibility of a national award. Barry was excited about traveling to a place he had previously visited only through books and television, a destination even more fascinating than the Carter family's Atlanta.

In the early evening at their Virginia hotel, they donned some un-usually formal apparel and left for the show. Then, as his mentor-turned-chauffeur guessed his way through the nation's capitol, squeez-ing the Buick, it seemed, through narrow passageways between famous statues and massive monuments, Barry sat covered with goose bumps, amazed at how a humble act of weaving could yield an experience such as this.

At one point Forrister mumbled his preference for a more leisurely trip, if only the school had the funds for it. But for Barry the hectic pace only enhanced his excitement. The Appalachian foursome arrived at the gallery late, with barely enough time for a photo of the three students beside their entries, and for each of them, including a good Southern Baptist boy, to sneak a glass of champagne at the tail end of the reception held in their honor. Then back to the hotel for the night, followed by the next day's anticlimactic return to familiar ground.

It was later learned that none of the three student artists had won a national award for their efforts, but for Barry the cake was sweet enough. The shawl not only pleased his own eyes, but it had pleased Mr. Forrister as well. And the trip to Washington had not merely pro-duced a pride from the display of his work in a famous building sur-rounded by concrete icons of the national culture. It had revealed to him the exotic rush of traveling far away from home.

His Washington trip was the climax of a quickly disappearing high school career. Academically he had remained an average student, but his role as yearbook photographer had led to the editorship in senior year. Moreover, his faithful attendance at the school's sporting events and his reliability as the official videotaper of basketball games per-suaded fellow students to vote him Most School-Spirited of the 84 members of the Swain County High School Class of 1983. And while it was of course fellow Almonoid alumnus Nat and not Barry who gar-nered the athletic awards, it was just as surely Barry and not Nat who was named Outstanding Student in Home Economics.

Life After High School

Life had passed quickly, until a Tuesday morning in March of 1995. The San Francisco air was quite chilly. But since it was the one day of the week in which Barry was free from both his jobs as waiter, he wanted it to be special. So he accepted the advice of one of his roommates to take in an event at the Exploratorium. After neatly trimming his short beard, he carefully selected a black turtleneck and brown sport coat for the occasion. Then emerging from his apartment on Fillmore Street, he walked to the trolley stop. Upon boarding, he noticed above the usual melange of trolley smells a singular odor, one that sent him careening back to his childhood. A certain brand of cheap perfume. His eyes reflexively, and of course in vain, sought out the ghost of Mrs. Taylor.

The stimulant ushered in a wave of nostalgia, causing Barry to ponder his life thus far, to recall times at Almond and Swain and events since. He thought about his 4 years at Western Carolina University, his degree in communications, minor in photography. Then, drawing a breath, he recalled the splendid postgraduation trip to San Diego, the new home of Nat Carter. A deep sense of contentment had encouraged him, and unemployment freed him, to stretch that visit to 6 weeks.

But what to do with what he had learned about himself in San Diego? Barry returned home to consider the next act in the drama of his life. He now thought of the role that Don—no longer "Mr. Forrister"—had played in the ensuing personal deliberations, of how Don's counsel, permeated with understanding, acceptance, and good judgment, resonated with the whisperings of his own inner voice. Listening to them both, he decided that happiness required another move outward, yet another rebirth, a risky return to the thrilling freedom of the southern California coast, to living on the absolute edge of the continent, farther from the leafy valley of his childhood than even the District of Columbia.

Barry recalled an incident on the day before he finally reached that decision. In rummaging through some drawers he had come upon an album of family photographs. Later showing them to some friends, he was puzzled by the absence of pictures of himself. The scenery, the house, the other family members were familiar, but where was he? Disturbed by this, Barry brought the pictures to his mother who insisted that the very young child upon whom the camera had so often been centered was none other than Barry himself. "You just don't recognize yourself because you've changed so much," explained Martha.

He knew she was partly right: It was indeed Barry Larson in those photos. His early existence was, after all, more substantial than a vague and complex set of rumors. But now he thought that maybe his lack of self-recognition wasn't due to any essential change in him. Maybe it was just that he could envision the larger person he was now becoming much more clearly than he could remember the smaller person he had been.

Barry remained in San Diego for 5 years, working as a teller and then a waiter, before joining some friends in San Francisco. There he now sat, silent in his fog of reverie until the trolley approached what had already become one of his favorite places in his new hometown.

Inside the cavernous hall the mellow sense of otherworldliness remained. The air was perfumed with the recorded sounds of cymbals, drums, and bells, mixed with guttural chants, a spiritual music not nearly as funereal as a dirge on an organ announcing an absolute end to something precious. Turning a corner, Barry was suddenly greeted by a flowing curtain of maroon, the robes of a dozen Tibetan monks. They appeared against a wall of what his brochure described as pure and sacred Indian cow butter dyed into various colors. Drawing closer, Barry saw that the agile hands of the monks were carving lavender-colored butter into hundreds of small lotus blossoms. But the blossoms were merely a small moment in a massive, ongoing labor of love—bright, arduously crafted mandalas of Buddha and of an array of saints, sages, and lesser deities.

Barry instantly understood the transient nature of these fragile and intricate creations. They would not last as long as they seemed to deserve. A brochure confirmed his suspicions, noting that although some butter sculptures are preserved for 30 years, most are attached to towering placards and tossed off cliffs, or left to wild animals, or sometimes consumed in a kind of Tibetan religious communion. Upon their completion in 2 weeks, these painstakingly crafted objects, too, would be destroyed. Nothing—everyone knows this—lasts forever. But for Buddhists, no fear or sorrow is attached to this apparent destruction. The sculptures-in-progress are not meant as beautiful objects but as precious experiences, and their destruction as simply one segment of a creative cycle. No danger that their physical disappearance will mark an end to their beauty; instead, it bestows meaning on the larger beauty of the cycle of life.

Barry was entranced by the leathery fingers of one aged monk—fingers dancing rather than flying!—as they gracefully and deliberately pinched off a piece of the butter and dipped it into a pan of ice water. As he watched, Barry felt the nearness of a great teacher, someone utterly silent whose presence seemed to insinuate itself into the core of his being.

On the ride home some other tiny thing, a small architectural detail on a building, suddenly reminded him of another such teacher. A few blocks after boarding the trolley he noticed an ornate edifice, his eyes moving to the top of a column painted a faint shade of pink. He thought about how he would have missed the effect of that detail on the overall scheme of the structure had it not been for someone whose passion for aesthetically pleasing details had in some ways taught him how to see and therefore how to live.

He also thought of how, since moving to California, he rarely used his camera. No longer compelled to freeze photogenic pieces of the world, he had come to place his faith in memories without a redundancy of media: how much more direct and interesting to compose experiences. It now seemed to him (although he knew that Forrister would disagree) that the camera attempted to create the impossible—something stronger than life itself.

Not that there were no decisive moments in life. To the contrary; Barry had come to resonate with these words of the great photographer Henri Cartier-Bresson: "Through the act of living, the discovery of oneself is made concurrently with the discovery of the world around us which can mold us, but which can also be affected by us. A balance must be established between these two worlds—the one inside us and the one outside us. As a result . . . both worlds come to form a single one. And it is this world that we must communicate."

But Barry had come to believe that the significance of a decisive moment, a brief aesthetic experience in which one is most fully alive, could be immediately available to each person with or without a camera. And that balance might be not only represented through an object of art but also presented directly in the mandalas of our actions, the patterns within the external manifestations of our experiences. In this way one's own life could become one's greatest artistic achievement.

He himself was indeed a work-in-progress, even though no project lasts forever. So, in the spirit of this city so defiant of the late-twentieth-century fog that shrouded its concrete hilltops and hollers, Barry focused on life. The creation of aesthetic moments required movement out into the world, and, almost 30 years after his birth, Barry was no longer naive about the dangers accompanying the trip. There would always be risks involved in the art of living. He knew that someday, hopefully in the far-off future, his own completed composition would be, figuratively speaking, sprinkled off a cliff, or used as the occasion for a communal gathering. And his new awareness was accompanied by neither fear nor sorrow nor hastiness. Instead the knowledge of his ultimate disappearance was a precious gift to the meandering present.

For Barry the risks included defying the expectations of others in order to honor his own evolving goals. For instance, he had become, to the chagrin of family members who wanted something more for and from their first generation college graduate, a professional waiter. While career goals might later change, for now he had chosen to ignore issues of money and status and power. His present work was sufficiently fulfilling.

He thought about the nature of that fulfillment, the (yes) *aesthetic* pleasures derived from a round of waiting dinnertime tables. Barry carved each night at the restaurant out of the flat flow of time into the rounded character of a drama. Challenges to his skills and talents gradually mounted as hungry patrons first trickled in, and then poured in. And at the evening's climax, at the apogee of the arc of time that was his shift, came the decisive moment when the waiter felt in fullest communion with all elements of his workplace, human and physical. This moment demanded a supreme sensitivity to every subtle clue about the desired pacing of courses at this table and that one, and the greatest number of instantaneous judgments about how best to balance the desires of the various visitors to his assigned territory. Then the denouement, as the evening eased back into its former stillness. It was, of course, only after the last coats and jackets were donned and the final tangible appreciations of his performance received that Barry, with a familiar sense of tired satisfaction, could light up a cigarette and call it a night.

It was indeed at the height of the nighttime rush that Barry felt most assured as he gave structure to the night in complex negotiations with all of his materials. This was the time when he felt most like himself, most fully alive. But this was also a time for channeling an overflow of energy present since birth. A cathartic moment that drained him of that excess energy, freeing him to navigate the following day relaxed. So Barry became less able than ever to recognize the younger Barry of those old photos. This was because, for the first time since birth, he had begun to live a part of his life at an unhurried pace.

Away from his workplaces Barry had learned to explore at leisure the textures and patterns in various California landscapes (the pink tint at the top of a single column of an ornate building was only one example). He found a passion so reminiscent of Forrister's deep love for the reverberations between minute details and an aesthetic whole. Similarly, each gesture toward another person seemed part of a larger picture, contributing to the unique composition of meaning that was his life. He had come to conclude that composing a meaningful life was more like patiently weaving a blanket than opportunistically snapping a photo. And he was ready to think that meaning can never be rushed, until an alternative phrase with a nearly identical sense cascaded down through the recesses of his mind and splashed noisily into the pool of his consciousness: "nothing beautiful ever hurries."

At very long last, Barry was studying those words.

He knew that his unhurried personal project was not a strictly private matter. The creation of himself in communion with the world was as visible to anyone who paid attention as were the movements in the making of a butter Buddha, in the composing of a finely colored silk print, in the dance of shadow and light in a photograph. The movements were lessons to be learned, offered by great teachers to anyone enrolled in the course of Life. In making those moves he might give to the world a small piece of the gift he had received from his own mentor.

Now as the trolley approached Barry's stop he allowed himself a moment of fantasy that described his aspirations more than reality. The city trolley became a school bus on which his whole world was riding, friends and strangers alike, everyone to whom he had dedicated his art, his life. One woman who resembled his old pal Carolyn Wilson was speaking to a young boy in the adjacent seat. Barry imagined her saying this:

I know a young man who was once like a trembling leaf of autumn staring into a wintry abyss. Who was once as terrified as a child pushed into the face of a corpse. A man whose fear led him to play very fast in order to avoid considering what he might become. But this young man was blessed with a teacher who could see into his soul, who taught him how to breathe the incomprehensible air of distant places, who gave him permission to search the world in order to find and make who he was, and to love what he made. A teacher who taught him about the patience needed in the seeking and the creating. Now this young man wants to be the same kind of teacher, one who teaches just by being who he is. And that is precisely what he has become. In fact, just knowing him could change your life.

THE MAGICIAN AND THE PAROLE OFFICER

Three different fonts are used in this story about the relationships between Forrister and a pair of high school buddies. The changes in font are meant to easily signal shifts across three distinct perspectives of events and sources of information related to these relationships. One is used to represent the perspective of Ben Dobson; a second for that of Paul Mosely. A third font represents a common perspective, shared by both former students. For Forrrister's take on some of the events described herein, see Part III of this book.

Otherwise, elements in the researching and writing of the story of Ben and Paul below resemble those of "The College Teacher" and "The Waiter." In manuscript drafts, I attempted to remain faithful to the themes identified by each former student (in separate interviews) and, as Ben put it, to the "spirit of our life experiences." Successive drafts were read by Ben and Paul, and the final manuscript approved. For further elaboration of methods and methodological rationale, see Part V.

The Snowfall

The snow had fallen persistently for 3 days into that new year, slowly expanding the possibilities for the two young men with time on their hands. For Paul Mosely and Ben Dobson it was the first winter break after high school graduation and each had resigned himself to a protraction of the holiday routine—chatting, snacking, killing time. But the quantity of snowfall had grown astonishingly, and the two pals were being drawn toward a frolic in the frozen blankness accumulating around them. Nothing more than a splendid opportunity for cheap thrills —this is how they saw it at the time—as a way of holding at bay those nagging images of the following week's return to academic drudgery. One of them—which one? the reader is free to choose—initiated the idea of the ski trip. The other decided to invite their former high school teacher along.

> Years later, Ben thought it was Paul who had done so.
> **Paul believed it was Ben's idea.**

But were not both aware that Don Forrister would feel awkward on a pair of skis? That performing acrobatics down a steep mountain slope was hardly his forte? Could they not foresee how they would guffaw good-naturedly at his pratfalls? Did they not know all along how, swerving hard to spray him with powder, they would split their sides in laughter? Had they not anticipated a day of role reversal on the slopes, a temporary transference of authority in which the physical prowess of the youngsters would devalue the authority of their former mentor?

Why a need to humiliate their friend and teacher? Their reputation as good-natured pranksters was already established, gained far off the slopes at the expense of Forrister and so many others. Most likely this would serve as gentle retribution for the shenanigans to which Don had subjected them a few months earlier, on a memorable August evening before the exodus. At any rate, it certainly was the first opportunity in the history of their relationship with Don for Paul and Ben to be truly in charge. So, still locked in late adolescence, they made the most of it.

Life in High School

Don had been their art teacher, but it was more than a mutual attraction to the arts that had pulled them into the zones of each other's lives.

As for many Swain students, the relevant magnetism emanated from the persona of Don Forrister.

Paul Mosely had somehow remained outside of its range for most of his high school career—until an evening late in his junior year. The occasion was the annual school talent show, and Paul had performed his magic act to much applause. Don had sought Paul out after the show and invited him to take his photography class the following fall.

For Ben it was a different story. At the beginning his regard for Forrister had been one of ambivalence, a curiosity about arts and crafts at odds with a slight aversion toward Forrister's eccentric nature. The initial introduction to art had come from his mother, whom the very young Ben had watched doing ceramics with her friends and needlepoint quilting with Ben's grandmother. His mother had also sent Ben for lessons with a locally prominent watercolorist, although the 11-year-old's interest had waned after several lessons. And a curiosity about photography had resulted from his close friendship with George Walcott, whose fascination with cameras emerged in seventh grade. But Ben was not even aware that photography was part of Forrister's curriculum until after enrolling in Art I. Most likely, it was the recommendation of his stern, conservative stepfather, who taught agriculture at Swain, that finally helped him decide. Ben's stepfather had spoken highly of Forrister as a teacher despite reservations about his unconventional physical appearance and unorthodox approach to life in general.

In Art II Ben had already begun to pursue photography avidly before he learned of George Walcott's fatal automobile accident. Badly shaken, Ben had burrowed even further into photography, partly as a tribute to his deceased friend. Don turned his attention to Ben's academic progress, maybe as a subtle means of consoling him. Ben would later recall this time as the birth of a deep attachment to photography, the art form beckoning him both as cathartic and as surrogate companion. It was a mind-altering time in which he began to develop a photographer's eye, if still a prelude to a senior year in which Ben's talent would flourish and a new set of social attachments would form.

Ben and Paul knew each other through classes and sports before entering into their final year at SCHS. Already, they had each effortlessly acquired an elite status, fellow nobility lounging at the top of the school's social hierarchy. If Ben was the handsome quarterback, Paul was the extroverted Student Body President, poised magician-entrepreneur, child member of Asheville's Biltmore Forest Country Club relocated to Bryson City as the privileged stepson of one of the town's few physicians. Despite being football teammates as juniors, the two Big Men on Campus found the school turf too small for both of them. Each, disliking the other's cockiness, had done his best to maintain a distance. Still, a common fondness for pranks meant that each was a strange amalgamation of royalty and court jester. And both tacitly acknowledged that an equal standing precluded each regal clown from being the butt of the other's jokes.

Perhaps the sudden bonding in their senior year resulted from the location of a suitable playing field for their silly games and a prominent someone—a teacher, no less—occasionally willing to serve as straight man. What they found was the photography course of Don Forrister, a venue in which two royal rivals became friends and coconspirators.

Their jokes were rarely as elaborate as a good magic trick: They seldom rose above the level of the Three Stooges. The adolescent antics were always intended to be benign, although once one of the Robinson brothers had taken unexpected offense at the "kick me" sign surreptitiously taped to his back while at the loom. A favorite moment was the first time they left campus for pizza during class time, sneaking it into the darkroom and inviting Forrister in for a bite. Their rewards were his double take and his sigh of relief as they informed him that their pack of coconspirators had included the school secretary.

As the year progressed, the secretary would always be informed before each of the increasingly frequent afternoon runs to Hardee's. An element of noblesse oblige was discernible: The rights to these trips were granted almost exclusively to star seniors. Still, each boy had also earned a reputation for trustworthiness. More than just jokers, each had a serious side.

> Paul understood that his perfect attendance award was merely one indication of the responsibility he felt to his new, widely respected stepfather; his temporary political ambitions were another.

Much too respectable to get "wasted" on the weekends, neither of these boys was a troublemaker, drinker, doper. So what was wrong with rewarding the winners of the world with some extra bits of freedom? The boys knew that Forrister also sensed the aura they possessed even if that played no role in his frequent willingness to bear the brunt of their tomfoolery.

> One advantage for Don in allowing them to kid around with him seemed obvious to Paul: it established a rapport that served to draw them closer into his sphere of influence.

It was also Forrister's way of signaling to them a tolerance for who they were: adolescents, after all, with a real talent for goofiness. They appreciated the tolerance. Forrister obviously believed that little harm could flow from accepting the inevitable immaturity in teenage personalities, as long as limits to inappropriate behavior were clearly established. And indeed, Paul and Ben were conscious of an invisible line that was not to be crossed. Whenever the ribaldry began to get out of hand, Forrister would emit subtle cues that suggested it was time to back off. With a deft touch of assertiveness, never sacrificing his cordial demeanor, he would remind the guys where the ultimate power resided.

This power, they knew, emanated from Forrister's twin possessions as a schoolteacher. The first was an auxiliary supply of authority from which Forrister rarely drew, available to every teacher in those earlier days and times. The second possession, the one they more genuinely respected, was Forrister's knowledge of photography.

Forrister would rarely impart this knowledge in a didactic manner. Instead he established opportunities for learning, issued challenges, gently critiqued their work, suggested alternative subjects, strategies, techniques. One important factor was the selection of a potentially fruitful site for the "shoot." For example, on one occasion the small class of five or six was led to a day care center to zoom in on napping children.

> Tiptoeing between the floor mats, Paul took a series of pictures of sleeping faces and floppy bodies from a multitude of angles. There were profiles, frontals, shots from behind ears and under chins, here a drippy nose, there a dangling tongue.

Or the visit to the Pepsi Cola bottling plant to focus on shadows, form, and texture.

> There Ben composed a photo with stark lighting contrasts of some long-necked bottles stacked in crates in a corner. He would later consider this to be his photographic hole in one, the only absolutely perfect picture he would ever take. The photo was displayed in contests across the state from Greensboro to Winston-Salem, and on the walls of his own high school. The two gold keys it earned would remain permanently on the walls of his parents' home in Bryson City.

Forrister was never satisfied with the obvious choices and would suggest unusual techniques, such as "burning and dodging," superimposing images from one negative onto another.

> One of Paul's sleeping babies became an apparition in a snowy creek.

Or Don would suggest placing developed film in a freezer to grow an intricate frostlike design. But these and other fancy techniques were always understood as a means to a communicative end. How could anger be captured in a photo? Or restlessness? Or serenity? Expanding their expressive abilities through photography was Forrister's paramount aim for Ben and Paul. But they both knew that one of them was more talented at this craft than the other.

Paul admitted to being rather conventional in his choice of subject matter and approach   while Ben was more "artsy."

To be sure, each had earned his share of ribbons. And each was attracted to the drama of the developing room where, in cavelike darkness, some chemicals were skillfully cajoled into revealing some occasionally astounding results of their efforts.

But even in the darkroom Ben's superior proficiency was obvious. He became, for example, the recognized specialist in rolling negatives. Ben rolled negatives with such sensitivity and dexterity—avoiding blotches by feel rather than sight in the close, inky room—that other students learned to trust him with their especially valuable rolls of film.

Paul understood that this was Ben's turf. When it came to videotaping, however, Paul believed that his skills surpassed Ben's. One assignment had been to videotape a commercial about an imaginary product.

On the day before the project was due, Ben invented the   (outlandish, thought Paul)   notion of pills that would cause dogs to grow into horses. Ben arranged for a shoot at the farm of a friend. The script was minimal: Farmer walks dog into barn. Cut. Two salesmen approach. "Hi, try our new instant horse growth pills." Cut. "Sure. Thanks." Cut. Farmer walks horse out of barn. Finished. Ben was not bothered that the script lacked sophistication and finesse.

Paul was secretly irked that Ben's commercial would receive credit equal to his. For he had chosen a more credible product, an imaginary soft drink named "Peak." And his project evidenced ingenuity and hard work: For a still shot, he sprayed aluminum pop cans, painted a mountain on a silk screen backdrop, and on another screen stenciled and painted the product logo. Then he directed an episode in which Ben filmed him, first, climbing up a steep mountain, spritzer mixed with sweat, and later, springing from behind a boulder to snatch a can that was balanced on top, ripping it open, and exclaiming: "PEAK! [short pause] Worth the climb!" Guzzle shot from a distance. And cut.

Later that year the Swain County Arts Program was invited, through the auspices of the Tennessee Valley Authority, to exhibit student handiwork at the World Exposition being held across the mountains in Knoxville. Ben and Paul were asked to videotape the demonstrations of crafts making by their colleagues at the fair, Laura Wyatt on the loom, Marsha Branson spinning wool, Susan Coolidge hand weaving, and so on. But what would later be recalled most vividly? Not their assigned tasks, but the brash and clever way in which they had crashed the most popular foreign exhibits. Armed with video equipment and passes that read "Tennessee Valley Authority," the pair had walked authoritatively to the front of very long lines and announced to the booth officials their readiness to videotape on behalf of the TVA. Skeptical looks were met with feigned outrage: "Weren't you informed that we were coming? This was supposed to have been taken care of!" The apprehension at the Japan exhibit arising from a "just checking" phone call to the TVA was transformed into amazement as they were graciously presented with thick press packets containing information about Japan and accorded the special guided tour for members of the mass media. They pretended to videotape throughout, never revealing that their recorder batteries had died near the beginning of the tour.

These were among the moments of senior year that would distinguish them from a background of weight-lifting classes, dating, and football practice. Finally, in May, school happenings momentous and mundane culminated in graduation. And following the ceremonies, Forrister had presented Ben and Paul with gifts.

Aware of one of Ben's Boy Scout hobbies, Don gave him a set of carved balsa wood rockets, which, when hooked to a car battery, shot high into the air and descended by an attached parachute. For Paul, there was a shiny black, 35-millimeter Nikon. When Paul, overwhelmed with surprise, protested that he could not accept such an expensive gift, Mr. Forrister assured him that he could and would.

Then began and swiftly evaporated the brief summer interlude of gatherings with family and friends, joyous celebrations of expectations met, and the sad and scary departures for sprawling college campuses where learned strangers waited with much more formidable challenges. Ben and Paul understood these few months as a time for casting off the simultaneously comforting and constricting exoskeletons of high school students in preparation for a new life phase. But this shedding left them feeling exposed and apprehensive, with only whatever reserves of knowledge and character they had managed, to that point in their young lives, to store deep inside themselves. The future was a scary blur. So, over the course of the summer, the two expended much energy in reciting the familiar particulars of their boyhood escapades and in clinging to the notion that their small hometown would always remain a sanctuary to which they could, if necessary, always return. Only in mid-August would the two graduates realize that neither of them really wanted them to leave. And that neither did their teacher.

On the Wednesday morning before their departure Forrister had surprised them with invitations to dinner at a restaurant in nearby Franklin. The dinner would be, he said, a bon voyage present to them both. His only instructions were mysterious ones: "Bring a change of clothing." Late on the following afternoon they converged onto campus where, prior to boarding Forrister's car, the standard gags about its cluttered and decrepit condition would be heard.

"Well," Ben muttered in mock disgust, "I would like to join you both but I can't fit inside this car."

But as the old Ford rumbled off toward the highway, the usual snickers from Paul dissolved into a more serious question on the topic.

"Man, why don't you get yourself a nice sports car? A red one, maybe a foreign convertible, a Saab?"

Paul had heard that Don had invested in some land in Jackson County, so he surmised that a spiffy new car would be affordable.

"Why would I want to do that? Bad investment. They depreciate instantly. I'd rather own some acreage that increases in value. Anyway, if I got a convertible, what would I do with Cavalry?"

Paul hesitated at this response, but Ben understood instantly that the mention of Don's beloved pet signaled an end to the discussion.

So he interjected a gratuitous joke about the 200,000 miles on the odometer.

But Paul thought only about how the mild May breeze would serve as a welcome freshener for the stale bubble of air in which they were encased.

Then, several miles after making the turn south onto Highway 64, the car veered suddenly onto the dirt road that climbed to the highest peak between the towns of Dillsboro and Franklin. Ben shot Paul a quizzical glance. Paul turned to look at Don. Don stared straight ahead for a moment and then pushed the brake pedal to the floor. Then he reached onto the back seat to dislodge two paper bags from between the stacks of free books recently rescued from the Boys' Club in Cherokee. Opening the first bag, he withdrew several items: pieces of lined white paper, three pencils, some large paper clips. Then out of the larger bag came three helium-filled balloons.

"OK," he said, "here's what we're gonna do. Each of us will take a piece of paper. The first thing we will write down is what we like about the other two. One thing I like about Ben is this, one thing I like about Paul is this. Next, each of us will write down what we don't like about the other two."

"I have to write something about Ben?" Paul looked quizzically at Ben as he asked Don the question.

"About me too. But wait, the third thing you need to write down is what you will change about yourself in the next 3 months."

"Change? What kind of change are you talking about?" asked Ben.

This quintessentially Forristeresque occasion was too close to—he didn't know what exactly—something that Andy Warhol or maybe Salvador Dalí would stage. Gags should not resemble this sort of surreal and excruciatingly personal event. This kind of weird episode stirred thoughts of that initial freshman reluctance to study art with Forrister. But Ben knew he was stuck here, with little choice but to play along.

Paul was more willing to participate. His only uncomfortable encounters with Don were when his free-thinking teacher had unintentionally challenged his strong religious convictions. He recalled the time that Forrister brought to class the *I Ching*, the Chinese book of wisdom. Students would ask questions and Don would interpret the answers. Or more recently, the day at Forrister's house in which Don had introduced Paul and Paul's girlfriend Laura to tarot cards. On each of these occasions Paul had felt conflicted: As an entertainer he was fascinated by the possibilities in these exotic rituals, but as a fundamentalist Christian he was concerned that these were not God-pleasing activities. To him, they lay in a spiritual gray zone, not in the blackest realms of Satanic witchcraft, but nevertheless invoking pagan sources for the light of knowledge that rightly belonged only to his Divinity. Don had of course honored his expressed wishes to refrain from such activities in his presence in the future. And this episode on the hill contained no sacrilegious offense. In fact, Paul had begun to enjoy it greatly.

"How do you plan to change your lives for the better as you head off to college?" Don elaborated upon his third item.

"Ha! I plan to enter a phase of complete debauchery!" said Ben.

"Well, write that down, then." Don ignored the poorly stifled cackles from both of them. "Then write down your name, address, and phone number. Each of us will wrap our piece of paper in plastic, tie it to a balloon, and send it off, and whoever finds it will be able to contact that person. And here's the deal. The other two will have to treat whoever gets their paper back first to anything they want—within reason, of course."

"Like what?"

"Oh, I don't know. Some fun event maybe. A trip to Six Flags. Or a piece of furniture from Pier 1."

This final clause in the rules suddenly added what felt like an agreeable element of a high-stakes gamble.

Ben, especially, was grateful, for now the exercise seemed lifted out of the realm of effete experiences-for-their-own-sake and attached to a purpose that somehow made it more manly and respectable.

"But listen, we also have to agree that, even if no one gets their balloon back after 3 months, we will each write to the others and tell them what we wrote down."

Why? Paul wondered silently. Maybe this is an attempt to ensure that we keep in touch. But is there really a need for that? Don would never leave Swain High, and Bryson City will always be our real hometown. But as he tied the paper to his balloon, carrying his temporarily private compliments and complaints, he began to imagine a future. In less than 2 weeks Ben would be matriculating at Appalachian State College, and he would be attending Guilford College in Greensboro. For the next 4 years they would rarely visit home. And few college graduates returned to live in Bryson City. Both of them seemed destined for a worldly success that would render them unaffordable to their little hometown. A desire for prosperity would see to it that they lived . . . who knew how far away?

In that moment of prescience, Paul could comprehend the vulnerability of the bonds of their friendship to the corrosive effects of time and distance. And more than that, he saw that Don's invention of this interlude on this mountain arose from a perfectly natural impulse to postpone the onset of the rusting. Maybe Don wanted to prolong—just a little—the time for teaching them his life lessons, the time in which the warmth of their proximity might still prevail over cold economics.

And warm air was indeed ascending gently from the valley to the west, lifting their balloons skyward.

Ben, suddenly ravenous for food, returned immediately to the car, failing to sense any great moment in the occasion or any point in dawdling.

Paul, however, followed the drifting specks of color for a few seconds longer. The exercise now felt like a magic trick. Forrister, master wizard of occasions, had made a small moment appear simultaneously whimsical and profound. Still, his own magic was even better. Abracadabra! His imagination had enabled him to see the present event from a point in the future, imbuing it with the nostalgic luster of a distant memory.

The food at the China House that night passed for exotic fare—water chestnuts, bok choy, soy sauce, slivers of pork, cashew nuts, mountains of rice, and an awesome dessert of vanilla ice cream with coconut shavings. Then, as the banter began to wane, Forrister announced the commencement of the evening's next phase.

The car was pointed toward the northeast and off they went. They drove, not over or beside, but necessarily *through* the little creek that led to Forrister's place, and

Paul recalled driving this route earlier that year to perform his magic act at Sarah's birthday party, and his amazement that even in the Appalachian mountains anyone could live in such extreme remoteness.

Nearing the house, Don suddenly asked about what kind of animal they each would want to be in their next lives. Ben replied that he would like to be an otter because they are serious and playful in equal measure. Don said that he would love to be an eagle, so that he could soar freely above the world. Paul disliked the question, mainly because his religion denied any possibility of reincarnation. He responded by saying that he would give it some thought.

Once in the living room, Don asked them to sit on the couch until he returned. He reappeared shortly with two blindfolds.

"Put these on and follow me."

Leading each of them by the hand to the porch, he told them to stand, eyes closed, facing the front of the house.

Ben received the first blow. Paul heard a gasp, then a shriek of laughter, and as he adjusted his blindfold to see out of the corner of his eye, and opened his mouth to howl in surprise, into it was injected a warm, slimy mass of dough and syrup.

The pies had plugged up every facial orifice of the two boys, who were simultaneously gasping and laughing, pulling the sticky mess from their hair and noses. Meanwhile, Forrister was laughing as hard as Forrister could laugh while expressing his appreciation to them for "allowing me

allowing him?

allowing him?

to do something that I have always wanted to do."

For Ben the meaning of this comment was open to interpretation. Maybe Don meant that he had always wanted to see if they could take a joke as well as play them?

But no time for interpretive exercises, for Don had led them to an arsenal of mushy strawberry cream pies.

To Paul they appeared to be the 99-cent variety sold at Ingel's supermarket, each a pile of fake whipped cream in a saucer of graham cracker crust. His suspicions were confirmed as one landed squarely on his mouth and chin.

Then he and Ben joined Don in flinging the pies, squishy projectiles zooming through the night air in every direction, until, smeared onto their heads, shoved down their pants, smashed onto their torsos, their bodies were coated with a sticky-sweet lather. Their howls of laughter penetrated deep into the dark thickets surrounding the homestead.

Soon Don vanished briefly to return with a garden hose that drew water from an underground spring. A fresh melee ensued over who would spray the frigid water onto whom in the chilly night air. Finally, after laughing themselves into a state of exhaustion, they changed their clothes, collapsed into the Mustang, and Don delivered Paul and Ben back to their respective homes.

Plopping into bed, Paul knew that tomorrow his parents would ask for details about the previous evening. He knew that his Mom had recently wondered aloud to Mrs. Dobson about the nature of this unusual sort of teacher–student relationship. Ben and Paul had reassured their parents, admitting that an eccentric such as Don would naturally be the subject of all sorts of unfounded gossip. Small town rumor mills are, after all, the most active kind, and Paul knew that Don took a risk in establishing friendships with some of his students, even if they were, technically speaking, his former students. He admired him for that.

Their relationship was uncommon partly because, even before graduation, it had encompassed regions of their lives that lay beyond the realm of the formal study of school subjects. But during the summer of 1982 had the line between students and teacher been erased? Had a mentor become merely an older pal, one with whom they could enjoy some harmless, fun-filled times? Not at all. Don—he who had on that particular evening designed for them, as he had many times through his classroom curriculum, an experience that transcended the ordinary flow of life—remained more than a friend. He was still Mr. Forrister, an artist-magician-teacher who could suffuse the transitory, minor articles of everyday existence—pencils, balloons, cream pies— with emotions and meaning that just might live forever in their hearts and minds.

Three weeks later, sitting in his dorm at Appalachian State, Ben opened a large manila envelope with Forrister's return address on the back.

On the same day at Guilford College, Paul received a similar package.

Upon opening his envelope, each of the freshmen withdrew a certificate with an inscription and an official wax seal at the bottom of a rectangular piece of cardboard carefully cut out of the top of a pie box. The certificate read:

PIE FIGHT

AUGUST 1982

BEN DOBSON—OTTER

DONALD FORRISTER—EAGLE

PAUL MOSELY—MAGIC

As autumn waned, it became increasingly likely that the balloons launched 3 months earlier were withered somewhere on a Carolina hillside, their secrets inside them. No prizes would be claimed in the contest Don had instigated on that breezy summer afternoon. So within days after the agreed-upon deadline, Ben and Don each received a letter from Paul keeping his promise to reveal what he had written on that mountaintop, the name of which he could no longer recall and perhaps never knew. Shortly thereafter, Don sent a similar letter to Paul and Ben. But they would wait in vain for any correspondence from Ben. He would write no such letter.

Ben could not remember ever actually making a promise to do so, and perhaps he never had.

Ben After High School

As if awaiting the arrival of the two men, the large doors into the Newark airport swung open wide upon their approach. Emerging into the cavernous building, they felt the mercifully cool air reach inside their damp clothing to chill the summer sweat. The two strode in absolute silence through the crowded terminal, one leading the other by subtle gestures toward a concourse where a jet bound for the Carolinas awaited their boarding. The tall dark-haired man in the uniform, Officer Ben Dobson, could not fail to notice the wide eyes above newspapers and magazines, people gawking at the handcuffs and leg-irons of the scruffy 20-year-old he was accompanying.

Ben imagined that the stories being hastily fabricated in the minds of the onlookers varied widely, with some no doubt implicating the shackled man in the most heinous of crimes. But two armed robberies were deeds dastardly enough to place someone outside the range of sympathy of this small-town-boy-turned-enforcer-of-the-law. His obligation, at any rate, was not to make judgments about the innocence or guilt of his traveling companion. As an absconder officer based in Charlotte, Ben took seriously his responsibility for retrieving anyone on his caseload of persons who had been captured after fleeing from a warrant of arrest by the State of North Carolina. Usually this meant driving to nearby towns and counties, but he had occasionally been required to fly to places as distant as Missouri, Michigan, and this time, New York City.

After less than a year at this job Ben was still not accustomed to the flutters of consternation caused by the appearance of a shackled man in an airport. He generally tried to evoke an air of normalcy by staring straight ahead, even as he covertly monitored the movements of the alleged felon beside him. On this particular occasion, however, a certain propensity—deeply entrenched, if usually under control in situations such as this—asserted itself. This was a disposition to focus on things around him of aesthetic interest. What attracted Ben's attention today as they neared the gate to their plane was an elderly woman sitting in a chair near a large window. He was drawn to the contrasts of the genuine creases in her leathery face and her sleekly synthetic surroundings. He had long shared with his high school art teacher a fascination with the character traits that seemed etched into the physical beings of the elderly. Forrister had been especially interested in Ben's grandparents, whose community near Fontana Lake had been flooded by the TVA in the building of a dam, and this old woman in the airport reminded Ben of a friend of his grandmother's named Thelma Proctor. He recalled the occasion upon which Don Forrister had escorted several students into the hills a few miles from campus to a large house where the members of the Proctor family were making molasses. Ben's sensitive photo of Mrs. Proctor smiling enigmatically as she worked, her facial features emitting contrasting waves of joy and sorrow, had later been selected for a competition.

He now sensed an analogous mystery in this woman's ancient eyes that followed the two of them as they passed directly in front of her. The cast of the afternoon light on her textured face seemed to divide it, Janus-like, into two halves of a withered oval, one side suggesting decades of severe devotion to duty and obligation, and the other evoking an opposing sense of lighthearted, almost childlike, playfulness.

Like an otter, he thought, equal measures of gravity and frolick. Ben's momentary hesitation was imperceptible to those observing him. His impulse— instantly dismissed, of course—was to abandon his youthful suspect, to stride over to the tourist sitting beside the old woman, to ask politely to borrow his 35-millimeter, and to indulge his photographer's eye.

Ben had not engaged in serious photography for several years. But even though unconsummated for too long, his attraction to the world's offerings of light and texture and form and color would sometimes, as on this occasion, be stirred from its dormant state. Ben was still a connoisseur of those qualities even if he had become celibate as an artist. And even the connoisseurship, a vestige from his days as a youngster when an aesthetic playfulness had somehow managed to coexist with his proclivities toward orderliness and conventionality, even that was gradually diminishing. For the nature of his job, indeed, the culture of his profession, had served to reinforce those latter proclivities at the expense of opposite ones. The playful imagination, a dangerous distraction in his line of work, must itself be shackled.

But now, suddenly self-conscious, he wondered whether the afternoon light through the glass shone on him as well as the woman, shone all the way down, revealing to an observant onlooker the subdued member of the pair of forces that had been confined to the deep recesses of his own character. Before disappearing into the tunnel to the plane Ben wondered how the old woman had managed to maintain the truce for all those years.

For Ben, the battle was nearly over by the time he graduated from college. In his first year of studies at Appalachian State he took the core coursework that allows freshmen to defer the decision about a major area of study and therefore of a lifelong professional identity. At least since his junior year in high school he had, in his imagination, donned various majors—geology, marine biology, business administration, as well as photography—to test their fit. At college the search intensified, the possibilities falling into two camps, identifiable as the solid and the secondary, or maybe the pragmatic and the artistic. Ben understood that these categories reflected two major components of his own persona. Geology and archeology appealed to the outdoorsy Ben, the little child who detested clean hands, the science student in love with Nature. But there was also the aesthete, the watercolorist Benjamin, with his undeniable talent for photography, his joy at finding in the textures of an old barn or the colors in a rock or the shape of a tree the means for expressing his innermost thoughts and feelings. Mr. Forrister's Ben.

But certain realities of photography as a profession would ultimately relegate it to a second tier of candidates. Decade after decade of wedding suits and dresses? A lifetime of families of four posing stiffly to impress posterity? He didn't think so. Even press photography did not approach Ben's notion of a desirable vocation.

His sophomore year would require a choice, and it—criminal justice—was more of a surprise to Ben than to some family members who had observed him throughout his boyhood. Ben's biological father, then an 18-year veteran of the Michigan State Police, had been separated from his family since Ben was 7. But Officer Dobson had remained in contact through biannual visits to Ben's paternal grandmother in Bryson City. Some vague, indefinable qualities of his father (in the authoritative aura of a natural dad?), abetted by other qualities in the exciting stories he told, aroused Ben's admiration and curiosity about police work. So, long after his father had returned north, he would visit the local sheriff's office or hang around the courthouse for hours watching justice being meted out. Years later, the more coursework he took, the more natural his choice of major felt to him. Still, photography remained a "fallback" possibility. Even without college coursework, his high school training had given him the basics needed for newspaper photography. If he ever had to use them. Forrister had expressed no disappointment over Ben's choice of career path: His reputation for not asking unsolicited questions about the choices of his former students thus remained unsullied.

But even after his final career decision Ben, like many of Forrister's other former students, would occasionally revisit Don's art classrooms. Bringing film for developing, he would advise Forrister's current students on darkroom techniques. He knew that Forrister enjoyed that, and he himself enjoyed how a return visit by a former football star became a small-town event. And while in town Ben would chat with his former teacher about the personal and academic concerns of college life.

After 5 years at Appalachian State, Ben graduated with an eye toward the North Carolina Highway Patrol. But all positions were filled and, disappointed, Ben moved to Asheville. There he bounced from one job to another, from sales work with a financial leasing corporation to inspector for Orkin Pest Control, to work with a finance company in Spartanburg, South Carolina, an hour down the interstate from Asheville. Ben remained in this precareer limbo until November, 1989, when he landed a position as parole officer. A few years later he became an absconder officer with the state of North Carolina, collecting mainly small-time thugs from here and there.

In 1991 Ben fell in love with a fellow parole officer. He married Karen Goodlad on February 15, 1992. On June 29 of the same year Ben also married the job of federal probation officer. To Ben, for Ben, both bride and career were ideal and permanent. On almost any evening the couple, a dog named Snacker, and photographs of their lives before, during, and after their wedding could be found in an ordinary house somewhere in the sprawling suburbs east of Charlotte.

Paul After High School

Meanwhile, in Asheville, 120 miles to the west of the Dobson residence, on one of those same evenings, Paul Mosely was performing a magic trick to a small audience. Looking into the mystery of his daughter Eileen's eyes, Paul surmised that she would be presented with a wild array of possibilities in her lifetime. While these possibilities might include the seeds of her empowerment, their dazzling richness might also be a source of puzzlement, or even fear, or may serve to blur the differences between the righteous and dishonorable choices to be made. Someone must be there to help her choose wisely. Someone to help her see the importance of honoring the inclinations (maybe already dormant in every beloved cell of her tiny body) that made her who she was. Someone with practice at doing just that: *He* would be there for her. But was the adoring father projecting the plot of his own life story onto hers? Since high school graduation, a significant part of that story indeed involved his listening to outside voices—of the Holy Spirit, and second, of Don Forrister—urging him to listen to his inside voice.

The major decisions in Paul's life had occurred later than for Ben. His college years were defined not by a wrenching choice of major but by travel opportunities. Sophomore year: a semester of study in Germany, exploring Europe. Junior year: on to Brazil. Senior year: several weeks in China in his senior year as a representative of Friendship Force, a cultural exchange program established to promote world peace. And then, immediately upon graduation, Paul traveled with his sister to New Zealand and Australia.

Paul declared a television production major in his junior year. TV production seemed a logical extension of the video making for which he had demonstrated a knack in Forrister's class. Furthermore, he thought he could fold his talent for magic into semieducational children's shows, thereby pursuing his avocation under the guise of a "real job." For his senior thesis, he had produced three episodes of Magic Magazine, an afternoon children's show on a local access station. And during his sojourn "down under," Paul had attracted sufficient attention "busking," a form of street-performance magic, to be invited for a brief stint on a Melbourne TV show.

Home from the diversions of travel, the graduate faced an unanticipated quandary. Although Paul had sent out resumes naively hoping to be offered his own television show, he was offered instead a position as a cameraman, a job he had already tackled as a summer intern, twice, at two different stations. He considered the work uninteresting and the offer demeaning. He turned it down. So now what kind of career? Continuing his occasional magic gigs, he managed to postpone an answer.

But as the months skated by, the question reasserted itself. How to achieve professional respectability without sacrificing job fulfillment? The former was important to him. Paul would look at his stepfather and see a doctor, look at his mom and see a real estate agent and nurse. His three siblings and two stepsisters? Another real estate agent, a salesperson, an X-ray technician, a paralegal, and so on, all adults in steady, conventional jobs. They, in turn, looked at him and saw—what? Someone who was squandering 4 years of a private college education for permanent adolescence? He imagined the questions his mother was fending off ("So what does your other son do, Mrs. Carlyle? Oh, and how old is he now?") and the patronizing consolations she was enduring ("Well, I wouldn't worry. I'm sure he'll grow out of that soon and get a real job.").

The desire for approval by his family (and the rest of the world) nagged at him. Ironically, that same need to be admired and loved fueled his fondness for staging magic shows, a need assuaged, as for thespians throughout the ages, through applause from crowds of strangers. At this critical juncture in his life, Paul received what he considered to be Don Forrister's greatest gift to him—the wisdom required for resolving this paradox.

"Impress yourself first, and that will impress others."

Forrister's message was conveyed partly through the attributes visible in his actions, wordlessly in decisions major and minor: Don's choice of clothes, car, home site, lifestyle, and so on. "Take me or leave me, but this is who I am." This, thought Paul, is what Forrister said silently to the world-at-large about himself. But Don's message was also transmitted through a Socratic kind of counseling (conversations, really, wherein Paul sought advice from an older friend) wherein questions were artfully arranged to guide Paul to wise conclusions.

One weekend in Paul's senior year Forrister had invited him for dinner at his home. After dessert Don's questions to Paul had included these: How are you going to use your television production major? Do you really want to do a kids' show? Do you really want to be something other than a magician? What if you could make as good a living doing magic? Then what is stopping you? What would make you feel that your parents had accepted you? And so on.

Paul's conclusions were twofold: first, that Don's sense of inner security had led him to a full and happy life, and second, that inner peace would not be derived from a career that was alien to Paul's sense of who he was. He decided not to enter any field primarily to please others. He would satisfy himself first, and incidentally, other people. His dilemma would be resolved, he realized, when success in a career as a professional magician incidentally pleased his family as well. So Paul began to refer to himself as a professional magician, but also began to develop a business around his vocational choice.

Meanwhile, affairs of the heart took center stage in his life. Paul had married Laura Marshall after 4 years of courtship. But a tumor had been growing beneath Laura's skull even as she and her fiancé were planning the events expected to yield wonderful memories for the coming decades. Stingy fate would afford the newlyweds only 60 days between wedding and diagnosis, 2 blissful months of illusions of a shared future. Now images of a white wedding dress and a honeymoon in the Canadian Rockies, too young to have acquired the protective carapace of memory, were crushed in the ordeals of brain surgery, radiation treatment, and chemotherapy.

Love had insinuated itself slowly into Paul but had grown its shoots down deep. The pain of their sudden uprooting was nearly unbearable. As Laura's condition deteriorated, she moved to hospice care in her family home in Washington, D.C., leaving Paul to confront his agony alone for hours at a time along Interstate 81. For nearly 5 months, a few days of work in Asheville were followed by a few days in Washington, followed by a few days in Asheville. During that time, the magician-husband's talents for artful concealment were tested as never before, as for the sake of his beloved, he hid his pain behind a mask.

On those 8-hour drives, Paul listened to tapes by motivational speakers on spiritual growth and surviving life's tragedies. And his hunger to make sense of seemingly senseless tragedy moved him closer to Jesus Christ. While full of sorrow and grief, he was able to find rest and peace in the darkest of times by understanding that God was in control. He had found his faith as a 9-year-old at the death of his father. The adult Paul believed that God was once again growing him in ways that would slowly reveal themselves. And Paul had shared with Don this conviction, hoping to challenge him toward faith in Christ and the power of the Holy Spirit.

After Laura's death, time would move him beyond his grief to the larger picture of his life that was unfolding. For nearly a year, Paul used his work as a diversion, traveling to trade shows in places as far-flung as Battle Creek and Phoenix. Paul would tailor his act to each company's products, selling, for example, Revco Scientific's carbon dioxide incubators with card tricks or Square D's push button electric switches with magic visual aids, patter, and sleight of hand. His performances were minicommercials that were extensions of the "Peak Cola" video project in Forrister's class, his introduction to the rudiments of delivering product and service information.

Then Paul met someone who shared his faith and priorities in life: He married Sharon McCaulliff. Sharon soon convinced Paul to open a small business in Asheville, a magic and costume shop. A year later the business had expanded, with four times the space, including room for a gift shop. Soon there were a host of subcontracted performers and a full-time salesman-magician to demonstrate an array of books, videos, and props. Later the business continued to grow, even adding a mail order catalogue.

Don Forrister had been right. In pursuing his dream, Paul had prospered. His shop was a success and his reputation grew. Indeed, what appeared to be a shop that enabled Paul to ply his trade as a magician was in reality a kind of prop for a tricky transformation. He had entered this converted house appearing to the world like an adult with arrested development. A year later he had emerged transmogrified into a respectable businessman.

He had also become thrice a father. Eileen, Sharon's daughter from a previous marriage was seven when Paul and Sharon married in 1992. In 1993, Priscilla was born; in 1994, Paul adopted Eileen; and in 1995, Catherine. Three girls. He was determined to set a good example for them all.

A Downhill Slope

Paul Mosely and Ben Dobson had survived bachelorhood as roommates for one year in that awkward period between college and matri-
mony, and then were pulled to different cities. In January, 1994, they
had not seen each other in over a year.

Paul was not certain whether Ben was still an absconder officer,   although Ben had heard about Paul's business success.

Paul believed that he had been largely correct about the corrosive
effects of time on friendship, but he was less certain about the enduring
consequences of teaching. For while he had also not seen Forrister for a
year, Paul believed that later chapters in his life narrative would indeed
evidence Forrister's impress. As he saw it, Don had given him many
things, especially the courage to choose a career that he loved.

And Ben agreed that Don had given him a special way to see the world, even
if he perceived it less acutely these days than he had in high school.

But high school buddies Ben and Paul now thought of each other
only occasionally, mainly when sharing with family members their
school-era memorabilia.

Sharon had laughed at Paul's piece of a pie box still mounted on their
bedroom wall. And a picture of a ski outing.

And, one evening, early in their marriage, while sorting through a stack of old
photographs, Karen had pried from Ben the story of that same outing.

But because even collective memories, like distant friendships, de-
cay slowly over the years, any version of what really happened on that
January day in 1983 is highly suspect—especially one in which a winter outing is portrayed as the apogee in a story of companionship between a teacher and two of his favorite students.

Was the role reversal moving their relationship inexorably down a
slope? In that time in the snow, their thoughts crowded around the
present moment, they could not see that possibility. Bedazzled by the
whiteness of that Carolina January, they found it quite impossible to
recognize what had once been glimpsed on a clear evening in the previous summer—that the appearances of their former teacher as a supporting character in their lives would become ever more sporadic. Now
they were blinded to the beginnings of a long good-bye.

So it must have been luck and not prescience that prompted Paul, fresh off the ski lift, to hail down a stranger, beckon him over, hand him his cherished Nikkon, and request a photo of the three comrades-in-sporting-gear, arms locked, mugging, grinning, skis and poles protruding in every direction.

Almost immediately, Paul understood that it was not the kind of picture that Ben would have taken. In those days, Ben would certainly have insisted upon more attention to composition and lighting.

And Ben knew that it was not the kind of picture that Paul would have taken. Even Paul had learned by then to value the spontaneous over the obviously posed.

And both knew that under no circumstances was it the kind of picture that Don would have taken. For a host of reasons, Don would probably have preferred no picture at all. But one was taken, more a snapshot than a photograph, the single souvenir of an afternoon spent cavorting together high on Sugar Mountain.

Years later, asked to produce a copy of that photo for a book as hard evidence of that outing, neither Ben nor Paul could find one.

THE "REAL ARTIST IN THE FAMILY"

I finally met Keith, the last of the four Robinson brothers, in a large warehouse-turned-residence somewhere near the Jimmy Carter Boulevard in Atlanta, Georgia. The building had been divided into one huge room and several smaller ones. The large room was furnished with funky period pieces and paintings that suggested taste more than affluence. Tall, angular, handsome, Keith introduced me to Marshall, his roommate, and then told his entire life story, barely pausing for breath. Here it is.

My first interest in the arts was as early as 5 or 6 years old. I can remember that my mother made all of the clothes for the whole family, and patterns were always lying about and I asked her once to draw one of the ladies off one of the patterns so that I could copy her drawing, and that was my first memory of drawing. Then when I started grammar school I drew a lot, mostly on my own. Looking back on some things that my mother kept I see that they were pretty darn good, I mean for a 6-year-old to understand surfaces, the way a face is round, trying to create light and shadow, using colored pencils.

I won my first art contest when I was 7, and things progressed from there. It was a drawing of an adult horse and a colt, just the neck and the head, and it was displayed in Cherokee—I have no idea why Cherokee—and I got a ribbon and the whole nine yards.

That was right after we had moved from Washington, D.C., where there were lots of entertainment available—movies, plays, and shows—to a place with very little of that kind of thing. It was the first time we had ever seen the mountains. Everything seemed so green, and there was so much to discover. We lived near a river and would explore by walking through the woods, climbing the mountains, always finding new things. I remember digging up wildflowers and replanting them in the yard. And it was then that I started collecting things. I collected everything from pieces of wood and pretty rocks to bottles from an old dump.

I would make little sculptures with pieces of these things, gluing them together, or painting the rocks and incorporating them into pieces of wood or whatever I could find. A paint-by-number phase went quickly because I was too impatient to wait for things to dry before moving on to the next color. So my parents bought me oils and canvass. But oils also dried slowly. So I went through all the different media, acrylics, oils, and watercolors, by the time I was 12.

I did most of this outside of school. There were no art classes at Whittier Elementary, but in some grades there was an art period. We never had a special art teacher, so we did only things like construction paper art, especially around the holidays. The teacher would create a prototype for us to copy—there was a lot of that, but no formal art training, no one to push me to do anything artistically in elementary school. The first person to do that would be Don Forrister.

I first met Don at the Job Corps office when I was 8 or 9. Don was the crafts instructor and he showed me things I'd never seen before, like pouring liquid into a mold and unmolding this thing that turned out to be an ashtray. Then glazing it and firing it and coming up with a beautiful finished product. And I remember taking out the slip, as it was called, that would get too hard to be poured into a mold, then working it as you would work clay, and Don didn't mind me doing that. Maybe because I was a son of the director, I don't know, but he allowed me to do to whatever I wanted. I went there often, sometimes every night, to Don's class, until the age of 16.

Then it was exciting as a freshman just running into Don Forrister in the halls every once in a while. It was difficult to treat him other than I had for 8 years, especially difficult to call him Mr. Forrister, but since the other students did, I felt it was important for the sake of showing him respect. But during freshman year I got involved in extracurricular activities—especially music—and so I could no longer see him every night.

Then as a sophomore I was able to take his class. In Art I class every student was given individual attention even as the whole class worked on the same project at the same time. But maybe because I had a history with him I was given the special opportunity of going a little further—once again, not being constrained creatively. That was nice.

First-year projects were very basic, of course. He gave us a basic knowledge of drawing and painting, although I don't remember painting at all very much, first year. We did projects, making and creating things, working in many disciplines from weaving to macramé. Most of our materials were either given to Don or things he found for very little money, like the yarns for weaving that came from an abandoned warehouse. He probably wouldn't like me saying this, but he climbed through the windows of this place where there were huge boxes of yarn just rotting and abandoned, so he just took it for his students. He also established relationships with one of the few factories in town, the jeans factory, where Don would get boxes of remnants of fabric or batting.

I remember the soft sculpture project. A lot of people were doing small things, but my piece was a really huge wall hanging, sort of flashy, if you will. The background was metallic gold and it was a peacock that was jeweled and sequined, with real peacock feathers for the tail. Then the whole thing was sculpted, it had texture and was really thick in places. I pierced the fabric through the batting and created these designs. It had embroidery on it. It was an elaborate monstrosity, but just one example of taking something that Don suggested, soft sculpture, to make my interpretation of it. And about that time our parents added onto the house a huge bedroom for the four of us, with Marcus and Derek on the smaller side, and Roderick and me the larger side. And over the years all of this work would come home with us and decorate our walls, like Roderick's batiks and my huge peacock soft sculpture.

Anyway, I have come to realize that we were not only learning about various media. I think we were also learning self-discipline. I believe Don put some thought into this. He believed that the line between creativity and discipline is very important. Can you see how having to learn how to create certain knots using twine or string and incorporating them into something you were making is a discipline thing? Yes, because you have to also use your mind as well as your hands.

Anyway, that was probably in my 2nd year with Don, my junior year. I remember winning contests in my junior year, mostly local stuff, or maybe regional. Every time I entered a contest I always won first place. Never anything else but first place. Unless I entered three submissions. Then I would win the top three places. We made jokes about it. I was in the newspaper every week. And Roderick was an excellent athlete, so between the two of us there were times when we were both in the newspaper for weeks. It was really funny. My father would open the paper and say, "Well, let's see who's in the paper today." I was also really involved in band and also academics. If I wasn't in the newspaper for winning some band award, or for winning some art award, I was in the newspaper for winning some academic award. Then I was the valedictorian of the senior class.

But only after a scandal erupted.

Well, you see, at Swain County High School they had what were called "marshals." The students with the highest grade point average in each of the classes—freshman, sophomore, junior classes—would serve as marshals at the seniors' graduation. That meant you wore a banner across your chest that said "marshal" and you were, like, one of the escorts for the class as they came down the aisles. I was a marshal my freshman year, I was a marshal my sophomore year, I was Chief Marshal my junior year. Meaning I had the highest grade point average in the class. So senior year I just knew I was going to be valedictorian. Well, without mentioning any names, there was a student in my class whose father was also a teacher at the school and whose uncle was the vice principal and whose other uncle was another teacher in the school, and so it was a very well connected family in the school. What they didn't realize was that my father was also a very powerful and important man and he had a very strong relationship with the superintendent of schools. Then at the end of the third semester the announcement came out that this person had been chosen valedictorian and that I was salutatorian. Well, I knew that, as my grandfather would say, "something in the milk is not clean."

I happened to know that this other person had dropped a course after the deadline and so should have received a WF, a withdrawal failure, and she did not. The whole thing was apparently erased from her record. When I got home that evening, my mother asked, "What's the matter?" I said, "Well, I'm the salutatorian." And my mother was, like, "something is not right." She called my father who was away on business and he said "Something is not right." So my father called the superintendent the next morning and told him that "if this business is not straightened out by the end of the day, I will be back on the next plane back to North Carolina to take care of it myself."

So I was called to the office that day and what was said was that a mistake was made and that they were very sorry, that I was the true valedictorian and this other person was salutatorian. You know, when you're a Black person in an all-White school system, you begin to be able to read things on people's faces. They don't have to say a word, but you can read it on their faces. And that whole room of faces all had a look that told me they were very displeased with what they were having to do, even if it was right. They were having to award me the status of valedictorian because I had accomplished a lot of firsts when there had been very few, maybe one or two, Black students before us ever, in the whole school system. And they had come to school and gone home and were never involved in any extracurricular activities. So I think that they just "had a craw-full," if you understand that expression. They had enough of Roderick and me in the paper every week, winning every award possible, winning everything associated with the school, and this was the coup de grace. "Not only has he won the Governor's Award for this and this award for that, but he is the president of the National Honor Society, the drum major of the band." The only Black person in the band is the drum major? I think they just had enough.

That was really the only time I felt discrimination at Swain County, but there was this place called Robbinsville where the sports teams would play ball. Because I was the drum major the band did not go to Robbinsville. The band director thought it was in my best interest and in the best interest of the band not to go. Because once I was booed. Booed by the fans because I was Black. So forget about returning to Robbinsville.

But I only told that valedictorian story to Don Forrister recently, in the last 2 years. He was shaken to the ground. He said to me, "I'm glad you didn't tell me that then. I'm glad that I didn't know anything about that back then." Because he had always had a good relationship with the other teachers that were involved, had to interact with them daily. Don is not the kind of person to remain silent. He would have had to say something and it would not have been good and may have cost him his job.

Don has real integrity. That's why Carolyn Wilson and I decided to dedicate the yearbook to him. All the past yearbooks were dedicated to coaches and to a math or science teacher, but never ever had the yearbook been dedicated to an art teacher. I said, "Well, I think we should dedicate the yearbook to Don Forrister," and everyone on the yearbook staff except for 2 people out of 12 or 14 had had Don Forrister and they all agreed.

And Carolyn and I were voted most talented in art. I don't know if she mentioned this to you in her interviews, but I had a mad crush on Carolyn Wilson and she knew it and it was bad because I "fancied" myself in love with her. I use those words because those are the words she wrote in my yearbook—that she "fancied" herself in love with me. I wanted to take her to the prom, but that was T.A.B.O.O.! Serious business! I asked her to the prom and she said she'd have to ask her parents and they said, "Absolutely not and that's that!" So we both went without dates, and I brought her a corsage and we were at the prom together.

Now, the year before—my junior year—I started thinking about college. Don asked me what I wanted to major in. I didn't know what I wanted to do with my life yet, although I knew that I wanted to incorporate art into whatever it was. But I had this fear that if I studied art in college and went on to become a fine artist that I would be poor, and I knew there were things that I wanted and places I wanted to see and that I needed money for that. My father suggested landscape architecture as a practical compromise. We had a friend in Washington who was a landscape architect and he sent me some information about landscape architecture, a list of accredited schools in the field, blah, blah, blah. I decided on the University of Georgia which has a highly rated program. I applied, was accepted, and, boom! I moved.

I took no studio art courses in college. None. I had art history, history of landscape design and the work was a lot more structured than in a painting or drawing course. But I did get to use what I learned in high school. How? Well, we were required in college to do illustrative plans, with a site plan, elevations, and then perspectives. I learned perspectives the correct way, by choosing and plotting points, and so on. But in designing things like gardens, in order to convey the essence of how the garden would feel, I always fudged. My perspectives were always drawings that were rendered. By choosing a couple of points and making the main architectural elements in those drawings work with those points, I was fudging because I knew how to draw, understood the placement of things and so could make it look perfect, even though it wasn't. The way the eye perceived it, it was correct, but using the ruler, it was not. That was because of the knowledge I had acquired in high school. And I was strong in the rendering aspect, when we had to color those drawings, make them beautiful. I used colored pencils, pastels, and watercolors in high school and I was very proficient in all of those, so my renderings were photographic, very beautiful.

I attribute all of that to Don Forrister. I'll simply say that I had never picked up a colored pencil before his classes. If he had not exposed me to those things in high school, I would never have known that I had a natural talent. It was because Don would buy me things with his own money. He bought me a set of Prisma pencils costing over a hundred dollars. The body of work that I created in high school was all in colored pencil and chalk. My work was like photo-realism. Don would send me home with slides and a projector, and I would project the slides onto my wall. Using the projected image and my tools I would make the pictures of apples in baskets look real. Don had taught me how to use the blending tools to blend the colored pencil so that there are no edges, and by using the natural oils in your fingers to smudge the colored pencil until it was smooth. The actual surface of the papers I was using for my drawings was smooth, and so I got a very slick finish. All these things I would have never known if Don had not taught them to me.

And they translated easily to my work in college. There I turned out a really beautiful body of work. And then, interestingly, my exit thesis, which was part written and part visual, tied my college and high school work together.

My college experience was just as rich as my high school experience. Mainly because I had the wonderful opportunity to study in Europe in a study abroad program. I was exposed to a whole new world, seeing things I had only heard about in Don's classes. Like the color of the sky in Tuscany. Have you ever seen the color of the sky in Tuscany? I went to Paris and the Louvre. Later in North Carolina Don wanted to hear everything.

"What did you see?" he asked.

"I saw everything," I said.

Then I applied for an internship. My college teachers saw my potential and thought I might be awarded an internship with this company called CORT, the number one landscape architecture firm in the United States. CORT, Incorporated.

And so out of thousands of entries in the United States, I was the top person chosen, and given a scholarship, actually given money. They paid my expenses when the nine others chosen had to pay their own. I went to San Francisco, to one of the largest CORT offices. We were working on EuroDisney at the time. I mean I'm still in college and I'm doing some of the illustrative site plans for EuroDisney. It was an amazing time.

I came back for my last year at Georgia in 1985 and did some catering work on the side. But through the internship I got a job with CORT as soon as I graduated. I worked for CORT here in Atlanta in 1986. July. August. September. October. November. Five months. And then I resigned.

Why did I resign? Because I hated it. In college I got to design and draw, to work on important projects, but when I got out into the real world of environmental design and landscape architecture, well, it was totally different. I would go into the office in the morning, make coffee for everyone, sometimes stop to pick up a box of donuts. I would sit in on an office meeting every morning, go to my desk, take up the project I was working on, then lunch, then back to the office. Then another cup of coffee and then fall asleep at my desk for at least an hour, not purposely, but I was not being challenged and I was bored to death.

I was given menial work because I was new, just out of college. It didn't matter that I was number 1 out of 10,000 in the nation, that was blah, blah, blah. I came to realize that they gave me a position because they had sort of promised these 10 students a job with their firm upon graduation. This was exploitation. They get the cream of the crop right out of college, put them in their firms across the nation, work them to death, and don't pay them very much.

So I quit.

And went to work at a clothing store. Very soon I became the manager. It was an Italian sportswear store that I was familiar with from Europe. The owners were two guys from South America who wanted to sell their franchise and get into something else. They knew that I wanted to design clothes and they wanted to introduce a line of clothes. They asked me if I wanted to be their designer. I was, like, "Oh my god, yes!" So still working at the store I was also doing these designs. All in leather—leather jackets, leather pants, leather skirts for women, leather coats, and so on, and so on. So I came up with this body of work, these really beautiful drawings rendered in colored pencil, pulling from everything I had learned from Don, and more.

And suddenly I wasn't Keith anymore.

Who was I?

I was Gerardo. Gerardo Bacaro.

In order to break into the industry in Atlanta, I took on the persona of a clothing designer. So Gerardo created these designs that these two guys sent to a factory in South America to have patterns cut and the clothes made. But when the long-awaited designs came back they were nothing that Gerardo had created. They told me that my designs would be much too difficult to make, too expensive to market, blah, blah, blah, and so they had created these other designs down in the factory and put Gerardo Bacaro's signature on the labels. And they were expecting me to go out and market this product as my own.

I thought of what Don Forrister would do in such a situation. And so I told them that I wanted out. We had signed corporate papers and I was only 23, and I didn't know what was happening. I only knew that I was, like, "screw you!"

I continued to work at the store, which had changed hands. And then it changed again, and I was fired. For racial reasons, quite frankly. And then I was faced with unemployment.

But right then somehow this regional fashion magazine found out about me. They wanted to do a feature story on me as an up-and-coming designer in Atlanta. I was excited but had no line and no money. My mother brought me her sewing machine and I spent my last dollars on some leather, made a pattern, and for the first time in my life sewed on a sewing machine. I made a leather coat because I had to be in this photo shoot the next week for this article. They did the shoot with the coat and it was, like, "Gerardo Hits Atlanta!"

I was an instant celebrity.

Then someone called me, someone for whom I had catered a wedding in my last year in college. Tricia Coburn was her name. She had seen the article and wanted me to come to Athens to do a party for her. And when we got together she said, "Oh wow, there are lots of things you can do. I need a new outfit to wear for the party, I want you to paint some finishes, because I also do glazed finishes and stuff, I want you to paint some finishes on some walls of my house, and I will need the food for this very large party." So I made her an outfit, leather skirt and suede blouse, to wear to the party, made her earrings, made the belt, made everything. I prepared and served all the food for this party, did the finishes on the walls. And all her rich friends were just outdone.

I slept at her house and the next morning at the breakfast table she was, like, "What do you want to do with your life?"

And I started to cry. "I want to design women's clothes and I don't have any money, blah, blah, blah."

And she said, "I talked to my husband about it and we're going to back you financially."

And so we went into a partnership together, and things started rolling. At my first show here in Atlanta I displayed my line of accessories, women's belts, earrings, and stuff. A smashing success. I was written up in *WWD*. That's *Women's Wear Daily*. All of these things were suddenly coming to me.

But those two South American guys found out about my success. I had changed the name of the company from Gerardo Bacaro to something similar when I started with the Coburns. So they tried to sue me. I was 23, and they tried to sue me! But Tricia's husband was an investment banker, and the Coburns hired a lawyer. It was, like, taken care of.

After my first show I had to create 700 pieces in 6 weeks. It was like a movie. I had a little run-down apartment in downtown Atlanta. I lived there alone. I turned one of the rooms into literally a sweatshop.

I bought a commercial sewing machine, had all these skins around me, and was creating these belts and jewelry. That's what I did. I got out the first line, and at the next show I was approached by a national rep for accessories who wanted to take my line to a show in New York. I didn't think I was ready but Tricia thought I was. So we allowed this woman to take my samples with her to New York. Most of my profits from my successful show in Atlanta were used to get me to New York. She took my stuff to New York, sold not one piece in the show, but had it knocked off, I mean copied it. Took all of my ideas and mass-produced it for her own company.

Boom.

Gerardo Bacaro was no longer.

Gerardo Bacaro was dead.

He died a premature death in 1989.

So what then? I took a job at a florist here in Atlanta. I worked my way up to shop manager. Meanwhile, I had both catering and flower clients of my own. I became manager over a lot of senior employees and I was given freedoms, allowed to come in late because I had freelance clients, blah, blah, blah. So there was animosity toward me. And when I was flown to New York for this floral job, all these employees rose up against me in my absence. When I got back I was fired.

So once again I had to find work. Which I did. Temporary stuff with a catering company just to find out about how the big companies did things. And hated it because everything they did was wrong.

Then for a while I took a job at a restaurant some friends had purchased. I completely redesigned the restaurant for them, revamped the menu, all new recipes, fabulous new cuisine.

Meanwhile, my personal life was a mess. I had bought a condominium with this friend who moved away to New York and left me holding this mortgage. Meanwhile, the list goes on of things that were occurring in my life. But all of them were growing pains and stepping stones to where I am right now.

And where I am right now is in business for myself. The name of my business is Gloriosa and it is a special-events production company. My company handles every aspect of parties, large and small, from the conception of the event, to creating all of the menus, to cooking most of the food myself unless they are really large events, and then I call a couple of chefs to help out. I do the flowers, and the designs, from backdrops to props. I do the painting. I do everything.

Sometimes I create plans for clients who want to see how a party will look. I do illustrative perspectives to show them the space with people in it, the decorations hung, the floral arrangements, and what not. So then I call upon my experiences from college and once again on Don for that skill and knowledge, that high school experience in color, technique, and how to use the tools.

Don and I have continued a relationship over the years. I see him at least once a year and each time is like a wonderful homecoming. It's usually at his home with him and Sarah. We share what we have been doing and they sort of thrive on it because, as you now see, my life is constantly changing from one thing to the next. But finally I have been able to report to Don that I've settled into a business that has been in existence for 5 years. And that I would not have been able to do it without what he gave me.

Seeing him is fun, too, because Don has always got some kind of project going on. When Marshall and I were there several months ago, Don mentioned that he had found an old Coke machine that had some bottle caps inside. So he was going to do a bottle cap sculpture, and wanted me, my whole family, everyone, to start saving bottle caps.

It's the least we can do, don't you think?

THE CHIROPRACTOR

The following is an excerpt from an interview with Ardley Hanson conducted in a McDonald's Restaurant in Bryson City, North Carolina.

One day Don took four of us out of the classroom without telling us what we were going to do. He was carrying a large bag with something in it. "Where are we going? What's in the bag?" we kept asking, and typically, he didn't say a word, just "Follow me." We went to the huge baseball diamond in the back of the school. Forrister stuck a pin in the ground, just a regular small pin. Then he told two students each to reach into a bag and take a handful of the substance and throw it into the air as high as they could. The substance was flour and when the students flung it upward we watched a million particles float down slowly to the ground.

"Think of these two fields and the area within them as the universe. Each particle of flour is a star in our galaxy, and there are untold numbers of galaxies besides our own. The head of the pin is the earth. And where," he asked, "are we in Bryson City?"

We were, I guess, a tiny speck somewhere on that pinhead.

Don would never tell exactly what he meant when we did things like this. But at that point in time, I took Forrister's intended meaning to be this: It was a way of shocking us into understanding that there is so much more outside of you. "There is a whole world outside of this tiny little town. So go look at it."

And I did.

And I am still looking.

WHAT DO STUDENTS TEACH?

Traces of Students in the Life Story of a Teacher

W HAT KINDS OF lasting lessons can *teachers* learn from their *students*? Part III presents a version of one teacher's life narrative in which tables are turned. Just as Don Forrister appeared as a significant character in his former students' stories, here some of those students dwell within his. Certain familiar events are revisited, and sometimes rewritten, seen from a different angle, even an opposing slant, thus suggesting the fragility of memories.

Composed out of lengthy discussions between Forrister and myself, this section focuses on the person who is Don Forrister, revealing the origins of his artistic nature and the wellsprings of his pedagogy, even the content of his dreams. It offers a deeper understanding of the interdependencies between teacher and students, of some of the ways in which they animate each others' lives.

Although the story is cast as a biography, written in the third person, it is autobiographical insofar as it recounts an honest version of life experiences from Forrister's perspective.

THE DREAM

Three-year-old Donald Forrister had a strange dream. In it, a cloudy substance whirled before him like the closing aperture of a camera lens, in a tightening circle, seeming to refuse the panicky child both light and air, threatening to close him off from his life. But at the very moment of his imagined asphyxiation the dream abruptly shifted, now resembling a pleasant out-of-body experience. Looking down from above, the child saw himself as a man dressed in a white toga, and carrying a tray up a long stairway to a princess or queen. A Lady of Power. But, before the man could reach the top of the stairs, the billowing cloud reappeared, obscuring his view and waking him.

The dream reoccurred often, and the young Donald would often resist sleep out of fear of its return. But over the years, its story slowly progressed until, in later versions, the clouds parted, revealing a white

Grecian temple that he was barred from entering. And the Lady remained invisible.

Then on a breezy day in March 1995, at the age of 47, Forrister decided to drive to a high point on the Blue Ridge Parkway to fly a homemade kite. On its tail Don had tied some paper strips upon which he had scribbled observations about his friends, messages he intended, in this odd fashion, to commit to Nature. The kite flew ever higher, bouncing in the wind like a white ball over song lyrics on a movie screen, until some quickly blackening clouds obscured it entirely. And before Don could release the kite, it broke away from his hands with astounding force. He would later only recall rising from the ground after an indeterminate amount of time.

The event affected Don in many ways. He was suddenly in possession of an intense energy that prompted him to write lengthy letters to nearly everyone he knew. In his classroom he would sometimes feel an overwhelming exhilaration, followed suddenly by a debilitating fatigue. And a new version of the dream appeared.

Now Don was able to move into the temple, gliding toward the inner chambers of the Lady. At first she was obscured by a series of screens—thin, pliable meshes of copper, silver, and gold. Slowly, however, each layer of mesh disappeared, until her face became fully visible. It was the most beautiful face he had ever seen, composed of tiny multicolored dots of light, like the iridescent points on the surface of a bubble.

Then she spoke to him, her words presenting a strange request. It was time, she said, that he trim his enormous collection of beautiful and interesting objects of man and nature. The accumulation of items had become cumbersome, no longer serving as resources for artistic, life-enhancing projects. Let some of those items go, and a weight would be lifted from him.

Upon awakening, Don felt a steady energy return, and he set about honoring the request.

GROWING UP AS AN ARTIST

Don had been collecting natural objects even before he began to dream. At the age of 3 he was living with his family in Carnover, a small town near Raleigh, North Carolina. He already loved the outdoors for its things of beauty and its open space. When had that love affair begun?

Since his birth he had lived in small houses with his mother and two older siblings, and occasionally his father. Each house seemed noisy and crowded to Don, and his family overbearing, with much harassment by his older brother and sister. He sought asylum in private, protected places—the woods. The forests were adorned with amazing things to be gradually discovered in quietude and isolation. There were intricately constructed bird nests, the soft blue oval eggs of robins, blades of grass with more shades of green than he could count.

He appreciated these unspoiled things in their own settings, but wanted to possess these treasures, to transport them from their natural settings to his bedroom, there to study them. The collection grew, filling every cranny of his room, until his mother imposed a moratorium on his gathering. Then Don decided to preserve these interesting objects by sketching them in their natural habitat.

This idea about drawing came from an unlikely source. His first art teacher—to use that term loosely—was his father. Harold Forrister was a millwright, someone who (his son vaguely understood) set up machinery in industrial settings. Pursuit of his trade meant traveling long distances to jobs too short in duration for relocating the entire family. So Harold would leave the other Forristers in Carnover (and later Murphy, further east) for weeks and months at a time. But during his visits home Harold, knowingly or not, contributed something permanent to the life of his second son.

Harold Forrister had produced two kinds of drawings in his life— mechanical drawings learned in trade school and sketches of horses. Don would sometimes sit beside his father and watch a pencil magically inscribe the form of a horse onto a sheet of paper. After his father left for work, Don would watch a how-to-draw program on television, on which the artist occasionally offered prizes to members of the viewing audience for the best rendering of his animal puppets. Don repeatedly entered these contests, with no luck.

Nevertheless, a proclivity had been born. At the age of 7 Don started taking pad and pencil into the woods surrounding his house, now practicing at retaining the likeness of the natural articles he would previously have relocated to his room. To be sure, he would never completely outgrow his love of collecting these items. But there were benefits in his sketching. One was that it increased the intensity with which he observed features of the woods. His concentration became like a tight beam of light that revealed subtleties in his leaves, dead insects, stones, and flowers. Once-secret hues and hidden textures began to disclose themselves to him. He would sit for hours in a green glen, admiring the formal beauty of Nature. There he felt a quiet dignity, a peacefulness, an orderliness, felt more control over his life, and over his materials. With this control and his enhanced perceptivity, Don's artistic talents grew enormously.

In school Don quickly achieved the status of Good Student, his polite comportment drawing him into the favor of his teachers. And as his elementary school years skipped away, Don remained a bit of a loner, never joining in other students' youthful conspiracies. He would remain in Murphy until high school graduation, except for a generally unpleasant 3 years in Denver, Colorado. His family had trailed after his father who had found work there in a missile factory. It was in Denver that Don first experienced art-as-school-subject.

The teacher was Mrs. Nieto, an energetic and regimented woman who unfailingly dressed in a white uniform and granny shoes. Rigidly enforcing a strict code of behavior, she offered endless lessons on marching properly down school corridors. But the otherwise literal-minded Mrs. Nieto often assigned projects of nonrepresentational art. Don, in the habit of carefully attending to discrete, observable, "real" articles, had difficulty imagining abstract formal qualities. So when the assignment was to cut a piece of linoleum into an abstract shape, Don simply copied the efforts of his classmates. Only time and practice would allow him to appreciate nonrepresentational forms in the visual arts.

There were other appealing attributes of Mrs. Nieto: Her high level of engagement was infectious, she rarely lectured, and her classroom possessed no heavy center of gravity, no teacher's desk toward which students' eyes must be constantly drawn. Instead Mrs. Nieto was possessed by a kind of centrifugal energy that propelled her outward onto the turf of her students. Roaming the classroom, she incessantly monitored the aesthetic choices of the busy students, commenting on their work, making suggestions about elements requiring additional consideration.

Later, in Murphy, high school was, like elementary school and junior high, a rather dim experience. Puberty arrived quickly and departed slowly, leaving few obvious footprints on his personal character. School was still a place in which to obey and to achieve. His grades were excellent: Adept at academic gamesmanship, he heard few complaints from teachers and parents. And he continued to draw.

Meanwhile, Don needed money for art supplies and life's other necessities, and so, beginning in the eighth grade, his summers were months of hard physical labor. For 3 summers he worked in tomato fields from 6 in the morning until 6 in the evening, trimming and tying the plants, and picking the ripe tomatoes. But what might have been drudgery to other adolescents was enjoyable for Don. He liked the feel of the hot sun on his back. He also liked the money. And he liked, as always, being alone with Nature, in a private space where he could, without interruption, enter into an increasingly elaborate fantasy world.

At 16 he moved out of his parents' home for a summer job down in the carpet factories of Dalton, Georgia. He was assigned to a windowless room with washing machines and dye beds. After an initial claustrophobia abated, Don began to enjoy the solitude of the washing room, where, undisturbed, he was free to travel through his mind to green pastures. Moreover, since Don now needed money for college, he would return to this job for 5 consecutive summers.

He knew in his senior year of high school that he would be attending Young Harris Junior College in Towns County, Georgia, not far from Dalton. He had, unprompted, entered a drawing in a contest for high school students. Shortly thereafter, Don received a call from Ezra Zellars, a well-known painter from Georgia and a Young Harris faculty member, expressing interest in Don's work.

Zellars would soon become an influence on Don. Don saw him as a "walking artist," removed from the world of clichés and conventions, someone who perceived the nearby in startlingly original ways, and expressed those unique visions in his paintings. Don was impressed, and soon believed that he too could live as a true artist. A few years later Don could imagine himself as a teacher.

For 3 months in the summer of his senior year in college, Don was an intern at the Job Corps Center at Cherokee, North Carolina. The Job Corps was a federal program for young men aged 16 to 22 in need of employment skills. Don's charge was to conduct a crafts program that included ceramics, leather crafts, drawing, and jewelry making. Don would later return to the Corps for a much longer stay, but only after his first trip to a foreign country. Through the graduate program at Western Carolina University, he had received a scholarship to study art history in Mexico.

The summer program was a mixed experience. Traveling to a variety of locations in Mexico, Don studied the fascinating ruins of ancient civilizations, but learned less about Mexican folk art than anticipated. Still, he was the recipient of two life-altering messages that summer. One came in a letter offering him a permanent position at the Job Corps. The second was a lesson delivered by an ocean breeze as he lay in his bunk on a warm Oaxacan night: He learned of the joy of being alone in a foreign land.

Traveling to distant locations had the same attributes as being remote in the woods. It offered freedom to be alone with his inner self. Abroad, he felt whole, more authentic, free to remove the mask expected by convention. Travel offered the fuller version of life previously experienced only in fantasy and forest. So peripatetic Don spent summers in the early 1970s backpacking through Europe.

TURNING OUTWARD AS A TEACHER

The sense of escape had grown even sweeter after he became a high school teacher in 1972. Now a minor sort of fame had added to the social obligations of the shy twenty-something. Everywhere in public were students, former students, families of students and former students, and school colleagues, all requiring polite chitchat in the video store or the gas station or the grocery line, all expecting his "teacher's face," all demanding "Mr. Forrister." But on his solitary ramblings on the European continent, alone amidst strangers in cafes, town plazas, and the great art museums of the Western world, he could be Don instead of "Don."

Accepting a teaching position a year after becoming a full-time instructor at the Job Corps, he decided not to quit the latter for the former. The program director, Delmar Robinson, had asked him to remain, and Don believed in the program's aims, in securing a place for art in the lives of those young men. And the artwork of the Black students was serving as a tunnel into an interesting culture. Moreover, he felt more secure with a fallback job. Art teachers were considered expendable in tight times. So, his work ethic in high gear, Don continued at the Corps, Monday through Sunday, 7 evenings a week, while teaching at Swain County High School during the day.

Of course, Don would not do absolutely anything for money. For example, he refused to pursue a masters degree simply to boost his pay, even at the prestigious Rhode Island School of Design. In the early 1970s he was offered a summer scholarship at the school. The following summer he returned, entering a masters program. But soon the coursework seemed disconnected from his high school teaching, suddenly the major focus of his life.

For this was a time of turning outward, when a portion of his indwelling and introspection was displaced by a concern for other people. Don had always considered himself to be a "good" person—"do no harm" and "live and let live" were benign beliefs at the heart of his ethical code. But the concept of goodness had acquired a more robust quality now, moving beyond slighter notions of kindness and decency.

In his early life he had prized only solitude in the woods. But now there appeared, at long last, empathy. That he was still obsessed with the personal security that emotional remoteness affords was obvious by the secluded location of his new house, his only neighbors being foxes and raccoons. Nevertheless, a more mature Don Forrister understood the selfhood of other human beings as continuous with his own. This meant, of course, that he was becoming a teacher who *cared* for his students and for this new vocation practiced on their behalf.

A sign of his growing devotion to his job was a willingness to donate hard-earned money to it. The old Swain High School was a small wooden building, its dilapidated condition bespeaking the relative poverty of the area. His small classroom was equipped only with a 12 × 4-inch carton of crayons. No paper. No pencils. No other art supplies. No school funds to buy them. To provide his students with the rudimentary materials of art, he had to purchase them with his own money.

At first he procured relatively minor items (although sometimes in sizable quantities)—watercolor paints, brushes, clay, papier mâché, wood for sculptures. In later years he would purchase major equipment, including pottery wheels and looms. Teachers everywhere, he thought, were generous creatures, coughing up pocket change to get the job done. But Don's generosity was exceptional: He was spending hundreds, and ultimately thousands of dollars, money that might have been more prudently stashed in a bank account or mutual fund. This, indeed, was another reason not to abandon the Job Corps: His second paycheck was supplying the materials for his high school art classes.

Some supplies and equipment were not purchased but collected. Don was, after all, a gatherer of beautiful objects since the age of 3, skilled at seeking out the raw materials of art. The activity of collecting was, however, now changing in character. Wrangling deals with supply store managers for materials that were aesthetically interesting but otherwise worthless was quite different from those joyous gleanings in the woods of his childhood. This was, he thought, hardly collecting at all—it was scrounging. He was on uncomfortable new terrain not for a shy person, too close to the entanglements of daily commerce, the world of the huckster, the salesman, the fund-raiser. He could take comfort only in a nobility of purpose, a sense that, with no quid pro quo involved, his integrity was not in question.

What to do with the gathered materials? The activities of teaching—planning a lesson, structuring activities, and so on—were also new to him, despite his education coursework in college. But he believed that his basic intelligence and the novel, sometimes bewildering, sense of caring would help him acquire the necessary skills. Beyond that, he relied on memories of previous teachers, especially Mrs. Nieto, whose energy he seemed to replicate naturally, as well as her disregard for territorial space in the room. He found himself delighting in critiquing his students' projects, but through a gentler form of questioning designed to provoke reflection about their work.

While he adapted teaching strategies from his own teacher, Don knew early on that his aspirations for his students were his very own. They were twofold. The first was to instill into his students an appreciation of that which made his own life worth living. This was a love of the natural environment, a sense of being awake to the aesthetic qualities in one's easily ignored everyday surroundings. The high art of museums, the masterworks of humankind could, of course, be enormously life enhancing, but Don believed in moving outward from the simpler beauty of the proximal toward the more complex and remote. He thought of the centrifugal inflorescence of flowers, the way that rose petals, for example, unfolded in descending order from the top. The reverse seemed nonsensical. It was, he thought, probably the same in all areas of academics, with an understanding of the strange opening only after the blossoming of the familiar.

The second aim was to nurture talents at recasting those formal qualities into pieces of craftsmanship and works of art. And again, he honored the local, the nearby, centering his programs around the kinds of arts and crafts he knew best, those from within the cultural heritages of Appalachia.

LEARNING FROM HIS STUDENTS

What were the raw materials with which he had to work? Each school term the character of each student slowly became visible. Each was unique, but, like the items he collected from the forests, with general attributes allowing for classification into one genus or another. Some students were like larvae that were bound to metamorphose into something grand. He wanted to be nearby when that happened. Others reminded him of unborn chicks pecking determinedly at the inside of a shell, to little avail, in danger of dying before being born, baby birds who needed his help in breaking out into the world. Still others were creatures so deeply camouflaged after years of obedience to the subtle demands of their social environments that a capacity for revealing their true colors seemed hopelessly diminished.

Early in his career Don had hoped to achieve his aims with every one of these beginning students. But he discovered that a school's organizational features can be educationally debilitating. Class size was one of these. In Art I, students could number 30 per class, placing limits on personal attention. He could not achieve his aims in one year, and not every student would be returning. An enormously complex winnowing process would occur. Who knew the real reasons why certain beginners would not enroll in Art II? Some had greater interests elsewhere, a few changed schools, some were untouched, maybe untouchable, by what art is and can do. Don resisted thinking of this attrition as his failure. He focused on those students who did return, on the cohorts of juniors and seniors with whom he would have a second chance.

Don was more attracted to some of his students than others. He cared for all—well, most—of his freshmen and sophomores, but had subtly recruited some into advanced study of art. These students possessed various attributes. Some seemed much like him, sensitive loners with a passion for the handiwork of nature. He was fascinated by others who shared his love of the outdoors: He saw the luminous qualities of the Appalachian hills in a few of the youngsters who were now filling the waking hours of his life. Still others possessed characteristics foreign to him—these were the self-assured, the gregarious, the poised. These were the students—the people—with whom he most wanted to share a gift, a form of experience, a way of life.

But this sharing must occur outside the strong walls of the fortress that was his private life. He had no close friends in his lonesome but not lonely existence. His 16 hours of daily work left no time for socializing or for a feeling of loneliness. His strongest attachment to a living thing was to Cavalry, a Weimaraner upon whom he lavished much attention. Don had become adept at the intricate craft of living beyond the heart of the human community.

Most colleagues could only vaguely perceive the circumstances of his life outside of school. This fuzziness, combined with Don's lack of deference to certain unwritten rules of campus comportment (manner of dress, with whom to lunch, proper length of hair, and so on), aroused considerable curiosity among some students, parents, and townsfolk. Their whisperings about his eccentricities would, on rare occasion, reach Don—only to be ignored, of course. He was, as always, who he was, never one to either flaunt or defend his personal life. Nor did he ever intend to make a statement, to teach subtle life lessons, by modeling what some students perceived as a steely integrity. This was simply, given the experiences of his youth, his preferred modus vivendi.

With each passing year, however, the solitude diminished. He did not aspire to guru status, nor work to gather a select group of students into a worshipful clique, as some teachers, especially in the arts and humanities, were wont to do. He merely obeyed a desire to lavish time and attention on particular students, much as they found themselves captivated by what they would call his "charisma." About this mutual attraction Don could say only that occasionally there was a chemistry; things sometimes "clicked."

Because Don saw the life of each of his students as a whole piece of cloth, and because his expectations for that life were rarely met by graduation, he often refused to abruptly end the mentoring. Unfinished business: These graduates, the people whom Cavalry trusted, became special cases. People whom he didn't avoid in the checkout lines, college students with whom he would correspond by letter, young housewives or businessmen whom he would invite to his house, or a museum or theater, to continue the lessons on the aesthetics of life.

The first significant batch of such students had arrived in the late 1970s and early 1980s. Among them was Carolyn Wilson. Sensitive, highly verbal, and physically attractive, Carolyn was the leader of a group of promising students, including, among others, Keith Robinson, Nat Carter, and Barry Larson. Most of them had a wide range of interests—music, books, science, ideas of all sorts. To Don, they seemed to roam like Renaissance people, across these fields of knowledge and connecting them, being stimulated, for example, by drawing a leaf to learn more about its physiology.

Don was especially intrigued by Carolyn's capacity for leadership. For example, Carolyn led her cohorts in creating a vocabulary they alone understood, binding them into an informal club. The often sarcastic tone to their banter served to camouflage the synergy between them. Don observed a competitiveness among them, but also a mutual support, in, for example, the heartfelt compliments upon special accomplishments. They seemed to stimulate each other toward greater achievements, and Don, as their teacher, wanted a piece of the action.

Carolyn was the kind of student for whom he felt he could make a difference. Two personal attributes defined her for Don—honesty and courage. Carolyn could be judgmental about others and brutally honest about herself. These were, he thought, marks of an artist: to know oneself intimately at an early age; to scrutinize the world and bravely inform it of what had been found.

Don had not yet considered the possibility that certain students might change the shape of *his* life. But the presence of these attributes of perceptiveness and candor in a mere adolescent was new to Don and it affected him deeply—or reinforced what was already there: a sense of the importance of living with integrity.

One additional quality became apparent in what would become an indelible memory of Carolyn. It happened on a drizzly March morning in Carolyn's senior year, at a time when some looms made their initial appearance in the classroom. On the previous afternoon, some students had asked Don about the source of funds for their purchase. Usually avoiding this sort of question, Don had confessed to often putting his own money into the program. Had Carolyn been in the group of questioners? Somehow she had learned of his response. Early the next day she handed Don an envelope. On the front was written "Loom"; inside was a 10-dollar bill.

Don knew of Carolyn's talent for manipulation and momentarily considered whether this was a cynical ploy for attention and affection. But soon comprehending the nobility of the gesture, he was deeply touched. His next impulse was to refuse this sizable gift from a student who could ill afford it, but decided not to deny her the right to contribute. That decision arrived at the precise moment his emotions took over.

It was not the first time that Don had shed tears in front of a student, and he belatedly imagined that they had startled, perhaps even confused, Carolyn. These were indeed tears of gratitude, but not for the money. Carolyn's gift was tangible evidence of one student's desire to match his intangible contributions to the cause of opening up her life. He suspected others desired the same. So the gift prompted Don's rededication to his program and his career.

One member of Carolyn's cohort was Barry Larson. Although 2 years younger than Carolyn, he had been drawn (Don was unsure of the origins of the connection) into her web of friends. Don was also intrigued by this boy who had jolted him into self-recognition with a book bag filled with assorted items of personal meaning—family photographs, shells, gifts from friends.

Barry had entered Don's course with a huge appetite for the aesthetic. Was it, wondered Don, a congenital condition? Although starving for photography, Barry seemed to find sustenance in almost any medium. In his first years he would engage in several art projects at once, finishing them hastily, as if a large quantity of work would disguise a feared lack of quality.

In a moment paradoxically calculated yet spontaneous, Don had called Barry's attention to this unfortunate tendency. He had summoned Barry to his desk to recite to him a poem about slowing down to make things more beautiful. He had attributed the poem to E. E. Cummings.

Don had first encountered that poem as an undergraduate, but later committed it to memory for two reasons. First, he wanted it, like the others in his growing repertoire, nearby for his own pleasure, the verbal equivalent of one of his gorgeous pebbles. But Don had also memorized the poem for Barry and had it poised for withdrawal at the right moment. Which had arrived. But Don would never be certain of the impact of that recitation. Barry's reaction was perplexing to Don, and neither had ever again spoken to the other about the incident.

Don had observed that when Barry did indeed focus on a single work, his artistry was superb. Was this due to a special significance attached to its making? That was the case, for example, with a hand-painted silk of the Smoky Mountains. Ultimately displayed at the Corcoran Gallery in Washington, it was arguably the most beautiful piece of work by any of his students thus far, and Barry had deservedly won a national award for it.

Don never trumpeted the awards of his students, hoping to avoid using their achievements in a crass manner, as advertisements for his program in the school and town communities. Of course, he could not prevent the awards from enhancing both his and the program's images. But his students should never engage in intensely personal artistic activity out of a lust for public approbation. Art was too pure, too intimate an enterprise, to be sullied by rewards such as ribbons and trophies.

Why then were the contests entered into with such frequency? Why the intense calculations over which-piece-by-whom-would-have-the-best-chance-where? Did the triumphs of Don's students offer vicarious gratification, pleasure from the ultimate victory that had eluded him as a youngster waiting in vain for recognition from those invisible people behind the television screen? Don believed otherwise: They were a powerful reinforcement of his basic message to them: "You can be more than you think you can."

No student had ever won more awards than Keith Robinson. Another contemporary of Carolyn Wilson's, Keith was perhaps Forrister's first student to understand that art was equivalent to living, someone who could see the aesthetics in clothes, in furniture, in the textures, flavors, and arrangements of foods on a plate. Don had known Keith as a 6-year-old boy at the Job Corps. One brother among four, Keith had been driven to excel in academics, especially the arts. Forrister knew that the resourceful and multitalented Keith would succeed in many ways.

Keith, Carolyn, and others made the graduation ceremony of 1982 difficult for Don. They comprised the most fascinating class of seniors he had encountered at Swain. They had touched his life and refreshed his hope of making a difference as a teacher. But there were promising reserves in the bull pen. For example, he could still look forward to the return of Ben Dobson and that self-possessed student-magician he had recruited into photography for his senior year.

From the very beginning Don had suspected that a Dobson boy would never pursue a career in the arts: The emphasis on financial security within Ben's family would militate against that possibility. But Don still wanted to rescue Ben's sensitive side from oblivion. The youngster's thoughts and feelings revealed themselves in conversations with Don about personal matters, and in the expressiveness in his drawings, paintings, and especially his photographs. And in his capacity for slipping into an inner world to escape the annoyances or travails awaiting him on the outside, Ben was, thought Don, second only to himself.

Thoughts of Ben prompted thoughts of Paul Mosely. Inseparable during their senior year, Paul and Ben shared a capacity to focus intensely, rigorously excluding extraneous thoughts from their activities. But while Ben focused on projecting feelings into photographs, Paul aimed at charming audiences with his sleight of hand.

Don had marveled at Paul's stage presence, understanding tacitly that his act represented many hours of practice. He detected a firm self-definition for someone so young, and a kind of creativity that might serve Paul well in his arts classes. But Paul turned out to be a dilettante, testing one medium and abandoning it for another. Although, by term's end, Paul had begun to show some promise in photography, Don did not feel he had fully succeeded with Paul. But who would ever know whether Paul had picked up some lasting pointers about, what? Painting? Videotaping? Living a good life?

Don was increasingly intrigued with the notion that one's life should be a work of art, something akin to a continuous stage performance. He was growing into an appreciation of how ritual and ceremony could disrupt the humdrum passage of time, lifting life above the routine. But as artistic events, these must be meticulously planned and staged, with coordinated details that heighten the experience and press it into memory. So it was with some irony, Don realized, that he could not fully recall the details of the piece of postgraduation performance art he had designed for Ben and Paul. Had they more accurate recollections of the occasion? It would be good if they had. We remember best, he thought, events of great meaning.

That event had begun with a ceremonial presentation of gifts. Why a pocketknife to Ben? The reason had disappeared with time. But Don clearly recalled the reasons for the expensive camera for Paul: Paul could afford to travel to exotic locations, and Don wanted to vicariously experience those journeys through his photographs. And it was a subtle means for remaining connected to Paul in the future.

Then in late afternoon came the event's next phase, designed to stand atop the first. Having climbed Baxter Mountain in Don's pickup, the trio engaged in a ceremony designed to project them into the future. The boys were directed to scrawl the answer to questions about their likes and dislikes onto papers to be inserted into balloons. The balloons were sent skyward, perhaps to be discovered by a hiker, perhaps to be slowly buried within layers of leaf-encrusted topsoil. If a theme of this activity involved the committal of their friendship to the everlasting world of Nature, it was secondary to the larger purposes behind the evening's activities.

Don wondered about the transparency of those purposes. Before the balloons were released, it was agreed that, after the woods had turned to red and yellow, and Paul and Ben had traveled to new locations, they would reveal to each other the answers to the questions. As with his gift to Paul, this was an attempt by Don to secure a promise for the future. His work with these two was incomplete. Each possessed unrealized potential: Ben's artistic inclinations were in danger of being swallowed up by another side of his personality; Paul had been under Don's tutelage for one short year. Now the outside world threatened to snatch away these items in his collection of interesting artifacts before he had completed their sketches. Ben and Paul would move, prematurely, beyond his control.

Had they gone to dinner next? If so, it had served, from Don's point of view, as an intermission before the final act. The play needed a light finale—a serious conclusion, perhaps, but not a maudlin one. So on to his house near Culver Creek, where he had hidden 20 cheap pies from the A&P. A pie fight would serve to fill in a hole in his own adolescence: Ever since the early days of television, he had wanted to experience the exhilarating mayhem of globs of cream flung at human targets. But with whom could he have ever shared the experience?

The pie fight was a success. Indeed, Don's aims for the entire evening had been met. It had served as Don's token of appreciation of their contribution to his professional and personal life. And he had ensured that their relationship would not end abruptly, that he would retain a place in their lives for a bit longer. Finally, he had exacted retribution for the pranks played on him during the year. The object of those jokes would demonstrate who was really in charge: *His* careful choreography called for Don to deliver the first shots at his blindfolded victims. He had reasserted himself as author of events, as teacher-artist in control of his materials.

But was another lesson lurking beneath the surface of the evening? The experience was a strange gift from someone with an eccentric way of being in the world. But it suggested that life could be lived as a form of art, a drama in which the playwright, disregarding recommendations from habit and convention, slices off pieces from the ordinary line of time, and fashions them into aesthetically bracing experiences. Maybe, from this and other experiences with Don, the boys had picked up a lesson or two about how to live. But then again, he reconsidered, maybe not.

Don's students were generally curious about his personal life. He had apparently acquired, at least among younger people, an image of a person of much integrity. But he resolutely avoided discussion of such matters, shying away from any inspection of his life as a kind of model. For several years the football coach, on behalf of the school's athletic club, had asked him to give a motivational speech on integrity. He was secretly flattered to have been chosen by students as someone they admired. But Don had repeatedly refused the requests, until they no longer came. He felt guilty about those refusals, but lecturing about living a moral life would have been, to him, a desecration of sacred territory, an obscene public airing of matters achingly personal.

He saw a paradox: Any person who would listen seriously to a sermon about listening to *oneself* in living one's life was bound to listen to *others* about how to live one's life. Good values, he believed, are not passed on by admonition or persuasion, but through a kind of moral osmosis, moving directly through the spiritual passageways between one soul and another. To him, it would be contradictory to convey such a thought in a speech, so he continued to teach these notions tacitly, through his everyday comportment.

Don understood that not all adults in the community shared students' appreciation of his comportment. Beyond the matter of living with Sarah, there was a kind of religious promiscuity, his penchant for attending churches of various denominations. He cared little for theology. Born into the Church of God, amidst the trances, the faith healing, and speaking in tongues, he had soon equated God with fear. Don was interested in the aesthetics of religion, in the ballet of formal ritual—which explained his preference for Catholicism over the chaotic "holy-rolley" religions.

Would the values that he lived somehow be transmitted to the few students he had allowed inside the circle carefully drawn around his private life? Barry, Carolyn, Paul, Ben, and Keith were students with whom he had become entranced, like the dazzling objects of the woods. He had pulled them into the core of his being and became a "significant other" in their lives. Perhaps it was his disrespect for formal roles that encouraged them to approach with their personal concerns a teacher whom many adults regarded as aloof, distant, and eccentric. This kind of bonding was new to Don, but he had felt honored by their trust and tried to meet it with sage and heartfelt advice, free of dictum and disapprobation.

These students would be "keepers." Decades after their departures from Swain, he would be as incapable of severing his bonds with them as he was of discarding the aesthetically interesting objects (called "opportunities for art lessons") that filled his classrooms and storerooms. Indeed, over the years the size of his collection had become the focus of negotiations with school administrators (as with his mother, much earlier). But Don had managed to maintain sufficient space at Swain, as he had in his life for his burgeoning collection of former students.

They were anomalies among his array of acquaintances, people whom Don greeted with genuine pleasure. They were the objects of continued attention, recipients of invitations to exhibits, or calls to dinner at his home. Continued contact was feasible with those who remained within the nearby counties. For others, letters and postcards and occasional class reunions had to suffice. He was eager to hear about unfolding life stories, secretly hoping that he might be a character significant to the plots.

But in the mid-1990s things had changed. The local school board decided to require fine arts credits for every Swain student. Enrollment in his courses mushroomed. For one semester each year, Don was now teaching only Art I. In the fall of 1997 he had taught the fundamentals of art to no less than 123 freshmen and sophomores in three classes.

These students were of a different tribe from those of previous decades. To Don, most had been victims of cultural crimes. Modern culture had, it seemed, done its dirty deeds with great finesse, insinuating itself into every nook and cranny of Appalachia. The old physical landscape had been smothered, some swatches of the natural vegetation under blankets of foreign-born kudzu and other areas besmirched by corporate America. Signs and buildings had moved the once unique character of the region onto a geography of nowhere, a place that bore the standardized look of turn-of-the-millennium America.

Worse, a way of being that was well rooted was also being strangled. The changes, Don thought, were telegraphed into being, transmitted silently and invisibly through the ether. The young were the most eager for the message, most easily distracted by the static of the popular culture. A new range of desires had been crafted for them far away and made palpable through television and the Internet. To assuage them, the kids had shed old behavioral patterns almost in unison, like an army of cicadas popping overnight out of their once confined selves.

Don's new students were both more and less worldly than previous ones—more materialistic, less observant of the world at their sides. Their rebelliousness was of a kind unfamiliar to Don. The Carolyn Wilsons and the Keith Robinsons had not rejected the traditional Appalachian culture, but hankered for additional knowledge to expand their worldviews. The newer form of rebellion was a sullen rejection of all but the MTV culture. For Don, it was a challenge to light fires in the hearts of these strange new creatures, many of whom had been unwillingly herded into the vicinity of the arts and crafts. And so the Arts I classes had became mere simulacra of the old, while Don taught fewer and fewer upper-level courses.

Educational conditions elsewhere in the school had also changed, although they affected teachers in other subject areas more than him. The onslaught of standardized testing had, it seemed, lowered the satisfaction level of many of his colleagues. They were placed into curricular straitjackets, forced to teach to standardized tests for an illusion of academic rigor. The emphasis on test scores and grades seemed to dampen student enthusiasm for learning. The emphasis on extrinsic rewards stifled an intuitive delight in knowledge, disconnecting learning from real meaning, from what made students who they were and from their aspirations.

These changes served to reinforce Forrister's tendencies toward physical and mental retreat. He began to ponder leaving teaching. In a few years, after 30 with the county, at the age of 54, he would become eligible for retirement. Then he and Sarah, also retired, might relocate. Maybe they would withdraw higher up an Appalachian hill, although soon that could mean meeting a new housing development descending from the other side. Their kind of Appalachia was rapidly disappearing. Their retreat might need to be more drastic, across the continent to an outpost in Montana or northern New Mexico. A second house in what was left of the Wild West for healing in privacy from the psychic wounds inflicted by the modern world? Could Forrister really remove himself, even for 2 seasons a year, from the land of his birth, where his collections of all sorts—his material possessions, his Swain alumni family, the geographical locations of his favorite memories—would necessarily remain? Sarah would come, of course, with her cat Thomas, as would Jet, Don's new Labrador. And some of his lifetime of memories.

But not all of them.

For he felt the power of the Lady's message about simplifying his life. His collections had become overwhelming. Like that strike of lightning, they energized, but ultimately served to debilitate. He would abandon them in the name of the Lady of the Dream. For the sake of Beauty he would write letters to the important people in his life, thereby entering what he would come to call the period of the purge.

THE PURGE

In the early months of 1996 Don Forrister made two lists. The first included the people he cherished most—Sarah, his four siblings, a few former students, local artists from potter to drawer to gallery owner. On the second list he identified the material objects most charged with fond memories—from childhood toys (softballs, jacks, cigar boxes) to the award-winning glazed clay goblets crafted in college. He wrapped each item distinctively and placed them together in an antique wooden box. Then, periodically over the next 2 years, Forrister would remove an object from the box and mail it to someone on his list.

To keep his memories alive, he must abandon them to other people. They must be moved out of the heart of their trusty guardian, to places where they might also be safe from the ravages of time and indifference. In those places memories of himself might also survive, longer than otherwise.

Preserving his positive contributions to the lives of his students was important to Don. But, even as even as he worried that his influences might not endure within a noxious modern culture, Don knew he could never have—and must never desire—absolute control over his students' experiences. Still, Don had spent his life as a teacher serving his notion of Beauty in a world entranced by other concerns. He recalled his years of collecting shiny trinkets and patterned rocks and shapely leaves. And he recalled the fascinatingly textured occasions with his students that were transmuted into the unique sculpture that was his life.

Had he inspired even a few of them to live in a similar way? Would they comb the hills for tiny gifts of Nature, or search for Beauty in the great green dumpsters of the world, or flock to the latest exhibition of the Masters, or even move into a classroom seeking out some shiny baubles for their own pedagogical artistry? He would never know for sure. Like every other teacher on earth, he could only hope.

Or was there something else he could do?

PART IV

WAYS OF TOUCHING ETERNITY

*Analyzing Some Enduring
Consequences of Teaching*

T HE FIRST THREE parts of this book paint a portrait of a high
school teacher who seems to have made a lasting impact on his
students. Part IV presents an analysis of the evidence contained
in earlier sections from two distinct theoretical perspectives. A phenomenological reading of this evidence supports the notion of Forrister as a singular hero, one who has indeed permanently altered the
lives of many of his students for the better. A second reading, drawn
from critical theory, is more skeptical about the long-range effects of
Forrister's teaching, pointing to extrinsic forces in the culture that may
have served to vitiate the power of his influence. This viewpoint serves
as a reminder to all teachers to be aware of these forces and the importance of collaborating with others against them. The reader is asked to
consider which of these conflicting points of view is more persuasive
and to think about the ramifications of this analysis for teachers and
students in other places and times.

AESTHETICS AND UTILITY REVISITED

Ferreting out the enduring traces of a teacher in the life stories of his
former students was an arduous task. Many of these traces were elu-
sive, easily hidden from the view of a biographer-stranger and even, I
have learned, from the learners themselves. Moreover, these elements
can reside anywhere on the broad existential landscape, within any of
the domains of human thought and activity. But however difficult it is
to uncover particles of evidence and to recast them in the form of biographical essays, it is even more challenging to analyze one's discover-
ies from a distanced, "scholarly" vantage point. Therefore, the analysis
below is necessarily tentative, partial, and incomplete.

It is fashioned from patterns already woven into this research
cloth—that is, in the text of my 1983 essay about the SCHS Arts program (Part I). There Forrister's program is observed in terms of its aesthetics and its utility. Initially, these two themes represented antitheti-

cal thrusts: The vocationally oriented objectives demanded by funding sources and inscribed into the formal curriculum seemed in competition with students' growth in personal expression. This expressiveness, resulting in "things of beauty," was important to Forrister and his students. Ultimately, however, my brittle dichotomy of pragmatics versus aesthetics melted away as I began to understand the coexistence of these seemingly opposite characteristics in the arts and crafts of Appalachia and in student engagements and products that were the tangible results of this arts program.

In this section, I return to the apparent dualism of utility and aesthetics. I reexamine it in light of evidence about the long-term outcomes of Forrister's teaching contained in Parts II and III of this book—evidence that is, I believe, both remarkable and inconclusive. More than a decade after their encounters with him, at least some former students seemed to have retained traces from both hemispheres—the useful and the beautiful—of Forrister's world.

The narratives of some students contained evidence of an enhanced ability to function effectively in the given scheme of things, balanced with a tendency to grow beyond others' expectations of them within a materialistic, individualistic culture. But other former students had apparently not achieved this kind of balance in their lives. The reasons for this are hard to fathom. Despite Forrister's considerable teaching talent and personal charisma, there were, it seems, things ignored, potential outcomes of education that were not addressed, and so left unplanted in the lives of his students. And there were important lessons, though well taught, that nevertheless proved impermanent as the lives of Don's former students meandered away from his into the powerful pull of an anesthetic utilitarianism.

The account of Forrister's legacy in this chapter outlines the contest between these two awesome forces—Don's personal magnetism and pedagogical prowess versus the hegemony of a utilitarian culture. It was a culture that could ultimately extinguish the gains made by an individual teacher who refused (rightly or not) to address its influences directly in his pedagogy.

In presenting two alternative, even conflicting, views of the long-term consequences of Forrister's teaching, the discussion below offers the reader a degree of interpretative space unavailable in the previous sections of the book. For, ultimately, it is indeed the reader who will judge whether and how Don Forrister has succeeded in touching eternity.

SOCIAL ADAPTIONISTS AND INHERITED SCRIPTS

In North America the institution of the school has often been viewed in narrowly pragmatic and utilitarian terms. For many citizens, and the public officials whom they elect, schools—and, by extension, the teachers within them—exist primarily as agents of the larger culture. Schools are expected to equip students with the skills, proficiencies, knowledge, attitudes, and modes of comportment necessary for economic survival and perhaps even prosperity. This educational orientation was inscribed within the official rationale of the SCHS Arts Program of the early 1980s (Part I). It was a rationale honored, no doubt, by many North Carolina parents and taxpayers: For a future artisan, commercial artist, or craftsperson, school is to learn how to make a living.

This rationale was, ultimately, too narrow to contain Don Forrister's hopes for his students. But Forrister-the-pragmatist did attempt to impart technical skills and knowledge useful in the arts and crafts–related jobs of the region, even if primarily through projects that enhanced the larger purpose of personal meaning making. It would be surprising if all of the technical know-how acquired in making batiks and rugs, in weaving, drawing, papermaking, photography, and so on, were lost by students upon departure from Forrister's program.

Indeed, at least a few of Forrister's former students identified particular artistic skills and techniques employed in their later work. Examples ranged from those used in Derek Robinson's sketching chores within his decidedly nonartistic job as state patrolman, to the pottery skills that a student named Sean Logan claimed he still possessed past the age of 30. But the most explicit descriptions of retained technique were provided by Derek's loquacious brother, Keith. He described his technical abilities with pastels, watercolors, and colored pencils in his landscape designs and renderings at college and in his work as landscape architect. "All of these things," said Keith, "I would have never known if Don had not taught them to me."

Another former student, elementary school teacher Cindy Greathouse, referenced skills and knowledge related to her teaching. They were elements of teaching to which she had been introduced during her "apprenticeship of observation" (Lortie, 1975) in Forrister's classroom. Forrister offered her, Cindy said, her "first exposure to a classroom that was open-ended and individualized." But Cindy best recalled Forrister's habit of focusing intensely on the single individual with whom he was conversing. She perceived his influence most strongly in the "listening skills" she came to employ with her own students.

Some of the educators, educational theorists, and laypeople who hold a profoundly conservative view of what schooling should provide, however, do not limit their educational aims to the acquisition of work-related skills. Their longings occupy a broader scope, encompassing what French sociologist Emile Durkheim (1934/1956) called the *social being,* an entity seen as rightful property of the prevailing culture. It is true that early-twentieth-century American sociologist Talcott Parsons and his contemporary, the educationist Franklin Bobbitt, like many of today's economic conservatives who comment on educational matters, stressed the importance of aligning education with the needs of business. But Durkheim's charging of the schools with the larger mission of transmitting the morals, customs, and religious beliefs preferred by the culture is more reminiscent of the calls by today's social conservatives for "character" and "traditional values" in education.

In this same vein, E. D. Hirsch (1988) and others have emphasized the culturally literate social being, the acquisition of common cultural knowledge by all American students. And Forrister's respect for art history translated into some exposure of students to this portion of a common cultural heritage. A few of Forrister's students recalled becoming acquainted (especially in Art I) with acclaimed artwork of the past. But Forrister was more interested in his students' capacity to relate knowledge about masterworks to their own work than in their acquiring it for its own sake. Students studied the styles and techniques of the Old Masters while composing their own pictures. Here is the recollection of Nancy Allport, Class of 1982:

> In the first year we did a lot more studying of older stuff. . . . We studied a lot of famous watercolors . . . watercolors and sculptures. That sticks with me more than anything else. I don't remember it in detail all that much, but I remember him talking to us about that. I remember when we were doing the watercolors, that's when we were having to draw our own pictures.

Nancy's inability to recall many precise details of art history was matched by several other former students. Specific details had blurred into the vague feeling tones that are the outcomes of what Harry Broudy (1974) called the "associative use of schooling":

> Often we are no more aware of what is in our subconscious cellars of memory than we know the contents of our attics, but given the right oc-

casion and stimulus we find to our surprise many items there that we had completely forgotten about. (p. 38)

Indeed, some respondents insisted that scenes in a TV program or paintings in a museum could still trigger a recall of images, ideas, or words associated with topics once covered in art class.

Other students continued to use traditional craft knowledge and abilities in their leisure time. Beverly King reported giving away the placemats, blankets, and table runners that she still wove on her own loom, especially "as a stress reliever on cold winter days." Likewise, Cindy Greathouse retained her knack for doing wall hangings and designing Christmas cards. Beverly, Cindy, and some other Swain alumni were conservators of the slowly disappearing Appalachian craft knowledge discussed in Part I.

The skills of a trade, the social being, the time-honored disciplines, the public traditions, the accumulated wisdom, the common culture—these are, indeed, important items for schools and teachers to preserve and transmit. Unfortunately, however, those who honor this list of items (identified as *social adaptionists* by Eisner & Vallance, 1974) tend to see them as content for transmission rather than as useful and necessary tools for cultural growth and personal renewal. Social adaptionists desire schools that adapt students to prevailing social norms, thereby reproducing the cultural status quo, schools that work to instill in students a reverence for an *inherited cultural script.*

A *cultural script* consists of the cultural formations that sustain and give meaning to the actions within the life story of an individual (Willinsky, 1989, p. 251). An *inherited cultural script* contains a formula for living in accordance with the norms of the prevailing culture. It offers a description of one's identity that is written by others and is thus marked by domination and control. These others may include the nearby—family members, acquaintances, local figures of authority—as well as denizens of the mass media. These other authors may, in turn, be under the sway of larger forces that are the actual sources of an inherited cultural script. The script's relative invisibility makes it difficult to understand how it positions an individual vis-à-vis the desires and expectations of the culture, and therefore to imagine and choose alternative courses of action.

Of course, no one is a disengaged aesthete who composes a life story in existential isolation nor a Prometheus who creates a life by dint of sheer will. None of us can claim to live in total independence and autonomy from the norms of the culture into which we are born, a culture that also provides us with the resources needed for functioning and developing as human beings. To some degree all of us plot out our lives in passive accordance with a given notion of who we should be. Still, some among us seem capable of avoiding total acquiescence to an inherited script, of achieving an identity with substantial personal integrity, while not ignoring responsibilities to fellow human beings. To the many students who loved and admired him, Donald Forrister was such a person.

DONALD FORRISTER AS STRONG POET

Don Forrister was, in fact, deeply conservative in many ways: in his regard for the traditional Appalachian cultural heritage, in his attachments to the physical landscape of the region of his birth, and in the way he lived certain values he had internalized as a child. These values included patience, diligence, independence, resourcefulness, individual responsibility, and hard work (Sean Logan's remark about Forrister being "almost a workaholic" was ratified by several other students; see also Part I). These values were not ornamental, acquired by mimicking the actions, or obeying the admonitions, of family members, teachers, or preachers. They lay at the center of Forrister's code for living.

Some of these traits, like the Appalachian environment in which they were shaped, predated and clashed with certain modernist (and even postmodernist) cultural formations that, even in the 1980s, were bringing changes to the social fabric and geography of the hills and urging alterations in Forrister's own life script. As a preservationist of what was left of the early, White, rural, Southern Appalachian culture, Forrister was, ironically, in many ways the opposite of a social adaptionist. Although he lived against the grain of a new order, he was never quite in harmony with the old. For example, Forrister was not conventionally religious. He attended Sunday services at any of several churches, most often Roman Catholic, the denomination offering the most aesthetically appealing rituals. (He refused to bracket off the officially sacred from the realm of aesthetics, the latter occupying such a prominent place in his life.) And there was, to the chagrin of some local religious traditionalists, his longtime cohabitation with Sarah outside of marriage.

As Carolyn Wilson pointed out, Forrister neither flaunted nor hid the nature of his domestic arrangements, although some students were quite curious about his personal life. Forrister simply followed his own moral compass sans display or defensiveness, followed it straightforwardly, within what appeared to many of his students as an unadulterated authenticity. Indeed, to those who knew him best, his modus vivendi appeared less like an odd eclecticism of traditionalist and modern values than evidence of his integrity and independence, proof that he was, indeed, crafting his own life story.

Forrister was resisting scripts offered by *two* identifiable cultures— one, in fact, a subculture whose traditional rural or small town script was preferred by some of his fellow Appalachians, and the other prevailing within the larger culture outside. To his students he was that rare person who avoided enacting a prefabricated life story, whatever its origins, but who was crafting an original script with an elegance and coherence all its own.

The philosopher Richard Rorty noted that Nietzsche long ago identified the source of that unfortunate tendency of living a foreign life script. It arose, said Nietzsche, out of insufficient knowledge of oneself as a unique individual. This was a failure, explained Rorty (1989),

> to see oneself as idiosyncratic, [but rather as] a specimen reiterating a type, a copy or replica of something that already has been identified. [It was] . . . for Nietzsche, to fail as a human being . . . to accept someone else's description of oneself, to execute a previously prepared program, to write, at most, elegant variations on previously written poems. (p. 28)

For Nietzsche, a good life is like an original poem insofar as disparate thoughts and actions are consciously shaped into a narrative unity, an aesthetic form, that bears the signature of the author. The admirable person is able to provide this coherence through strength secured in honoring his or her own emergent ends and purposes. That person has what Nietzsche called *style* (cited in Polkinghorne, 1988, p. 154). And style, it seems to me, is the primary attribute of what the philosopher Harold Bloom (1973) called a *strong poet*, someone who, like Forrister, refuses an easy acceptance of life prescriptions written by others.

There was also an existential stylishness apparent in some (although certainly not all) of Forrister's students, a proclivity toward defining for themselves the nature of their "social being," a tendency toward writing strong poetry with the instruments of their selves. And one place that we may find profound traces of this teacher is the deep recesses of character of his former students, as revealed through their specific choices of how to act. Evidence that Forrister was a source of their courageous decisions, a person who helped them make certain independent moves on their own initiative, pervades their life stories.

THE GOOD PEDAGOGUE AND SELF-IDENTITY

Some courageous decisions made by students involved unexpected career choices. Barry Larson decided to ply a trade—restaurant waiting—less prestigious than the careers approved within the life script preferred by family members. Forrister can be credited with bolstering Barry's determination to ignore that script in favor of Barry's own. Likewise, Paul Mosely, the son of a medical doctor, was encouraged by Forrister to follow his own vocational inclinations to become a magician. And Ardley Hanson found support from Forrister in pursuing chiropractic studies.

Chiropractics had been Ardley's goal since high school. The seed was planted after the 16-year-old experienced binocular vision after running track. He decided "for some reason" to visit, not an oculist, but a chiropractor. When the treatment was effective, "I knew then what I wanted to do with my life." His sense of gratitude was soon supported by ethical reasoning. Researching the field, Ardley was attracted to the "moral approach" of treating the fundamental causes of physical problems, rather than "oversimplifying them" or masking them with painkillers.

Even then Ardley had viewed chiropractics as an unfairly maligned, "nonconformist" line of work. It was Forrister, "one of the five most influential people in my life," who emboldened him to

> do what you think is best. Don't worry about what everyone else is thinking, or [let them] influence what you do or say or how you perceive this project in art, or whatever. . . . That helped me not to worry about the fact that I am in a nonmainstream profession.

But perhaps Forrister's most important influence involved, not students' vocational choices, but their decisions regarding personal issues of lifestyle and ethics. Here are a few examples:

• Roderick Robinson, an African American student, attested to the comfort he felt in approaching Forrister about whether to continue dating a White girl. Roderick described Forrister's response and his own reaction:

> He told me to follow my heart. He told me to follow my heart. He told me to do what I felt was right. It was one of those situations where . . . anyone else . . . would have frowned upon it, but Don . . . said, "You have to follow your heart." . . . Don and my parents

taught us [him and his three brothers] how to be open-minded, to give people the benefit of the doubt, don't categorize one particular race of people based on what you hear.

• Carolyn Wilson, guided by an ethical sensibility acquired, she averred, from members of her family as well as from Forrister, resigned her secure position at a high school where colleagues were, in her judgment, being treated callously by the administration.

• Sean Logan turned to Forrister when others were unable to comprehend the depths of his addiction to alcohol. Although the addiction did not disappear immediately, Sean insisted that Forrister's counseling helped: "Alcohol might have taken a big toll without him, but I could talk to him."

• More than one frightened student facing issues of sexual orientation alone within starkly conservative families and communities were able to confide in Forrister, and sometimes *only* in Forrister. Their testimony echoed that of Roderick who received understanding and reassurance concerning the issue of interracial dating: "I don't think that in small Swain County High School there was another place I could go where I could express myself and not have anyone be judgmental about it."

A remarkable number of Forrister's students were indeed willing to reveal a significant portion of their private lives to Forrister. Accessible to those students, he was trusted with their heavy-hearted secrets. They welcomed his affirmation of what their inner voices were insisting they must do in order to succeed as human beings, in order to grow into their inimitable selves. They drew from him (and sometimes others) the courage to write their own poetry, to live their lives with style.

This was educational territory lying far beyond the more familiar ground of technical proficiency, of the utilitarian skills and knowledge demanded by social adaptionists. This was pedagogy in the ancient Greek sense, wherein a slave-teacher, while walking a student to school, would help him place the technical and the academic into the contexts of the wide outside world, teach him character, guide him toward a good and virtuous life.

This is not to suggest that Forrister foisted on his students a tight definition of virtue, that his own strict notion of a good social being was subtly advanced. Nor is it a claim that Forrister was a "role model," in the narrow sense of that overused term. To the contrary, the patterns in the lives that his students chose to lead following their tenure with Forrister were clearly distinguishable from the patterns within his own. For example, most (although by no means all) of his former students were significantly more materialistic than Don. Most were more conventional in dress and appearance. Some had become fundamentalist Christians—I know of none who adopted Don's religious eclecticism. Only a few became teachers or artists themselves. And yet many had achieved Forrister's impressive degree of personal integrity, his tendency to act in accordance with personal proclivities that sometimes ran counter to prevailing orthodoxy. Forrister promoted self-knowledge within his students so that each might act wisely in constructing a unique self-identity, rather than moving to replicate his own.

Such knowledge is, indeed, necessary to self-creation, a point that is also, as Rorty (1989) reminded us, Nietzschean. But what if Forrister had advised his students, not to "follow your own heart" and "do what you think is right," but to "follow my lead and do what I think is right for you?" What if he had modeled a way of life narrowed by a prevailing cultural script? What if, existentially blindfolding his students, he had attempted to lead them to knowledge of *his* self rather than to awareness of *their own* selves? Suppose he had tried to impress upon them the adoption of his life script, subtly suggesting the copying of life poems that he had already composed. Such a pedagogical thrust would not only threaten the students' acquisition of self-knowledge and therefore their capacity for self-creation, it would, through the attempted replication of Forrister's self-identity, threaten the idiosyncratic nature of his own life and subvert his own status as strong poet.

But what is *self-identity*? Pragmatist and neopragmatist philosophers have suggested that the *self* is neither a material nor a spiritual substance, but an *idea* that is constructed by a conscious human organism. The idea is *achieved* over the course of a lifetime as a person interacts with features in his or her physical and social environment. Self-identity thus accumulates through a *hermeneutical* process: A person constructs the self through interpreting the meanings of various experiences and integrating these experiences into a historical unity. Or as Ricoeur (1981) suggested, self-identity is the result of an ongoing story in which the events of one's life are woven into a *plot*. The plot of the stories that we tell to ourselves about ourselves can possess a structure that is somewhat unified. These plots, our personal histories, thus provide a degree of coherence to our self-identities, a semistable view of who we think we are (and who we think we are not) in relation to the people and things in our universe.

Of course, as many postmodernists would have it, our identities, woven into the plots of our lives, are never absolutely seamless, nor are they static. Instead they are ambiguous and amendable, even for persons who honor an inherited script. Even for rigid and conforming individuals, the plot of their life stories shifts and thickens as it accommodates new information about their selves in relation to the world. This information that leads to growth in self-identity may result from questions that arise within life experiences. The responses to these questions may prompt a redescription of the self (Rorty, 1989), the kind of redescription that is crucial to the writing of strong poetry.

PROTECTING SECRET PLACES

Phenomenologists insist that one dimension of the self—its private side—is formed within a *secret place,* that secluded region of lived experience, especially childhood experience, which lies "beyond the world of institutionalized life" (Langeveld, 1983). Within this margin of experience the child may live in solitude and safety, often losing himself in imagination and fantasy. Feeling at home in a secret place, the child may begin to imagine a self that is singular, distinct from others in the world. He may begin to read between the lines of the life script that might otherwise seem impenetrable and closed to scrutiny and question. And, for Langeveld, this sense of a secret place is retained into adulthood, when it is more likely to be shared with significant others.

Forrister's cherished places of childhood lay within the hills and forests of North Carolina, which had granted him solitude and safety and where his infatuation with Nature grew into ardor. The aesthetic qualities of the mountains, and the objects of art and craft in which they were transmuted, would become a lifelong passion. Indeed, Forrister's life story (Part III) has suggested the origins of a robust imagination within those splendid secret places that he, as an adult, strove to share with his students.

To the consistently conventional, the robustness of that imagination may cause the adult Forrister to appear eccentric. Some will surely read the description of his dream (Part III) as confirmation of that view. Others may wrongly judge him as reclusive, still residing in a far-off place. It is true that Forrister maintained a certain distance from most of his colleagues, foregoing most faculty social events, refusing to partake in campus gossip. But recall Forrister's eager involvement in the local arts community and in the lives of his students. If not exactly gregarious or conventional, Forrister could hardly be considered monastic or wildly eccentric. Rather, his persistent efforts to maintain the integrity of his art program represented a lengthy struggle to sustain a personal educational vision that ran counter to the prevailing adaptionist mind-set.

Part of that vision was to protect the secret places of his students.

Forrister was aware of their rich fantasy worlds, what he called the "comfort zones" to which some of his students resorted, "especially [those from] really poor backgrounds and family lives." A rich imagination, for Forrister, was generally incompatible with predictability and gentility. Indeed, he admitted his attraction to a healthy rebelliousness in some students (e.g., Carolyn Wilson). These rebels were also often sensitive and perceptive, and this combination of fierce independence and acute aesthetic awareness marked them as candidates for an education in the arts. So Forrister (sometimes) recruited them into his program to equip them with additional resources for maintaining an internal aesthetic playground, for guarding the silence of their secret spaces against the noisy distractions of the larger culture.

Protection and enlargement of students' imaginative capacities requires some knowledge of their character. Indeed, John Dewey (1938/1963) insisted on a teacher's awareness of students' life journeys, on knowing, that is, "where the child is coming from." But securing this knowledge requires travel backward in time, into students' life histories. This movement may result in what van Manen (1977, p. 213) called *co-orientational grasping*, an engagement in which the teacher empathically adopts the perspectives of his or her students.

Empathic understanding of one's students does indeed require knowledge of their life stories. Forrister's knowledge of Barry Larson's freneticism could have only come from studying Barry, from close observations of his comportment and informed interpretations of his actions within the context of his youthful life plot. But only a teacher who cares deeply about teaching expends the time and energy to study his students. And in the recollections of his former students, Forrister's caring was a recurring theme. Sometimes his care for them lasted beyond graduation, more as friends than as mentees, into their adulthood.

Nel Noddings (1984) has offered a relevant view of the "caring teacher." One element in her ethic of caring is *confirmation*, wherein the caregiving teacher "see[s] the cared-for as he is and as he might be—as he envisions his best self" (p. 67). This "seeing" occurs through observations of students and through honest *dialogue* (Noddings's second dimension in an ethic of caring), through which a teacher achieves the kind of intimacy evidenced in Forrister's relationships with many of his students. An important factor in achieving this rapport was (as mentioned) personal in nature, a trust and reassurance born out of qualities such as honesty, tolerance, and acceptance. Another factor was the organizational structure of his classroom, the arrangement of its physical setting.

This structure (described in Part I) facilitated movement from student to student and gave Forrister the opportunity to offer them his intense, undivided attention. While teachers who lecture from a podium in a factory-like setting may, in some sense, "care" about their subject matter and their students, they are hindered by a setting not conducive to the personal dialogue, confirmation, and cooperative atmosphere that Noddings called for. In his less institutionalized setting, Forrister was better able to observe the meanings being created within artistic endeavors. He was free to guide students toward the outward expression of their innermost thoughts and feelings, even to co-inhabit the secret places publicized in their artwork. Being with them at those moments of self-recovery was, indeed, an opportunity for the deepest sort of co-orientational grasping.

But to what extent did Forrister's "care-full" efforts to protect and nurture the imaginations of his students succeed *in the long run*? I have described how some former students managed to surmount their inherited scripts to make ethical life choices. But did the appreciation and/or production of works of art by Forrister's former students continue beyond graduation? If so, did they help sustain a proclivity to write strong poetry? The answers to these questions are, I fear, complex and equivocal. In elaborating upon my responses, I move briefly to the field of educational psychology.

THE CRITICAL SPIRIT: DEGREES OF TRANSFER

What I am wondering about is called, in educational lingo, *transfer of learning*. The question concerns the degree to which learning can be transferred from one setting to another, from one in which content and skills are acquired—for example, Forrister's classroom—to places of everyday life outside of that setting, years after the act of learning. At least three schools of thought can be identified among educational psychologists who explore the transfer of learning.

One group maintains that students can acquire abstract, generalized thinking skills that enable transfer to occur, skills learned without reference to specific subject-matter domains. If, for example, students acquire a set of generalizable problem-solving skills in an academic setting, they become better problem solvers in other settings, regardless of the nature of the new problem to be solved.

Other theorists believe that transfer of generalized skills is impossible since skills are bound to, and must be taught in, the precise contexts of their application, through immersion in the elements of subject matter to which they apply (Beyer, 1987). Transfer is hindered when few similar elements exist between the learning situation and the situation in which the learning is to be applied.

Focused primarily on cognitive skills, both of these schools of thought see the development of thinking ability as resulting exclusively from the transmission of technique. Both address the question of whether the learner is capable of (rather than inclined to or interested in) transferring what has been learned. But the approach of Brell, drawing on Dewey (1933/1960), is different. Brell (1990) suggests thinking about transfer not only in terms of procedural norms but also (and more important) as a process that is dependent on the *disposition* of the individual "to strive for intellectual, emotional, and behavioral integrity, or what is sometimes called the *critical spirit*" (p. 87). He elaborates:

> A concept of critical thinking as transfer . . . [implies] that teaching for transfer is less a matter of transmitting knowledge, skills, strategies, and principles of thinking . . . than of fostering in students from the start an inquiring disposition, by which I mean a "readiness" to consider the bearing of apparently discrete frames of reference on one another and toward the construction of a more integrated world view. (p. 66)

Brell suggests that for a critical spirit to be born and thrive, students must learn to *value* it. They must develop a desire to probe into the "givens" of a situation, a willingness to imagine more than obvious, taken-for-granted, conventional perspectives, and thereby enlarge the number of "discrete frames of reference" and available courses of action. They must be ready to consider how the relationships of these perspectives to each other can offer a "more integrated world view," a fuller sense of who one is in relation to the world, and ultimately a more robust life story. They must be willing to engage in a quest for deeper personal meaning, the kind in which Forrister was himself engaged. How might such willingness have been transferred to his students?

I doubt, with Brell, Dewey, and others, that a critical spirit can be taught through a direct form of instruction. Rather, it must be fostered indirectly, with subtlety and persistence. In the sciences, this process begins by creating "doubtful situations" in which students desire to find answers, and in the humanities, "by having students generate and compare alternative interpretations of . . . points of view that intrigue them" (Brell, 1990, p. 68). In the arts, a critical spirit may be enhanced though suggestions about novel ways of apprehending familiar phenomena. Forrister's former students attested to his penchant for doing precisely that as he roamed the classroom, posing questions about aesthetic choices, wondering aloud about color, design, texture, "constantly challenging you," as former student Sean Logan put it, "to do something different, something more original."

Forrister created conditions within which intriguing aesthetic problems would arise (rather than posing preformulated problems) and created conditions for imagining solutions to the problems. "He would ask questions more than give you the right answer," observed Sean. Exuding love of surprise, Forrister aimed to create doubt and uncertainty, disturbing superficial satisfaction with a middling drawing or sculpture. Or a mediocre existence: Consider his unexpected recitation of a meaning-laden Cummings poem to the youthful, unfocused Barry Larson.

Forrister's lessons for Barry about carefully observing details within larger contexts had transferred across the years, reaching maturity long after Barry's graduation. Moreover, this learning outcome had generalized to his most important composition: the story of his life. Barry had grown to see the process of choosing and arranging particular actions as analogous to composing a photograph. This sense of aesthetics even permeated his life at work.

Barry's work as a waiter seemed to possess some of the formal qualities of an *aesthetic experience* (Dewey, 1934/1958). Aesthetic experiences possess a vitality that distinguishes them from the flat flow of ordinary life. In aesthetic experiences a person feels a unified structure in that flow, progressing in an organized fashion from the initial acceptance of a challenge to a fulfilling denouement. New perceptions arise as a person experiences his environment aesthetically, perceptions of relationships between familiar phenomena and new ones seeking a place. Dewey called this act of perception "an act of reconstructive doing" wherein consciousness becomes fresh and alive. It is this freshness and vitality that lives at the heart of every aesthetic experience. Indeed, as Dewey insisted,

> experience, to the degree to which it is experience, is heightened vitality . . . [and] because experience is the fulfillment of an organism in its struggles and achievement in a world of things, it is *art in germ* [italics added]. (p. 19)

Barry did not view waiting tables as a jumble of discrete tasks tangential to the aesthetics of his everyday existence. Nor was work an anesthetic activity from which to flee through his imagination (as it occasionally was for the adult Ben Dobson and the young, tomato-picking Forrister). Barry's love for finding and placing detail within a larger pattern gave vitality to his otherwise mundane work, with the small moments of each shift arduously crafted into the eidetic form of a concerto or play. On that public ground in a San Francisco restaurant the private space he had carried from the verdant hills of North Carolina seemed secure. That secret place, laden with innately satisfying formal attributes, opened here onto the arena of his practical work. As with Forrister's pedagogy or Barry's own earlier craft making, the private imagination had poured itself onto a public arena. Work had wedded play. Beauty had married utility.

How had Forrister supported that relationship? His use of the Cummings poem was one example of Max van Manen's (1991) notion of *tactfulness* in teaching. Tactfulness means "touching" someone, rousing them from slumber into greater personal awareness while respecting and preserving their personal space. This kind of tactfulness can bring coherence to the scattered pieces of a self, prompt (as Brell would have it) the construction of a more integrated worldview, and thereby encourage personal growth. What Barry's story suggests for van Manen's phenomenological construct is that a seed planted by an act of tactfulness may itself lie dormant within the consciousness of the student, with growth and learning occurring serendipitously at a propitious moment years hence.

And what does it suggest for Brell's theory of learning transfer? The story, although a singular one, confirms the power within the kind of transfer associated with the development and valuing of a critical spirit. For Barry, the transfer may have been occurring for years without his awareness of it. But in a San Francisco trolley car, after confronting some Tibetan monks with qualities reminiscent of Forrister, he finally recognized his disposition toward striving for integrity in his life and realized its major source. The message of the poem heard years earlier became suddenly available to Barry: "Take time to compose your artwork—and your *self*—well." The meaning of a poem offered by a teacher to an adolescent in an Appalachian schoolroom had finally been grasped by a thirtyish adult on the opposite side of a vast continent.

Transfer of learning accomplished? A larger idea of self achieved? Apparently. But the work of Carl Bereiter suggests that if Forrister's pedagogy was indeed the primary impetus of that achievement, then he is a rare specimen of teacher-as-hero. Bereiter (1995) described the phenomenon of *heroic transfer* as follows:

> [T]he hero is someone who sustains a purpose or value despite adversity and lack of social support. . . . Heroic transfer undoubtedly does exist.

There are people who credit some teacher with having instilled in them a disposition or aspiration that stayed with them and influenced their behavior throughout life. But this is [a] chancy . . . business; it probably depends on just the right input in just the right emotional context, at just the crucial moment in a person's development. (pp. 30–31)

Or, in van Manen's terms, heroic transfer requires a rare degree of teacherly tact. But narratives of several former students attribute to Forrister's tactfulness long-term dispositions similar to Barry's. Carolyn Wilson's knack for keen observations, acquired under Forrister's tutelage, continued to enhance her abilities as a writer. Ben Dobson's awareness of the colors, forms, and textures in his physical surroundings also remained long after graduation. For still other students, a disposition to write strong poetry was apparently gathered less from Forrister as schoolteacher than Forrister as person.

Indeed, a central element in Forrister's ability to promote a critical disposition was his presence as a strong poet, as one whose modus vivendi contrasted with elements of the prevailing social code. Forrister as math teacher or football coach could perhaps have effected the same heroic dispositional transfer, *if* he were a math teacher or coach who lived a life that fostered doubt and uncertainty, prompting his students to imagine alternate possibilities. Indeed, Forrister seemed at times to intentionally sprinkle his life with works of performance art in which his students were given roles. How else to characterize, for example, that evening of celebration with Paul Mosely and Ben Dobson (Part II)?

But these aesthetic experiences also underscore the *limitations* of Forrister as hero. However intriguing, they were, for students, rather passive aesthetic encounters, initiated and designed by someone other than themselves. Indeed, as adults, few of Forrister's former students consistently engaged in making art. The artistic publicizing of secret places was rarely practiced in busy adult lives. The disposition to do *that* had not successfully transferred across the dramatically changing vicissitudes of life that had pulled them away from the influence of Donald Forrister. The most potent episodes of "self-recovery" (Greene, 1977)—the kind of artistic engagements present in Forrister's program—were largely things of the past.

Forrister himself was chagrined over the waning of the artistic urge in many former students. Of course, not all of them had abandoned the quest for personal meaning or were no longer attracted to the works of great visual artists for some emotional and intellectual white water in their lives. Some continued to scrutinize their natural surroundings or infused their daily activities with kinesthetic forms and rhythms. Others attended concerts, plays, and museums. Nevertheless, for Cindy Loggins, Barry Larson, Kathy Shue, Ben Dobson and others, the abandonment of serious engagements with the loom, camera, easel, and sketchpad meant the end of at least a certain kind of self-recovery. Why was this so? I offer next some clues gleaned from the life stories that suggest the powerful forces operating to limit the transfer of a disposition to make art and therefore to question the conventional and to write strong life poetry.

CRITICAL DISPOSITIONS VERSUS CULTURAL IMPERATIVES

Ben's life story illustrates a prolonged struggle between two components of a complex persona, two contrasting professional identities, and, ultimately, two opposing notions of what constitutes the "good life." The sensitive, artistically talented side of Ben, the side appreciated and nurtured by Forrister, seemed to defer to a side determined to relegate photography to a supporting role in his life. In college the influences of his lawman father secured a victory for a more practical professional identity, pulling Ben into the world of criminal justice, even as vestiges of his innate aesthetic sensibilities endured in his daily routines.

This is not to suggest that Ben Dobson was certain to find less personal fulfillment as a lawman than as a photographer. But part of Forrister's hopes for Ben was the continuing development of his photographic talents. He wanted to give him a permanent space for making sense of the often mind-numbing activities of everyday work. But Ben's attendance to daily routine had ultimately caused an abandonment of photography as once appreciated and practiced. Incidents of making meaning through photography, plentiful in high school, seemed virtually nonexistent in Ben's later life.

Ben's story suggests the limitations of any dedicated and talented high school teacher who fights alone in the struggle against the routine and the mundane. It seems that the soul of the child, and of the adult he is to become, belong, after all, not solely to the student or to his teacher but to a wide assortment of claimants. Some are best described as cultural forces that pull both students and adults toward the conventional and the anesthetic.

For former Swain students, the enticements offered by the culture were primarily (although not exclusively) pecuniary in nature. Several insisted in interviews that, however talented, one could barely survive in a job in the arts and crafts. Indeed, the flight of many Swain graduates to broader economic pastures in Asheville, Charlotte, and Atlanta attested to the persistent economic malaise in their small town. To them, remaining in Bryson City meant consignment to the lifestyle of Robert Fricke, whose determination to remain a local artist had meant a lack of steady employment in Bryson City or elsewhere. Even in the larger cities pursuing an arts-related career was a formidable challenge, as the story of Keith Robinson illustrates. Or consider the case of Annie Chrisler. After graduating from an interior design school in Charlotte at the top of her class, and brandishing what she described as a "killer portfolio," Annie could not land a job in her field. Frustrated, tired of "selling wallpaper to little old ladies," she returned home to live with her parents and become a cosmetologist.

But for many Swain graduates, as for most of their American contemporaries, salary was an important criterion in career choice. Indeed, a march toward materialism had achieved unprecedented momentum in the late twentieth century. A hyper-acquisitiveness ran rampant, thanks in part to clever new strategies in mass marketing. Selfhood was more closely linked to material possessions than to an ethic of sharing in a common world. A robust popular culture was seducing people (young and old) into living scripts prepared on behalf of interests other than their own.

The cultural scripts in circulation honored work in the corporate business world and smart entrepeneurship (see the story of Paul Mosely) over the helping professions or those in which elements of the prevailing culture and one's place within it are explored, questioned, and critiqued. The strength of this materialist imperative helps explain the brevity of the deliberations of some of Forrister's students over whether to become (or remain) a "starving artist" or to choose a more lucrative trade or profession.

The degree of acquiescence to those scripts by ex-students varied widely, and precise measurements of Forrister's influence in each case is impossible. Given the power of the allure, it is compelling that occasionally some degree of heroic dispositional transfer had apparently occurred. I have noted the evidence of remnants of Forrister's spirit of artistic inquiry living on in the hearts of strong poets who had scattered far and wide.

Carolyn Wilson had resisted the lure of affluence in favor of a deep moral imperative. She had found contentment in her family, her modest lifestyle, and her part-time teaching job at a community college. The humanitarian aims of her teaching, her chosen mode of self-creation, strongly reflected those of Forrister's. Cindy Greathouse was similarly moved by Forrister to "realize what a good teacher is." During her junior year Forrister served as a model in the imprinting of her first self-images as a school teacher and inspired her later efforts at passing on an artistic spirit to her own students.

Other alumni had sought a middle ground, aiming to dissolve a dichotomy between material satisfaction and existential style. For instance, the enormously intriguing (and continually self-re-creating) Keith Robinson persisted in his efforts to parlay his artistic talents into some sort of profitable business. But still others were inclined to act out a life script that narrowly defined success as the accumulation of wealth. I am unable to forget my conversations with three former students, otherwise modest people, who bragged openly of their financial prowess, eagerly divulging the amounts of their sizable annual incomes.

There is, of course, nothing inherently evil about prosperity. But such remarks suggest the capacity of an individualistic, materialistic culture for establishing priorities that run counter to the collectivist moral and political character of strong poetry. Within a robust definition of that term, students living with style are seen as primarily social beings and moral agents, responsible citizens whose public spaces open into shared communities.

The philosopher Charles Taylor (1991) has noted that genuine growth of the self must take place within "a moral space, a space in which questions arise about what is good or bad, what is worth doing and what is not, what has meaning and importance . . . and what is trivial and secondary" (p. 28). One recalls that some of Forrister's students (like Forrister himself) often operated within such a moral space, carefully considering the place of ethics in their life stories. Again, Carolyn's story is a profound reminder that personal integrity and social responsibility need not be conflicting attributes. To the contrary, each individual contributes to communal growth whenever she redefines herself in a truly moral way; and conversely, an individual is fulfilled only through enlargening the community's sense of what is possible and virtuous.

As Dewey (1916/1966) reminded us, the renewal of self and community is best facilitated within a democratic culture, within a just and caring society. The more equitable the distribution of power in a society, the more likely that strong poetry will be shared and composed. But democracy cannot easily survive a steep imbalance between individual goals and attitudes of altruism, compassion, cooperation, and civic responsibility (Goodman, 1992). As Lesko (1988) wrote, "Indi-

viduals need to be concerned with the public realm, and a just society needs strong, autonomous individuals to keep it responsive, self-
critical, and dynamic" (p. 10). So one question for a teacher might be
this: How can one instill in students a critical disposition that (a) enables them to perceive imbalances in the culture and (b) engages them
in redressing those imbalances?

But this question was not part of the personal and pedagogical
agenda of Donald Forrister as depicted in the first three parts of this
book. Therein, Forrister may be viewed as typical of the kind of "good"
teacher portrayed in the mass media, but one whose work may be critiqued as supporting an individualistic and acquisitive culture over a
more socially just and economically democratic one. Consider, for example, critiques of the images of schoolteachers portrayed in the popular culture by Ayers (1993), Dalton (1995, 1999), Edelman (1990),
Kellner (1989), Mitchell and Weber (1999), and Ryan and Kellner
(1988).

What dimensions of the portrait of Forrister in this book resemble
the "good" teacher of popular books and Hollywood movies? At least
insofar as he did not wholeheartedly participate in, nor fully appreciate, the prevailing school culture, Forrister was an outsider. He was a
loner, as popular with his students as is Mark Thackery in *To Sir with
Love*. He was popular because he cared deeply for students, related well
to them, and learned from them, as did, for example, Miss Johnson in
the book *Dangerous Minds* (Johnson, 1995) and the film of the same
name. Like Forrister, Miss Johnson spent her own money on school
supplies and materials. Forrister was popular, and in a sense, effective,
because of a passion for his subject matter, as was John Keating in *Dead
Poets Society*. Forrister was also popular because he sometimes used unconventional pedagogical strategies to reach students, as did the title
character in *Mr. Holland's Opus*. And he was popular partly because of
his refusal to adhere to social codes involving dress, appearance, collegiality, and personal lifestyle. He occasionally bent rules to accommodate student needs (e.g., his decision to use funds designated for vocationally oriented crafts to purchase paints for his talented student
artists), much like the teacher of the book *The Water Is Wide* (Conroy,
1972) and film *Conrack*.

Another dimension shared by Forrister with teachers of print and
film is a reticence or refusal to enter the realm of the overtly political,
to foster in the lives of his students a disposition that is critical in the
strong sense employed by those intellectuals known as critical theorists. One of those theorists has argued that in order to accomplish that,

real and "reel" teachers need to move beyond noble-minded solitary efforts toward more radical narratives (Dalton, 1999). Dalton offered the following about the character Conrack, a teacher:

> My point is not that [Conrack] did nothing for the children in his class. . . . [Conrack] shakes those children from a listless slumber, helps them connect with their world, and helps some of them dream of the world beyond the salt water that divides them from the mainland.
>
> [But] that one teacher projected as a light in a darkened schoolhouse is not enough. Without the power of a collective force, Conrack probably did all that he could do, and the character is right in realizing that his solitary effort is not enough. . . . (pp. 47–48)

What *would* be enough? For most critical theorists, general cultural oppression is not effectively resisted in the long run by the kind of resistance evidenced within Forrister's sly subversion of the formal, vocationally oriented curriculum (Part I), nor in his tendency to privatize aesthetic activity. For them, critical dispositions must include more than an impulse to re-create an individual self. It must involve a willingness to intervene in the larger forces of domination that may ultimately determine the nature of that self. For Forrister and other teachers, this would mean moving beyond hopes for a chancy and fragile heroic transfer of value systems, into real praxis. It would mean engaging in the kinds of dialogue with students that bring them to an understanding of the forces that can vitiate the strength of the life poetry they write.

For an arts teacher to enact this sort of critical pedagogy, overtly political progressivist educators might recommend emphasizing the moral and political dimensions of art itself, especially by attending to the politics of imagery within the popular culture. The arts and crafts of Appalachia had always played an important part in Forrister's curriculum. Popular art, as part of the larger popular culture, might become a more significant element in that curriculum, not merely as a source of images or aesthetic qualities to be infused (already often the case) into their own artwork, but as material for critique. The subtle and pervasive aesthetics of the Internet, billboards, movies, television, apparel, architecture, and so on, might be rendered more visible; an investigation of the interests served by the qualities and images contained therein might be undertaken. The relationships between those interests and students' own proclivities for an acquisitive lifestyle might be explored.

What may be needed is a study of art that serves as a means for awakening both the student-artist and his or her audience to the every-day antidemocratic cruelties and injustices that would otherwise remain just beyond their fields of consciousness. And connecting art to issues of power in this fashion would be to refuse the artificial separation of a private, aesthetic imagination from a larger capacity to envision alternative social arrangements, ones in which those power imbalances inscribed within inherited cultural scripts are redressed.

For, indeed, the hills of Appalachia are no longer a rural sanctuary from the forces of modern and postmodern life. They have become part of a larger cultural terrain, contested ground, it seems, upon which fierce battles rage for the souls of its inhabitants. A materialistic, utilitarian culture is now an obvious threat to the potential and actual beauty to be found in lives of productive, socially responsible, idiosyncrasy. In this way of thinking, the strong poets who were and are Donald Forrister's students, creatures with a disposition toward carving out such lives, may become an extinct species if the battle is lost.

QUESTIONS

But however frustrating for those who—arrogantly, perhaps?—believe that they know how to save that species, the strong poet who is Donald Forrister has a right to prefer his own style of living and teaching. His life story embodies a refusal to draw a link between art and politics in his curriculum, deeming such a drawing as dangerous—especially to art, which might be sacrificed to a single political perspective, but also for his students, who might be indoctrinated rather than educated in a self-defeating pursuit. Such a pursuit is also scary to him because of a self-perceived lack of expertise in the area: "probably something that I would not know how to handle and it might get out of hand and . . . cause a lot of problems."

We must accept—and perhaps celebrate—the fact that Donald Forrister can only be himself. Formed early in life, core elements of his teaching persona are unlikely to change. He is unlikely to alter fundamentally his view of the nature of art and of his approach to teaching. And if so, then how is his teaching to be finally, officially judged?

Why should we not honor the perspectives of Forrister and his students over the one preferred by critical theorists? Have his students not offered powerful evidence of the heroic results of Forrister's teaching? What about the stunning poetry embroidered within their life stories, as they, inching toward middle age, credit him with the continued strength and wisdom needed to pursue their quests for personal meaning? Has a disposition to use good judgment in acts of self–re-creation not been etched indelibly into their life scripts, transferring to novel sets of existential circumstances? Will such transfer not continue until the final chapters of their stories are written—or even beyond, ad infinitum, as they teach in his manner? Is it a mere cliché to suggest that a teacher who is responsible for the continued personal growth of even one ex-student has succeeded immeasurably? Or that, in such a fashion, a teacher has truly touched eternity?

Then again, did Forrister really succeed in promoting a form of heroic transfer? Or has youthful devotion to artistry been diminished by an array of cultural formations? Haven't hopes for workspaces that are also arenas of personal re-creation been dashed? Haven't marriages of beauty and utility been unable to withstand the corrosive agents of a brutally individualistic and utilitarian culture? Didn't Forrister's reluctance to investigate the nature of those agents leave his students unable to resist the culture's enticements toward convention and individual aggrandizement? Wasn't Forrister's definition of caring too narrow in its omission of a strong critique of that culture? Hasn't that meant a failure to touch eternity?

These many questions I leave to the reader. Together, they evidence a deliberate stance of ambiguity, an attempt to delicately balance my messages concerning the work and lives of Forrister and his students. My refusal to privilege one interpretation of the realities of the characters in these life stories is designed to afford readers some interpretive space. Some will find this degree of textual freedom disconcerting, irritating, or anxiety-producing—especially those with strong ideological leanings.

But I expressed very early my affinity for heuristics over authorial certainty. For these are the consequences of the epistemological preferences that have shaped the writing of this book, of my postmodernist views regarding the politics of textual conversations. My aim was to encourage various participants—writer, characters, as well as readers—to engage in conversations about what constitutes good teaching and living, with no voice privileged over another. In the final part of this book, I elaborate upon these and other issues of epistemology and method involved in the researching and writing of this sort of narrative-based study.

PART V

RESEARCHING, WRITING, AND READING NARRATIVE STUDIES

Issues of Epistemology and Method

THIS BOOK IS DESIGNED to stimulate thinking about the enduring outcomes of education. To that end, I have attempted to avoid posing as an omniscient researcher-author performing a soliloquy for a silent—or silenced—reader. Instead, I have employed an experimental, postmodernist approach that honors the life stories of schoolpeople, that displays researcher judgments that change over time, and that invites participation by the reader. The text aims to promote polyvocal, conspiratorial conversations between the writer, the protagonists of those life stories, and the readers of the study, thereby furthering a fundamental, but often neglected purpose of educational inquiry.

What do I mean by "polyvocal, conspiratorial conversations?" And how can readers be encouraged to participate in them? How is this participation important to the furthering of that fundamental purpose of inquiry? And what, precisely, is that purpose? These questions lead us into an exploration of how this kind of text might move readers to interrogate their previously held notions of what constitutes good teaching and educational significance.

A QUESTION OF PURPOSE

Let us think of texts of educational inquiry pragmatically, as tools crafted for particular purposes. In the design of a useful tool, form follows function. Similarly, the formal qualities imbedded within a useful evaluation or research text should flow from the intended function of the inquiry, the purpose that it is designed to serve.

What are the purposes that educational inquiry might serve? A classic distinction in the field of program evaluation suggests one answer to this question. Michael Scriven (1967) distinguished between formative and summative purposes or roles of evaluation. These two purposes, noted Scriven, are directed at different audiences who are likely to use the evaluation text in different ways. *Summative evaluations* provide a terminal, overall appraisal of an educational program, for ex-

ample, informing decisions about promotion and rejection of person-
nel and courses. Summative evaluation is often an act of responsibility
to the person(s) and product evaluated, or to taxpayers (p. 55).

Formative evaluations, however, are designed with a different role
and audience in mind. Focused on improving an ongoing program,
they aim to discover deficiencies and successes in the intermediate versions of the program. Formative evaluation may be used as a tool of
enlightenment and empowerment for the people affected by that program (Cronbach, 1982; House, 1980) and other programs. An evaluation or research text might do so by raising significant questions about
various dimensions of the evaluated program.

Exploratory, formative evaluations differ significantly from declarative, summative evaluations in the kinds of truth claims they advance.
Indeed, the difference between the epistemology that underlies summative evaluations and that of nonauthoritative, formative evaluations corresponds to the epistemological differences between traditional social science and postmodern art. I will explain.

Cronbach (1982) noted that the primary purpose of social scientific
research and evaluation is to *reduce uncertainty,* to seek literal truth
within a particular paradigm, framework, or worldview. The desire to
know a "real world" with certainty is a persistent one, dating back at
least to writings by the Greek Parmenides, and found later within the
writings of René Descartes (Diefenbeck, 1984). But textbooks on educational research and evaluation still evidence this penchant for the
indisputable, their authors fretting about the potential contamination
of objective findings about the "real world," a soiling to be minimized
only through the most rigorous applications of the scientific method.
As Krathwohl (1993) put it, "of all knowledge sources, only science
and the reasoning authority routinely seek and survive testing and
challenge" (p. 50). In other words, only science and a Cartesian logic
can contribute to uncertainty reduction. And it is indeed important to
secure knowledge that approaches certainty if one's research or evaluative purpose is summative in nature.

But some theorists no longer partake of the modernist belief
that absolute knowledge of an objective reality can be achieved by
researchers. These *post*modernists even disagree that objectivity must
stand as a kind of "regulative ideal" toward which social science must
always strive. Instead, they see studies of human phenomena as more
subjective and humble enterprises. Abandoning an obsessive quest for
certain and total knowledge that transcends a fallible, human perspective, they opt for an epistemology of ambiguity that seeks out and celebrates meanings that are partial, tentative, incomplete, sometimes

even contradictory, and originating from multiple vantage points. Such an epistemological stance seems appropriate to a project of educational inquiry whose role or purpose is the *enhancement of meaning,* rather than a reduction of uncertainty. It seems suited for a formative, post-modernist study, such as the Swain Project, that is designed to raise important questions about the nature of the educational process.

So is the Swain Project an endeavor of postmodern social science? Should this nontraditional research and evaluation project be called scientific at all? Some postmodern theorists would prefer to retain the label of science for this sort of study, even if features associated with modernist social science are missing. Some have experimented with research texts that aim to erase, ignore, or straddle the line between science and nonscience, arguing that conventional distinctions are illusions. Scientific texts, suggested Latour (1988), are as open to interpretation as literary texts and, insisted Vattimo (1988), as rhetorical as literature. Indeed, all scholarly texts exhibit a narrative structure (Nelson, Megill, & McCloskey, 1987).

Such genre-blurring, called the "third stage of qualitative research," remains fashionable in many fields of the human studies (Denzin & Lincoln, 1998, p. 18), resulting in what anthropologist-storyteller Clifford Geertz (1983) calls an "omniform social science." Articles in educational journals such as *Qualitative Inquiry* and *International Journal of Qualitative Studies in Education* and books such as those in the Ethnographic Alternatives Series serve to blur the boundaries between the social sciences and humanities (Ellis & Bochner, 1996). Elsewhere, Lather (1997) vacillates between calling her postmodern feminist study about women with AIDS a "different kind of science" (p. 233) and the work of a cultural critic who "assumes an intermediary position between artist and scientist" (p. 239).

Scientific papers with a quasi-storytelling format are sometimes performed at professional meetings, instead of read in a traditional argumentative manner (Denzin, 1997). Ethnographic performance texts consist of poems, short stories, or dramas (Denzin, 1997). Auto-ethnography (including "evocative" [Ellis, 1997] and "heartfelt" [Ellis, 1999] autoethnography) has emerged as a genre that blends ethnography with autobiography. Other researchers have explored the intersections between ethnography, cultural studies, and fiction (Banks & Banks, 1998). Meanwhile, the written word has yielded to other media for communicating findings—slides, film, photographs, paintings, musical lyrics, and so on.

Perhaps because many postmodernist innovators began their careers as ethnographers and sociologists (rather than as artists, literary critics, or art theorists), they see themselves as engaging in "eccentric" (Lather, 1997, p. 236) kinds of *social science* rather than in experimental or revolutionary forms of *art* (literary or otherwise). An inability to imagine research as art, or literature as research, may also indicate a lingering sense of art as "intuitive" rather than empirical, "subjective" rather than, as Ricoeur (1981) would insist, very much *of* the world.

I claim that at least part of the Swain Project crosses a recently obscured boundary into the territory of the literary arts. The life stories around which the study centers exhibit literary characteristics. Moreover, since the Report, as a whole, aims to raise questions about the complex phenomena of teaching and learning, its function resembles that of imaginative literature more than even postmodernist social science. I will elaborate.

Jerome Bruner (1986) posited two basic forms of human cognition, the paradigmatic, or logico-scientific, and the narrative. The deep structure of paradigmatic thought is "most purely (and plainly)" revealed in science (especially theoretical physics) and in mathematics, while "the great works of fiction that transform narrative into an art form come closest to revealing 'purely' the deep structure of the narrative mode of expression" (p. 15). Each kind of text is fashioned in accordance with an intended function. Design elements within logico-scientific texts promote the primary purpose of engaging in paradigmatic thought—reducing uncertainty—by approaching, if never quite attaining, objective truth. Narrative texts (especially fictional ones), however, are designed to do what good art does so well. And what is that? According to the novelist James Baldwin (1962), the greatest achievement of art is the "laying bare of questions which have been hidden by the answers" (p. 17).

What design elements operate within the "deep structure" of a work of literature? It is nigh impossible to delineate them precisely and completely. Barone & Eisner (1997) have listed some qualities that make texts of educational inquiry *arts-based texts:* the presence of expressive, contextualized, and vernacular forms of language; the promotion of empathic participation in the lives of characters; the creation of a virtual reality; the presence of aesthetic form; the presence of the author's personal signature; and perhaps most importantly, a degree of textual ambiguity.

The stories in Parts II and III of this book exhibit most of these characteristics. For example, the language is largely contextualized rather than abstract, more vernacular than technical. This language is employed to re-create the lived worlds of protagonists and to encourage readers to dwell momentarily within those worlds. Moreover, the individual life narratives tend to exhibit Aristotle's (1961 edition) eidetic story form—they have a beginning, middle, and end. I discuss later how the text presents the reader with virtual realities. I will also reveal the nature of my signature as project director and author of the book.

Still, the report fails to exhibit certain of the arts-based features mentioned above. It is not pure poetry. Nor is the text, taken in its entirety, rounded out into the syntactic shape of an Aristotelian story. And even the individual life stories (and edited interview scripts) do not approach the level of metaphor-laden imaginative literature. Moreover, the nonstoried, analytical chapters of the report tend to state rather than express meaning, to denote rather than connote.

Nevertheless, while falling short of participating in Bruner's ideal deep structure of fictional literature, the Swain Project leans more to the narrative/artistic side of the research continuum than the paradigmatic/logico-scientific. Inasmuch as I moved onto the ground of this project as an arts-based educational researcher, my aims are indeed heuristic: to stimulate reflection and discussion about certain fundamental educational issues; to lay bare the questions that have been hidden by certain implicit, taken-for-granted answers about education and inquiry; to foster "brooding about the issues involved in telling [schoolpeople's] stories" (Lather, 1997); to reduce the commonsensical certainty about what it means to be educated.

Perhaps these aims could be more effectively promoted in a traditionally structured piece of imaginative literature—a novel, a play, an anthology of consistently fictional short stories—than in the verbal collage assembled here. Perhaps the more prosaic and analytical chapters too obviously expose implications best left submerged within more literary life stories. These are textual issues that I leave to the reader to ponder. But I do believe that the Swain Report exhibits the design element most crucial in a narrative text for achieving the heuristic aim of a work of art. That is the element of textual ambiguity. And if it does, then it may achieve the status of what Michael Bakhtin (1975/1981) called a *novel*. I will explain.

EPICS AND NOVELS

Bakhtin reminds us that not all stories are innocent. Some, while possessing many of the design elements mentioned above, are merely disguised as art, promoting an aim unlike that identified by James Baldwin. These stories belong to one of two primary genres of stories, the *epic*. Epics, for Bakhtin, are stories that seek to suppress a variety of discourses by converging upon a correct, final interpretation of events. Epics include cultural narratives such as myths, fables, and legends. Or they may be works of propaganda that support a cultural script, authoritative stories that tell us in a dogmatic fashion how to live our lives, identifying "correct" endings and scripted purposes for living. They are, wrote Bakhtin (1975/1981), "constructed in a zone of an absolute, distanced image, beyond the sphere of possible contact with the developing, incomplete, and therefore, rethinking and re-evaluating present" (p. 17).

Writers of epics, like many social scientists, deplore ambiguity. Other writers have coined alternative labels for epics. For Belsey (1980, p. 91) *declarative texts* attempt to impart knowledge by shutting out voices other than the author's and limiting the interpretive options of readers. Likewise, Phillips (1994) wrote of "narratives that need to be true (or close to the truth)." Sometimes narrative must be "correct":

> [w]hen something of significance hangs in the balance, when further action or intervention is called for, when policy is about to be made, and so on . . . we are more likely to act successfully if we act on the basis of correct information. (p. 17)

Unambiguous texts emitting an air of final authority are indeed suited to a decision-making process that is convergent, terminal, summative. An inquiry text serving that kind of function must be designed to yield, not imaginative speculation, but decisive declaration about what is (and is not) true, good, and beautiful—or, in our case, educationally useful. As an epic, this book would aim to reduce uncertainty about whether and how Forrister's students had become educated human beings. It would offer authoritative answers about the quality of Forrister's teaching from a single, consensual point of view, rather than raise important questions concerning the attributes of good teaching. But it is not an epic.

Standing in opposition to epics are stories that possess the characteristic of novelness. Novelness is sometimes (but not always) found in the modern novel. For Bakhtin, the novels of Rabelais and Dostoevsky manifest it to the highest degree. But novelness is not confined to that kind of literary text. Novelness, for Bakhtin, is an attribute of any text that promotes a dialogue between a set of views or cultural frameworks. Literature with novelness is polyphonic, respecting the variety of languages found within the dialogue between the author of a work, its various characters, and its readers. Each of these contributors to a set of textual exchanges speaks with a distinct style and from within a unique existential situation, through utterances shaped by specific social and historical forces (Holquist, 1990, p. 88), and no voice, including the author's, is privileged over others.

These sorts of exchanges serve as constant reminders of *otherness* in speech, as they celebrate a diversity of voices offering varied interpretations of phenomena (Bakhtin, 1975/1981). Often conflicting, the voices heard in the textual conversation may raise important questions about topics under discussion, challenging the reader to rethink the values that undergird certain social practices.

This book, taken as a whole, is obviously not a novel in the usual sense of that word. However, I have aimed to imbue it with a Bakhtinian sort of novelness, as a number of distinct voices engage in a kind of dialogue about important educational matters. Whose voices are these? In the remainder of Part V, I explore dimensions of the dialogue involving the writer, the people whose lives are represented in the text, and readers—and examine their relationships to the heuristic aims of this project.

AUTHOR OR WRITER?

The origins of this book can be traced to the 1970s, during my tenure as a high school teacher in New Orleans. In my 3rd year of teaching, I began to ask myself what were, as I would later discover, Big Questions in the scholarly field of curriculum studies, a field in which I would later professionally reside. Questions such as, What is worth teaching and learning, and why? And after those few years of seeing my students advance down the academic assembly line, exiting at graduation, moving out of my sight and my life, I began to wonder about the difference I was making in their lives.

I would occasionally encounter former students at class reunions or in department stores or restaurants, but the situation would invariably preclude my posing any penetrating (and awkwardly self-serving) queries about how *their* lives might have been saved by *my* pedagogy. I understood that these were questions best asked by a relative stranger, perhaps an educational researcher or a journalist. By the time I had become a credentialed educational researcher myself, the intellectual space occupied by these questions had been given over to others. But they would later return to center stage, serendipitously, as a result of some educational consulting work.

In 1982 I received a request from a representative of the Rockefeller Brothers Fund to write an essay about one of the recipients of their Awards for Excellence in Arts Education Program. This program sought out for recognition America's best public school arts teachers. My essay resulting from this request, published in *Daedalus, the Journal of the American Academy of Arts and Sciences,* is reprinted as Part I of this book. During its writing I became acquainted with a remarkable person and teacher.

In 1990 I relocated, moving from Kentucky to Arizona. I had lost contact with Don Forrister, although the *Daedalus* essay was, for a decade, required reading in my qualitative research courses. Students occasionally requested updated information on Forrister, asking about his current whereabouts and his program. These questions rekindled my own curiosity about Forrister, and I added the following queries to the list: What about his former students? Had he made an indelible impression on their lives? What might be the significant and enduring consequences of his teaching?

The Big Questions had returned with a vengeance. And the idea for this book was born: a longitudinal case study that would document the robust, wide-ranging, long-lasting consequences of Don Forrister's teaching.

Telephoning Forrister, I asked whether he was amenable to a further invasion of his professional privacy. He immediately laughed his consent. After I elaborated on my intended focus, he volunteered a list of students who had been present during the period of my earlier research. In the spring of 1995 I sent introductory letters to several former students, followed by phone calls, to arrange interviews on my first visit to North Carolina since 1983.

Over the following years I made several return trips from Phoenix to the Southeast, meeting with former students in a region ranging from Atlanta, Georgia, to Raleigh, North Carolina. There were also visits to California, primarily to interview Barry Larson. I would begin initial interviews by reviewing some of the points made in my introductory letter. Of course I addressed confidentiality issues, explaining that, despite pseudonyms, actual identities would be easily detectable by friends and family members. Intimate details of their lives would be on display.

Gradually, my interview tactics grew more sophisticated, ultimately including a request for a succinct indication of the kinds of influences, if any, that Forrister had had on their lives. I was searching for a central theme around which biographical revelations might be structured. Responses to this question varied greatly, with some former students (for example, one Robinson brother) asserting that Forrister had been only a marginal presence in their lives, and others detailing significant life changes resulting from their experiences with him.

Following this "grand tour" question, I asked the interviewees to dredge up childhood memories and then to move forward chronologically, always keeping in mind the focus provided by their opening observations. For example, a theme identified by Barry Larson involved Forrister's metalesson about living life slowly in order to appreciate it. The details of his hasty delivery at birth (as related to him by family members) thus became thematically relevant to his educational biography.

Interview transcriptions followed initial visits. And the long and arduous process of writing commenced.

The Swain Project was, in this manner, born out of my personal curiosity about the nature of the educational process. It was not co-originated by my informants; I was the sole instigator and director of the project. I was also the primary composer of this final report, even if I intended my voice to be merely one within the chorus of the text.

Aware of the influence of my own interests in producing this work, and of the directorial and authorial power I have wielded in its construction, I insist that it be regarded as any research or evaluative text—formative or summative, novel or epic—should be. What I have written in this book must, I mean, be viewed with suspicion. Although I have not written an epic text, I am a child of a modern Western culture in which the author, standing above suspicion, has traditionally written out of a position of privilege. This privilege rests in part on a broad acceptance of the foundationist epistemology described earlier. "*Author*-ity" in the modern era has been supported by a tacit acknowledgment of a special access to supposedly objective (and therefore politically disinterested) truth, beauty, and virtue. The privileges of the modern author flow from a presumed ability to reduce uncertainty through the skills of reason and science possessed as a professional. The modern author's agenda—to enlighten, instruct, and to instill moral values—therefore tends to be honored by other children of the culture, including readers.

The persuasive power of modern authorship flows from an acceptance that the single, literal reading of a textual object intended by the author, is indeed possible. Rosenau's (1992) description recalls the author of a Bakhtinian epic or a declarative text:

> The modern author in society is a "legislator" . . . a specialist, a professional, an intellectual, or an educator. . . . [T]hey know and decide things by weighing the "positive" and the "negative" and determining what is "true." [They] arbitrate in the sense of choosing between opposing points of view in controversy. What they select becomes "correct and binding." (Bauman, 1987; quoted in Rosenau, 1992, p. 27)

Postmodernists, as noted, strike a different intellectual pose. They refuse the modernist notion of authorship. Skeptical of the existence of an unconditioned truth, they repudiate the idea that any human can attain direct knowledge of it or should always strive to approach it. The modern author is thereby cut off from the source of his privilege, his instructional agenda dismissed, his persuasive powers sapped. Indeed, his very existence is, metaphorically speaking, placed in jeopardy.

Roland Barthes (1977) did indeed declare the death of the author, since the reader was now viewed as free to draw his or her own meaning from the text. Perhaps what has truly perished is a modernist faith in the possibility of authoring a text that is objectively true and morally and politically neutral. For postmodernists, every text is inevitably tinted (but not tainted) by the perspectives of the author, and inevitably bound to issues of personal meaning, history, and power. In other words, the ideology that supports a text is the result of human choice which "cannot be made without reference to a value, set of values . . . or interests" (Cherryholmes, 1988, p. 4). And the symbol systems, the forms of language, the means of expression employed in the text? They too imply human choice. They too signify the presence of values and interests.

News of the moral weight of language was heard initially from speech act theorists, who remind us that all speech is a form of action. When one chooses one's words, one chooses how to act. Wittgenstein (1953/1968) similarly reminded us that language devices are tools for constructing views of reality. When we employ alternative languages, we are moving to alter that reality. This action necessarily implies a choice of values, which, in turn, reflects the interests of the actor, or author. Writers such as Habermas (1970) and Lyotard (1984) later noted that those interests are present in doing research, itself an inevitably political act.

The claim that all human inquiry is fundamentally political disturbs the modernist author's agenda of delivering a truth relatively untainted by human interests. But postmodernists stand accused of advancing their own political agenda (Phillips, 1994), even if their professed stance is one of "ideological openness" (Lather, 1986). Would not the presence of such an agenda suggest a stance as authoritative as that which the postmodernists critique?

Wicomb (1991) is helpful in resolving this dilemma. She wrote of her decision "to amend my title, to erase the word *author* and replace it with the word *writer*. . . . As a writer [unlike an author], I do not have an agenda. But like everyone else, I [inevitably] write from a political position" (p. 14; see also Smith, 1987). A writer's *agenda* (like that of an author) implies "a disregard for writing as a process of discovery." Agendas focus on attaining a prespecified, standardized end product, on having one's intended readers adopt the finished and static political stance of the author. For Wicomb, however, the writer can have no finalized views. She prefers to talk of an "education" of the writer within the process of discovery that is writing. In this view the writer is incomplete and developing, a student of her own writing and its relationship to her position within a political space.

A postmodern researcher-writer often reveals facets of this education. Indeed, anthropologists (since Malinowski, 1922) and sociologists (perhaps since Hammond & Bellah, 1964) have offered autobiographical accounts of their fieldwork. This is an account of my own efforts. And changes in my perspective over time can also be ascertained by comparing Parts I and IV of this book. These writings may prompt the reader to hear me, the researcher-writer, as a frail, human voice, engaged with informants and readers in a textual conversation.

But sometimes a voice is, like that of a ventriloquist, "thrown." In the Swain Report, my writer's voice is most audible in the analytical Parts I and IV. But I also assume responsibility for the life stories of Forrister and his former students. And the question of who is speaking in a biographical text is, perhaps, even more complex than in most ethnographies.

In biography, as in ethnography, "the devices, the construction scars, the brush marks are all more or less invisible, at least to the unwary eye" (Geertz, 1988; cited by Pinar & Pautz, 1998, p. 68). In each case, identities are crafted and constructed, selves that are "rhetorical figures and performative assertions enacted in specific situations within fields of power, history, and culture" (Kondo, 1990). The personae constructed by biographers or ethnographers are indeed situated selves, rhetorical figures employed in the interests of the writer, within a "constructed cultural account" (Pagano, 1990). The language devices I employed as a biographer, the representational strategies adopted, the grammar and vocabulary used, the selection of people to interview, the kinds of personal information elicited from them, the nature of an interview process that influenced how informants talked and what they revealed (Briggs, 1986), the choices of which stories to include in (and exclude from) the collection, the juxtapositioning and sequencing of stories—these are but some of the construction devices that subtly shaped the identities of characters in this report.

The Aristotelian format and literary language of the life stories were rhetorical strategies employed to persuade the reader, albeit in an artful way. *Literary persuasion* may appear benign insofar as it avoids the declarative text's implicit denials of an authorial agenda. But because its powerful formal properties order and distort reality (K. Gergen & M. Gergen, 1986; Sarbin, 1986), the literary text is at least as suspect as other discursive forms. Holquist (1990) wrote about such order:

> In a literary text, the normal activity of . . . giving order to chaos is performed to a heightened degree. . . . [E]very time we write or read a literary text we give the greatest degree of (possible) order to the world. (p. 85)

But my own aspirations for this text bear repeating. They were not to trick readers into viewing the portraits of characters as neutral representations of reality, but to rhetorically persuade them to ask questions about important educational issues. I fashioned this book in accordance with that aim, ordered it to include more than life stories crafted within a literary language and a diachronic format (Polkinghorne, 1995). The stories in Parts II and III, arranged upon a textual stage, were sandwiched between critical essays.

The whole text was arranged, therefore, to allow meaning to develop while avoiding the literary deceitfulness of *narrative smoothing* (Spence, 1986). Narrative smoothing is evident in a seamless recounting of events that flows in a synchronic pattern from beginning, to middle, to inevitable denouement. Chronologically structured, the individual life stories may indeed appear tidy and slick. But the larger picture of Forrister and his teaching emerges from within a patchwork of impressions pieced together in the full text, one whose representational format results from unusual "textual gymnastics" (Schwandt, 1997, p. 307). This format is in the experimental spirit of postmodernist books such as those edited by Tierney and Lincoln (1997), Jipson and Paley (1997), Ellis and Bochner (1996), Diamond and Mullen (1999), and others within and outside the field of education. In these works textual staging calls attention to itself as artificial, the result of a desire to destabilize the notion of *author*, and to avoid the illusion of realism.

The writers of those books purposely subverted their own authority by engaging in the kind of relational arrangement found in fictional texts. Iser (1993), quoting Culler and echoing Bakhtin, suggested that

> fiction can hold together within a single space a variety of languages, levels of focus, points of view, which would be contradictory in other kinds of discourse organized toward a particular empirical end. (p. 9)

Indeed, narratives are similarly "shaped by particular patterns of inclusion, omission, and disparity," and their "selectivities, silences, and slippage [are] . . . sources of valuable insight, not problems of distortion" (Popular Memory Group, 1982). Iser (1974, p. 15) coined the term gaps to refer to carefully positioned omissions and silences that the reader must fill in with personal meaning from outside the "composed apparition" (Langer, 1957) that is the text. These empty spaces in the text require that the reader actively participate in the (re)construction of the textual world, thereby further subverting authorial privilege and suggesting that interpretive power must be shared for the text to achieve its ends as a novel.

In a sense, the writer of a text-with-novelness moves to persuade the reader to engage in a textual conversation that may be ultimately dangerous, disturbing, disruptive of comfortable, familiar notions about the world (Foucault, 1977). The presence of indeterminacy and ambiguity, and the loss of familiarity and certainty, may result in profound anxiety for the reader. The author is no longer present, speaking with finality, advancing a final agenda. As the reader reconstructs the illusion of the text, she may uncover what phenomenologists call an *otherness* (Poulet, 1986), an alternate consciousness, a "mind" behind the effect, a "fellow being" at least partially responsible for the virtual world now re-created.

The fellow being who is the writer—here, yours truly—may still be a sneaky character, a shadowy Other with a grab bag of literary tricks designed to lure and entice. But I hope that, having revealed a few of the construction scars in this text, I have been sufficiently obvious in the abandonment of my authorial pedestal. For my political position as a writer is one of power sharing; my aspirations, of a heuristic rather than a propagandistic or declarative sort. Quite obviously descending onto the textual stage, I aspire to be merely one suspect among the many who now participate in the interplay. To elaborate on this point, I turn to some others whose voices are also heard in the textual conversation within the Swain Project, the "suspicious characters" of Don Forrister and his former students.

PARTICIPANTS AS CHARACTERS

Let us not romanticize the "natives" who inhabit a research text such as this one. Indeed, are the characters whose selves are presented and examined in a narrative work any more or less truthful than the researcher-biographer? With many other commentators on this subject, I think not. Grumet (1988) has accurately described stories as "masks through which we can be seen," with every telling of a story a "potential prevarication." In the telling, personal interests are omnipresent.

Moreover, human beings are only able to "construe their lives within the confines of linguistic and social conventions" (K. Gergen, 1988, p. 102), conventions that are designed to evoke particular responses in an audience (Martin, 1986).

If Parts II and III of this book were a collection of strictly autobiographical essays, protagonists would still be wearing masks (fashioned in conspiracy with the writer-interviewer), suspiciously engaged in the (re)crafting and (re)shaping of their identities. The resulting rhetorical figures would still vary in accordance with those "specific situations within fields of power, history, and culture" (Kondo, 1990). Moreover, in autobiography, multiple versions of the *self* are simultaneously in play. There is, for example,

> the self then, the self now recalling then, the self now interpreting the self then from the present self's perspective, the self now thinking of possible future selves, a possible future self looking back now to the present self seeing it as in the past. (Cortazzi, 1993, p. 13)

And to this postmodern cauldron add issues of memory. Here are three questions by Wieder (1998): "How do people select their memories? What cultural processes do they follow? What happens to experience on the way to becoming memory?" Questions such as these have prompted cognitive scientists to investigate the fragility of autobiographical memory (Brinthaupt & Lipka, 1992; Conway, 1990; Schwarz & Sudman, 1994). Their findings advise against one version of an autobiographer's self fully trusting another version.

Notions of a nonunitary self are consistent with the thinking of various postmodernists. For example, feminist postmodernists tend to view the self as fluid, shifting, developing, emergent (Bloom & Munro, 1995; De Lauretis, 1984; Smith, 1993). Their view is supported by theorists whose emphasis on discontinuities and disruptions undermine the possibility of an integrated and consistent self-identity (Barthes, 1977; Derrida, 1978; Foucault, 1973). Freeman (in Brinthaupt & Lipka, 1992) has suggested that these postmodernists are following Hume in his denial of the possibility of an idea of selfhood. And they follow Nietzsche (1887/1968) who first hypothesized about the self as multiplicity.

In my view, these theorists have performed a valuable service in problematizing the modernist notion of a totally static, consistent, unified self. And in this project the self of the chief protagonist, Don Forrister, is viewed through the positionings of many other selves. Looking through the experiences of many former students, the texts of my essays, and Forrister's own recountings an identity emerges, albeit not an entirely seamless and coherent one.

But have postmodernists overreacted somewhat in favoring the differences over the similarities between various versions of a self? My own views on this matter reveal my pragmatist proclivities. I resonate with the attempts of William James, George Herbert Mead, John Dewey, and Richard Rorty—as well as Bakhtin and some narrative theorists—at a dialectical healing of the apparently antithetical concepts of a unified self and a fragmented one.

Mead (1934/1960), for example, would not abandon the notion of the self as an "idea" constructed by a human organism, developed and modified through a lifetime of interactions with facets of one's environment. The organism strives for coherence, integrating into a historical unity the experiences in which the interactions occur. The identity, the "I," that results from this integration is, indeed, the crowning achievement of a conscious organism.

James (1890/1960) noted how crucial memory was to this process:

> The identity which the "I" discovers can only be a relative identity, that of a slow shifting in which there is always some ingredient retained. The commonest element of all . . . is the possession of the same memories. However different the man may be from the youth, both look back on the same childhood and call it their own. (p. 372)

So memory, that easily maligned process, nevertheless plays a vital role in binding together a selfhood. Memory, however fragile and untrustworthy, turns out to be "self-serving" in more than its tendency to skew reality according to a particular set of interests. It also serves the self in its own construction. Memory is the glue that holds meaning together, that allows for a life story to be fashioned and related. Without it there would be only discontinuities, only multiple versions of a self, no plot to transform an otherwise unrelated series of events into a life story (Ricouer, 1981).

The plot of a life consists of "ingredients retained" that are shaped into a story form. In Western culture (unlike some others) the form is often Aristotelian. Polkinghorne (1988) noted that "the self is that temporal order of human existence whose story begins with birth, has as its middle the episodes of a life span, and ends with death" (p. 152). We may be privy to (a version of) the end of the story of the deceased. But for someone still alive (e.g., a character in the Swain Report), the plot is open-ended, allowing for what may be called *life assertions* to move it forward. These are actions that draw upon accumulated memories of prior activities for their meaning and in turn contribute to the meaning against which future actions will be regarded. The creation of new passages in a life story, like the meaning making in reading a written text, is an interpretive process. And the interpreter, maker of the meaning, is a version of the self of the actor or reader.

A totally fragmented self can make no such meaning. A self with no history, without memory, has no future. A "self now" that is totally alienated from a "self then" cannot act. While one is never precisely the same person today as yesterday, without at least a semistable identity, a core of self-recognition, a sense of "I," one is dysfunctional. As the pragmatists (and others) would have it, a sense of self is a tool for meeting fundamental human needs of sanity and survival. They also emphasize the contribution of radical critique and reconstruction to the health of a self, the importance of occasional reinvention through powerful acts of the imagination. But after deconstruction of the self there must follow reconstruction; a sense of continuity and a degree of trust between various selves must be woven like a thread throughout the story of who one is.

For Bakhtin (1975/1981), that same thread can be used to bind together loosely my own selves with the selves of others. Bakhtin, triumphing over a false dichotomy, suggested that personal existence is simultaneously unique and unified. On one hand, meanings given to events in the world inevitably vary according to one's position in the world. My pain and my death will indeed be mine—they occur within my own existential location. On the other hand, notions of pain and death (and other life events) are comprehended by others; paradoxically, my selfhood is, to that extent, shared, existing in relation to others', as their selfhood exists in relation to my own. Sharing the event of existence means that selves and others are inevitably bound together in dialogue. To engage in this dialogue is not, argued Bakhtin a matter of choice, but essential to self-construction. Holquist (1990) explained Bakhtin's point:

> I am always responsible for the response [to others and to the world] that is generated from the unique place I occupy in existence. My responses begin to have a pattern; the dialogue I have with existence begins to assume the form of a text, a kind of book. . . . Bakhtin conceives of existence as the kind of book we call the novel. . . . [F]or all of us write our own text, a text that is then called our life. Bakhtin uses the literary genre of the novel as an allegory for representing existence as the conditioning of authoring. (p. 30)

As mentioned earlier, Bakhtin described novels as texts that can promote dialogue that results in an educational process. They can enlighten the reader as to how others author their life stories and give
order to the world through their growth, self-development, and reconstruction. Within those stipulated terms, the Swain Report is a
"novel" designed to accommodate the tales of situated selves transformed. As characters in their life stories, former Swain students did indeed become reconstructed selves, often from life-altering experiences
with their teacher.

Moreover, in this collection of life narratives, each self engages in
the reconstruction of selves in addition to his or her own. Insofar as
some characters (inevitably) include others in their own life stories,
they may themselves be viewed as biographers. And conversely, the
selves of the (auto)biographers are elsewhere reconstructed. This is especially true for Don Forrister, whose persona is reconfigured through
the prisms of the stories of many former students, as well as his own
and mine. And indeed, the oversight of the researcher provides an additional layer of complexity. I am (even as writer and not author) the
biographer of teacher and students, even as they tell stories about
themselves and others.

The resulting intratextual discourse is, therefore, novel-like: enormously complex, varied and rich, with impressions from each of the
accounts ricocheting about, here conflicting with, and there reinforcing, other impressions of the characters in this research text. This discourse circles around to meet itself, recalling the perspective on narrative of the Pueblos and other Native Americans, described by Silko
(1991) as one of "story within story; the idea that one story is only the
beginning of many stories, and the sense that stories never truly end"
(p. 84).

I have detailed many of the ways in which the (re)constructed
characters here serve as rhetorical figures deployed in the interests of
the writer and informants, within a cultural account collaboratively
fashioned (Pagano, 1990). Next I elaborate further on those details.

Writer-Character Negotiations

The idea for the Swain Project, again, was mine. It was not born out of
a struggle in the life of a member of a marginalized group, in the tradition of emancipatory-minded stories (hooks, 1991). Nor did it result
in the kind of collaborative text exemplified by Nespor and Barber
(1995). In that research project, the authors supported the efforts of
parents of special education students who "saw [the work of the au-

thors] as a way to strengthen and extend their political voice" (p. 51). Several of those parents had tried to write about their experiences on their own. Among Forrister's former students only Carolyn Wilson had considered writing about her relationship with her mentor.

As originator and director of the study, I held gatekeeping power, control over whom to invite into it. Of course, invitees could refuse my request. Except for two, all contacted Swain alumni ultimately consented, although with varying degrees of eagerness. Many were pleased that someone had chosen to document what they perceived as Forrister's extraordinary talents and his place in their lives. They already held, prior to my invitation to collaborate, personal "reasons to *need* the research" (Nespor & Barber, 1995, p. 51). So a tacit research bargain was struck. I brought writing skills and access to publication venues; participants contributed autobiographical data and interview time. I received the information needed to achieve my formative research or evaluation purpose; they acquired a venue for honoring their teacher—and for reconstructing their selves.

To repeat, disguises were donned by those engaging in the self-reconstructions. Respondents wore discursive costumes suited to the project; the contents of their revelations were shaped by the contexts in which they were elicited. Relevant dimensions of these contexts included the following: the interview setting (a respondent's living room, a small-town McDonalds at breakfast time, a formal tea in the lobby of the St. Francis Hotel, and so on); the perceived power differential between the interviewee and researcher; the race, age, gender, social and cultural background of each; the participant's images of the book's potential readership (family members, friends and neighbors, Don Forrister, distant scholars and other strangers).

Drafts of life stories were sent to informants for feedback. These "member checks" were *not* conducted to meet a traditional criterion of confirmability, nor for establishing the kind of validity that is critical to declarative texts. They represented an ethical gesture more than an epistemological one, an action designed to honor the rights of informants to read and react to our jointly constructed versions of their life stories (Schwandt, 1997).

Each story was crafted around a theme identified by the informant. The theme related to prominent shifts in life plots that arose out of their relationship with their teacher and served to structure the interviews and the emerging story. The theme served as a *qualitative control* (Ecker, 1966), a means of determining the autobiographical details to be elicited and included in (and those to be ignored and excluded from) the developing story. This choice of theme was sacred, untouchable:

Never did I attempt to influence an informant's judgment about the nature of Forrister's significance in his or her life story. The details needed to document this significance were another matter.

While fashioning early drafts of stories out of transcripts, I would sometimes fill in holes in interviewees' responses, pulling from my own imagination small descriptive details needed for composing a vivid story. In doing so, I remained faithful to the theme desired by the interviewees. Upon later remission of the draft to the informant I was sometimes surprised at their inability to recall the precise details of an event or setting. I would then ask this question: "*Could* it have happened like this?" Note that I did not ask: "*Did* it happen (precisely) this way?" This line of questioning represented an attempt to share power in the writing, and not, I insist, an author's arrogant appropriation of a life story. It was the work of a writer interested in producing a full-bodied account of a life that would serve the heuristic purpose of prompting questions in readers about teaching and learning.

The question of whether these fabrications of detail diminish the trustworthiness of the storyteller is addressed later as we consider the reader's role in reconstructing the text. But first there are additional issues of potential power imbalances between writer and characters. They concern the text (Part IV) in which I deconstruct and analyze the reconstructed selves of those characters. Given my choice to do so, could such a textual arrangement be egalitarian? truly polyphonic? If so, how were issues of power surrounding textual format and design resolved fairly?

Format and Framing: Life Stories and Life Histories

Some narrative theorists refuse to allow stories of schoolpeople to stand naked, alone, unadorned by the social-historical contexts only theorists can provide. They believe, that is, in the textual supremacy of life histories over life stories. These narrativists—primarily critical theorists—are concerned about the power differentials that may exist between informants and the larger culture. Since forces in the larger culture can overwhelm and distort the apparently innocent version of a life story, the researcher-author must intervene to redress this power imbalance through critical analysis.

Consider, for example, Goodson's (1995) insistence that life stories are inherently uncritical, partaking of a script composed elsewhere, by others, with the purpose of maintaining the maldistributions of power within the larger culture. Stories told by members of marginalized groups may thus be, ironically, potentially *dis*empowering, participating in a "tyranny of the local" (Harvey, 1989) and a "specificity of the personal" (Goodson, 1995). Life stories, that is, may reaffirm a narrow and distorted account of events that fails to recognize and problematize certain elements of social context and social process. Disseminating stories that are naive, unmediated by theory, critique, and social commentary, may serve to unknowingly fortify patterns of domination. For that reason, argued Goodson, "stories need to be closely interrogated and analyzed in their social context" (p. 90). By providing a dialogue of action within a theory of context, he suggested, we turn life stories into life histories and begin to see them as "social constructions which allow us to locate and interrogate the social world in which they are embedded" (p. 98).

As a critical theorist, Goodson may be charged by some with demanding a narrowly ideological form of cultural analysis. But educationists of other political stripes have also worried about the ability of stories—insofar as they are merely descriptive rather than scholarly, theoretical, and analytical—to stand successfully alone. For example, Elliot Eisner, proponent of educational criticism, a form of research and evaluation in which the researcher-evaluator brings the tools of art criticism to educational matters, agrees that storylike descriptions are insufficient.

Eisner (1991) suggested that the descriptive dimension of an educational critique provides readers with vicarious experiences of events, the equivalent, in Goodson's terms, of the life story dimension of a life history—or the "filling" of the Swain Report sandwiched in between analytical Parts I and IV. For Goodson, naive stories should not constitute the entirety of a narrative research text. Likewise, for Eisner, description—or storytelling—is "almost never adequate without interpretation" (p. 97). Educational critics must explain the educational significance of what they have described, "illuminating the potential consequences of practices observed and providing reasons that account for what has been seen." They must augment the descriptive element with explicit interpretation and evaluation, even employing social science theory for the sake of "satisfying rationality, raising fresh questions, and deepening the conversation" (p. 95).

Other theorists oppose the use of academic language in narrative texts, preferring to privilege the voice of the informant in a life story over the commentary of an outsider. For them, placing a vernacular, literary, anecdotal, narrative portrait into a paradigmatic envelope is demeaning to the narrator or storyteller. Such framing represents for them a form of academic arrogance that does violence to the meanings expressed by participants.

Even within a postmodern zeitgeist, however, refraining from paradigmatic thinking and writing is difficult for many educational researchers. As Lincoln (1997) remarked, "Most of us are unaccustomed to writing in literary, non-scholarly genres [that are] unlike what we have always done" (p. 47).

In crafting the Swain Report, I attempted to play two games at once. On the one hand, I assuaged a felt need to speak in an analytical voice about motifs confronted within my conversations with former students. On the other, I wanted to honor the life stories of participants before transforming them into life histories.

So I experimented with a format in which life stories were presented extensively and physically distanced from the commentary of the researcher. I desired a format that, while not mimicking the genre of the modernist novel, offered sufficient space for a Bakhtinian sort of dialogue between characters and writer. I wanted a variety of voices to be heard speaking in their vernaculars, in "primary speech genres" (Bakhtin, 1975/1981), unmuffled by the scholarship of the author, outside of his tight theoretical framework built with an academic tool kit.

Ultimately, framing did occur. A researcher, even one with a formative aim, has a right (or duty?) to offer his observations about the educational phenomena being studied. But my critical commentary would reside in chambers of its own, in separate chapters, respectfully distanced from the tales told by informants. The result was, I hope, a reasonable compromise between the recommendations of two opposing camps of theorists on the issue of narrative framing. By turning a collection of life stories into a collective life history through critique, I have perhaps avoided charges of trafficking only in the local and the personal. In providing textual breathing space for the voices of individual characters, by refusing to drown small snippets of their narrative poetry in a sea of scholarly prose, I hope that my presentation is relatively free of modernist arrogance and authorial privilege.

The strategies I employed are not intended as a final solution to issues of representing characters in research texts. My approach is not a model for replication elsewhere, but an attempt to be creative and fair, given the contingencies of this particular project. I hope that it will encourage others to engage in their own textual experiments, thereby contributing to a limited bank of currently existing strategies.

But if in some measure I have succeeded in honoring the perspectives of informants-turned-characters, have I also drawn readers into the textual conversation? Indeed, why should wary readers, whose voices are so important to my formative aspirations, commit themselves to the discussion? Why should they trust the writer and characters as coconversationalists? How might they benefit from joining in? And should readers assume positions of privilege over writer and characters?

IMAGINING THE READER

In a certain sense, the writer is also a reader. "One's writing is," wrote Agger (1990, p. 178), "always silent dialogue." But other readers of this report, with different life stories and membership in different communities of discourse than my own, will use it in ways unfathomable to me. No psychic, I strained mightily to envision an "intended readership" (Iser, 1974) for guidance in shaping the text. Who might be willing to "cruise" (Barthes, 1975) the text? And who are the readers who might find it sufficiently seductive? Might they encounter disturbing insights upon rummaging for items to bring back to the places where they live? How might they then use—or abuse—those items? Only in a few rare cases will I ever know.

This section of my text is, therefore, suspended within a fragile web of desire. I, the writer, will divulge what I hope occurs in the reading events. I hope for polyvocal conversations with no overbearing participants. For conversants who are, at least initially, mistrustful of each other, adopting a postmodernist attitude of wariness over potentially hegemonic authorial tendencies, of skepticism over the seemingly innocent tales of earnest characters. But I hope ultimately for readers who are able to conspire together with writer and characters toward a more sophisticated set of questions about the potential outcomes of teaching and learning.

We know that epic texts that share some of the formal features of the novel can lure an unsuspecting reader into their ideological webs. Characters may appear to embody various forms of otherness, but ultimately submit to authorial intentions. Postmodernists, therefore, understand the need to be *revolutionary readers* (Belsey, cited in Wicomb, 1991), readers who are reluctant to relax their critical faculties, even in the presence of an experimental text, composed by a well-intentioned writer, peopled with (apparently) autonomous characters, with novelness as its aim.

Some readers of the Swain Report may read it closely, literally, "correctly," as final fact. Others may read it boldly, read all or some of it as imaginative literature, or as a form of literary nonfiction. I hope,

as writer, that it performs for some readers a heuristic function, ultimately doing what literary art can do. Indeed, a revolutionary reader
can assert a readerly prerogative and think of the Swain Report as if it
were a work of imaginative literature. While still distrustful that writer
and characters will reveal the truth, a revolutionary reader may nevertheless join in a useful conversation with them. How so?

A reading event may be played out in two acts, two phases that are
dialectically intertwined. In the first phase, the reader inhabits the
worlds of the characters (here, Forrister and his former students). In
the second, the reader is shocked into thinking about the meaning of
phenomena (here, educational) observed when transported into a
familiar nearby world. Let us explore each of these phases in some
detail.

Reconstructing the Text

What if the Swain Report were a purely imaginative piece of narrative,
a *fictional* work in the traditional meaning of that term? In the first
phase of reading imaginative literature, say literary theorists, a reader
reconstructs the author's text. The reader, in this phase, is hardly revolutionary as she silently attends to the vision of the writer, re-creating
a world previously assembled by the literary artist. These re-creations,
wrote John Dewey (1934/1958),

> are not the same in any literal sense. But . . . there must be an ordering of
> the elements of the whole that is in form, although not in details, the same
> as the process of organization the creator of the work consciously experi-
> enced. Without an act of re-creation the object is not perceived as a work
> of art. (p. 54)

In re-creating the illusion of the literary text, the reader attends to
those textual details—elements of aesthetic form and experiential
content—that corroborate and reinforce each other and contribute
to the unity of the textual world under reconstruction. In this phase of
the event, the reader, in Ricouer's (1976) term, attends to the *sense* of
the text.

Phenomenologists have alluded to a "literary attitude" that is
adopted by the author in constructing the hypothetical world of a fictional narrative and by the reader in reconstructing it. This attitude is
"literally inserted into the real world . . . in a process of restructuring
[items and elements that exist in the real world]" (Iser, 1993, p. 4). This

restructuring, argued Iser, is the result of three fictionalizing acts. The first two are the *selection* and *combination* of elements "from a variety of social, historical, cultural, and literary systems that exist as referential fields outside the text" (p. 10). These "real world" elements, manipulated by the writer, do not merely represent reality but serve as pointers to things not in the text. Selected empirical elements combined within the text serve an important literary purpose. For the reader to be lured into the reconstruction of the text, the apparition to be reconstructed must be plausible, credible, believable, possessing a sense of fidelity—qualities often associated with good narrative and qualitative research (Bruner, 1986; Grumet, 1988; Lincoln & Guba, 1986). A text that conveys a sense of closely observed reality (whether psychological, sociological, or physical) is more likely to succeed in the seduction of the reader.

For Iser (1993, p. 11), the third act is the text's *self-disclosure* of its own fictionality. This disclosure is accomplished through a range of signals, formal properties of the text that are usually associated with literary genres (see, e.g., the list above by Barone & Eisner, 1997). The presence of these attributes, argued Iser, serve to invoke "conventions . . . which form the basis of a contract between author and reader, the terms of which identify the text as a literary fiction." It is this disclosure that places the world represented in the text within brackets, "thereby indicating the presence of a purpose that proves to be the observability of the world represented" (p. 16).

Other types of texts, argues Iser, omit different sorts of signals. In reading and writing texts that do not disclose themselves as fictional, such as works of paradigmatic social science (Bruner, 1986), no literary attitude is adopted. In Iser's view (but as we shall see, not in mine), the paradigmatic text cannot be temporarily bracketed off from the ordinary stream of consciousness. In a paradigmatic textual event there is no representing reality in order to point to something else, no recasting of existing structures in the real world for the sake of conveying meaning. There is simply a mimesis, an earnest attempt at verbally replicating those structures of the real world.

But Iser's (1993) sorting of narrative texts into two primary genres, the fictional/literary and the nonfictional/nonliterary, is puzzling in its rigidity. He admits that fiction is often broadly conceived to include all items, textual and otherwise, fashioned by human beings, thus playing a role in nonliterary activities of cognition and behavior (including works of social science that attempt to disguise their fictional status). But Iser ultimately chooses a more exclusive definition of fiction. The literary text's self-disclosure as fictional means that its "function must be *radically different* [italics added] from related activities that do not mask their fictional nature" (p. 12).

For Iser (1974), the text offers its implied readers a "frame of possible decisions" (p. 55), ordered through "means of communication by which the reader is brought into contact with the reality represented by the author" (p. 57). These include the subtle signals that suggest the text's status as fictional or nonfictional. But how will the reader decide to use a text in which the signals are insufficiently clear for discerning the attitude preferred by the writer? What of texts that blur the boundaries between genres, texts that contain both paradigmatic and literary features? What about narrative-like texts that are labeled nonfiction, but that read like fantasy? Or what if my own implied readers, savvy and rebellious, reject their implied status outright, ignore the attitude I have subtly assigned to them, and choose to read the text robustly, in an unapproved and illicit manner? For answers to these questions, we move beyond the initial phase of the reading event to the second. In this phase, the reader turns away from the textual illusion to ascertain the meaning of the reconstructed world for the one in which she is actually living.

Dismantling the Textual Illusion

In certain unfortunate textual events the reader succumbs to the enticements of the text to remain in the initial phase of reading, never advancing to the second. I can think of at least two kinds of such reading events. In one the reader dwells in an aesthetic remove, within a sublime world of fantasy that is, according to the formalist critic Northrup Frye (1967), best understood as "the negation of reality" (p. 169). Some texts—romance novels, for example—are indeed designed to ensnare the trusting reader in the impossible world they have been persuaded to reconstruct. Docile readers are content to lounge forever within such a place that offers escape from the tensions and troubles of daily life.

But other storied texts also attempt to persuade anxious readers to cling to a (re)composed apparition. These are epic stories that overtly advance a narrow moral stance or political ideology. In reading these texts, one is enclosed in a reconstructed world, either a literal world with details selected and arranged to advance a conventional version of the truth, or a scientifically sanctioned one, or one that is the singular vision of an expert–author-as-legislator-of-reality (Rosenau, 1992).

Like the romantic story, the epic suggests that the reader remain silent in the face of the text. Both suggest that the reader dissolve her self into the illusion she has re-created.

Other sorts of literature—for example, the Bakhtinian novel— entice readers to revolt, to break that silence, to dismantle the textual illusion for their own purposes. Revolutionary readers recall the insistence of postmodernists from Barthes to Derrida that even texts of well-intentioned authors possess a surplus of meaning as supplied by a hegemonic culture. Unpacking and inspecting that surplus is essential if there is ever to be achieved a degree of trust of the "others" (writer and characters) who appear within a text. Moreover, since the self of the reader is bound within that same domineering culture, she must regard that self as partial, incomplete, and evolving. The reader is, therefore, just as suspect as writer and characters, her voice no more or less privileged in the textual conversation. Paradox reigns here: Only when a reader is self-doubting can she be persuaded to question her own perspective and engage in the kind of dialogue that may lead to a textual event with what certain pragmatist philosophers call *critical utility.*

Traditional pragmatists such as William James (1890/1960) conjoined notions of truth and utility, arguing that whatever is true is useful and whatever is useful is true. For James, a belief is to be considered true, and therefore valuable, only insofar as it yields a "completed function in experience" (p. 48). The kind of function performed by an epic text is the attainment of a convergent truth, to be used for final, summative purposes. In reading and writing epic texts one hopes and aims for conventional forms of utility, the referential reliability of information to be used in making judgments about the fate of actual persons described in the text.

But critical utility, a function that may be identified with Bakhtinian novelness, represents a modification by *neo*pragmatists of the utility criterion. Premised upon what Cherryholmes (1988) described as "visions of what is beautiful, good, and true" (p. 151), critical utility is concerned less with the narrow truthfulness of statements and observations than with the values that support them. A text is critically useful insofar as it causes readers to question certain values (including educational values) previously considered beyond questioning.

The value-saturated nature of literature has been recognized by philosophers throughout history, from Aristotle to Charles Taylor. Ricouer (1992), for example, likened works of literature—those "thought experiments we conduct in the great laboratory of the imaginary"— to "explorations in the realm of good and evil. . . . In the unreal sphere of fiction," he wrote, "we never tire of exploring new ways of evaluating actions and characters" (p. 164). And Iser (1974) equated the critical utility of a novel with its tendency to transgress against prevailing social norms. Within the novel, norms, set into new contexts

> act as . . . the subject of a discussion which . . . ends in a questioning . . . of their validity. This is frequently brought about by the varying degrees of negation with which the norms are set up in their fictional context—a negation which impels the reader to seek out a positive counterbalance elsewhere in the world immediately familiar to him. The challenge implicit in the negation is . . . offered first and foremost to those whose familiar world is made up of the norms that have been negated. These . . . readers of the novel are then forced to take an active part in the composition of the novel's meaning, which resolves around a basic divergence from the familiar. (p. xii)

Although Iser was referring to the modern novel, his words also apply to postmodern texts such as the Swain Project that are not easily classifiable as fiction or nonfiction. Critical utility may indeed be achieved by revolutionary readers of this work who choose to take a literary attitude toward it. They may honor Fish's (1980) insistence that the literary attitude is "always within our right to assume toward properties that belong by constitutive right to language" (p. 109). And as Pagano (1991) noted, assuming this attitude in reading possibly nonfictional narrative may direct our attention "away from the troublesome, and possibly repressive, questions of truth and falsity" (p. 198).

While reading nonfiction as fiction can be beneficial, does the opposite hold? What of Iser's (1993) warning that "inappropriate reactions will ensue" when the reader of a fictional text fails to assume the fictional attitude (p. 12)? Or what if the reader mistakes a text composed toward formative aims, one that meanders along a fiction/nonfiction continuum, for a declarative text with summative intentions? Indeed, might not Swain protagonists become victims of an unwarranted trust by the writer that readers will not use a novel as an epic? What if revelations about Don Forrister were used, not to promote a reimagining of the potential outcomes of teaching wherever they may occur, but as a dossier, for making decisions about Forrister's future status as a teacher? Readers already familiar with the actual characters represented in the text may be especially prone to such a misconstrual. Warning: the danger of Pagano's "repressive consequences" is indeed present in reading a text like the Swain Report.

Swain characters—Forrister and alumni—were, to varying degrees, aware of this danger. For while I often attempted to conceal their identities by the standard means of pseudonyms and misleading physical descriptions, the fictionalizations were quite incomplete. They understood that friends, family members, and others might read the book, not for its intended purpose of "playfully explor[ing] what understandings and meanings the story makes possible" (Jardine, 1992, p. 56), but in a literal fashion that could affect attitudes and actions toward them. Therefore, each interviewee no doubt calculated responses to questions with the book's potential audience in mind.

I can only remind such readers that this book was composed in a postmodern spirit, and like all life narrative, is rife with exaggerations, distortions, inconsistencies, contradictions, and imaginary constructions that disqualify it as a final, factual rendition of people and events. Elements of the "real world" have been selected and recombined—that is, manipulated—so that they do not merely represent reality but adumbrate that which is *not* in the text.

Distance from the "real world" of Swain County may increase the possibility of seeing more of that which is not in the text. A stranger to the people and landscapes represented may be prone to read the book nonliterally. While not trusting the reconstructed text as a mirror image of reality, such a reader may still resonate with its portrayals, putting it to use as an *imaginary*, as an opening into a possible world. Having reconstructed the virtual world first constructed by the writer, the reader may then depart from the textual realm and dismantle it to see what it offers. Searching for a "reference" (Ricouer, 1976) for the text—or what Barthes (1975, p. 24) calls a "something else"—the reader takes the text home into the world of her daily experience to see what it might say about familiar conditions, conventional practices, and the values and ideologies that support them.

Revolutionary readers of the Swain Project report may likewise "pragmatize the imaginary" (Iser, 1993). In the second phase of the reading process, they will have disassembled the world of Forrister and his students and used it critically for their own purpose of value negation. Extracting meaning from the text, they may come to question the usefulness of stale, tired ideas about what should count as educationally important.

THE CONSPIRATORIAL CONVERSATION

For the Swain Project text to be critically useful, for it to promote uncertainty and value negation, it must, as suggested earlier, serve as a catalyst for a polyvocal conversation, a narrative communion of writer, characters, and readers. But how are these participants to achieve sol-idarity when the prevailing attitude is one of mutual suspicion? Let me underscore the radical shift in attitude necessary for successfully read-ing a postmodern literary text, if it is to serve the formative purpose of a Bakhtinian novel. This requires an ultimate suspension of mutual mistrust in favor of an open sharing of ideas and ideals towards a fu-ture that is both desirable and possible.

An *author* may suspect that the reader will not know how to "prop-erly" read the text. Perhaps he fears that the reader will remain in a state of restrained consciousness, incapable of deciphering a message subtly embedded within a literary form. So the author may decide to declare (rather than express) that message, thereby shifting genres from novel to epic, and his status from writer to author. A *writer*, how-ever, holding the reader in high regard, is pleased to think that she will dismantle what has been constructed and reconstructed.

The writer (but not the author) presumes strong, revolutionary-minded readers who disdain subservience. As writer, he may still in-tend to persuade the reader—but not to adopt a "truthful" vision (moral or empirical) inscribed into, and sanctioned by, the text. The writer re-sists the compulsion toward propaganda, toward self-righteously trick-ing or bludgeoning the reader into accepting an agenda, however mor-ally and politically enlightened. Writerly persuasion is of a different order, aiming to entice the reader into wondering about what has been previously taken for granted.

My intention here was to persuade readers to question prevailing notions of educational significance. I did so by inviting several charac-ters into the conversation, a teacher and his former students. But the selves reconstructed here need not be seen as trustworthy representa-tions of real people. Elements within these life narratives were care-fully selected and recast into a form designed for the critical purpose detailed above. Upon dismantling the text, the reader may regard them, in a critically useful fashion, as analogues of students and teach-ers who inhabit the nearby world of the reader. This choice is possible because Bakhtin is, I believe, correct about the shared dimension of our beings enabling us to apprehend that to which a text with novelness alerts us. By manipulating elements of the "real" world, the text-with-novelness (including the experimental, postmodern kind proffered here) enables us to observe that which has not been observed before—ways of being, qualities of life, exhibited by actual people in situations analogous, but never identical, to the ones portrayed. Like a teacher portrayed in literature, drama, or film, the character who is Don For-rister of Swain County may call to mind other teachers with whom readers are familiar. These actual characters then become the objects of scrutiny and may themselves be reconstructed within a polyvocal textual engagement.

In such an event we are reminded of how astoundingly liberating an act of story sharing can be. For on that occasion of narrative communion the vigilant reader takes the offer of perceiving certain phenomena in a strange new way. She accepts the invitation of the writer to seek out the analogues of rhetorical figures and to remake "real" selves in the new light of the text. In other words, she enters into a *conspiracy* with the storyteller-narrator and those characters, a political and value-based conversation about the relationship between current conditions and a more desirable state of affairs, between *what is* and *what should be*.

Readers of this book may find themselves asking any number of new questions. Questions about whether the selves reconstructed herein—those of Don Forrister, Barry Larson, and so on—do indeed resemble any characters observed outside of this text. Questions of what a broadened and deepened sense of educational possibilities might mean for their own pedagogy. Questions of whether teachers must collaborate with each other in order to ensure that their aspirations for their students are not undermined by a materialistic, individualistic culture. Questions of how to do so.

If these or other educationally significant questions arise within conspiratorial conversations generated by this book, then what often is—narrow and shortsighted notions of educational outcomes—will indeed have become closer to what should be—teachers and schools dedicated to the endurance of the cognitive, the ethical, the aesthetic, and the useful, within lives that stretch out far beyond graduation day.

REFERENCES

Agger, B. (1990). *The decline of discourse: Reading, writing, and resistance in post-modern capitalism.* New York: Falmer.

Anyon, J. (1982). *Aspects of resistance by working class and affluent fifth-grade girls to traditional sex-role demands.* Paper presented at the annual meeting of the American Educational Research Association, New York.

Aristotle. (1941). Politics, Book 8. In R. McKeon (Ed.), *The basic works of Aristotle.* New York: Random House.

Aristotle. (1961). *Poetics* (S. H. Butcher, Trans.). New York: Hill & Wang.

Asheville (NC) Citizen. (1982, April). Swain jobless rate climbs.

Ayers, W. (1993). A teacher ain't nothin' but a hero. In P. B. Joseph & G. E. Burnaford (Eds.), *Images of schoolteachers in twentieth-century America: Paragons, polarities, complexities* (pp. 147–156). New York: St. Martin's Press.

Bakhtin, M. (1975/1981). *The dialogic imagination: Four essays.* Austin: University of Texas Press. (Original work published 1975)

Baldwin, J. (1962). *The creative process.* New York: Ridge Press

Banks, A., & Banks, S. (1998). *Fiction and social research.* Walnut Creek, CA: Alta Mira Press.

Barone, T., & Eisner, E. (1997). Arts-based educational research. In R. M. Jaeger (Ed.), *Complementary methods for research in education* (2nd ed., pp. 75–116). Washington, DC: American Educational Research Association.

Barthes, R. (1975). *The pleasure of the text* (R. Miller, Trans.). New York: Hill & Wang.

Barthes, R. (1977). The death of the author. In R. Barthes (Ed.), *Images, music, text* (pp. 142–148). New York: Hill & Wang.

Bauman, Z. (1987). *Legislators and interpreters: Modernity, post-modernity and intellectuals.* Ithaca, NY: Cornell University Press.

Belsey, C. (1980). *Critical practice.* London: Methuen

Bereiter, C. (1995). A dispositional view of transfer. In A. McKeough, J. Lupart, & A. Marini (Eds.), *Teaching for transfer: Fostering generalization in learning* (pp. 21–34). Mahway, NJ: Erlbaum.

Beyer, B. K. (1987). *Practical strategies for the teaching of thinking.* Boston: Allyn & Bacon.

Bloom, H. (1973). *The anxiety of influence.* Oxford: Oxford University Press.

Bloom, L., & Munro, P. (1995). Conflicts of selves: Nonunitary subjectivity in women administrators' life history narratives. In J. Hatch & R. Wisniewski (Eds.), *Life history and narrative* (pp. 99–112). London: Falmer Press.

Brell, C. (1990). Critical thinking as transfer: The reconstructive integration of otherwise discrete interpretations of experience. *Educational Theory, 40*(1), 53–68.

Briggs, C. (1986). *Learning how to ask.* Cambridge: Cambridge University Press.

Broudy, H. (1974). *General education: The search for a rationale* (Fastback #37). Bloomington, IN: Phi Delta Kappa Educational Foundation.

Brinthaupt, T. M., & Lipka, R. (1992). *The self: Definitional and methodological issues.* Albany: State University of New York Press.

Britzman, D. (1991). *Practice makes practice: A critical study of learning to teach.* Albany: State University of New York Press.

Bruner, J. (1986). *Actual minds, possible worlds.* Cambridge, MA: Harvard University Press.

Casey, K. (1995–1996). The new narrative research in education. *Review in Research in Education, 21,* 211–253.

Center for Improving Mountain Living. (1981). *County development information for Swain County.* Cullowhee, NC: Western Carolina University.

Cherryholmes, C. (1988). *Power and criticism: Post-structural investigations in education.* New York: Teachers College Press.

Connelly, F. M., & Clandinin, D. J. (1990). Stories of experience and narrative inquiry. *Educational Researcher, 19,* 2–14.

Conroy, P. (1972). *The water is wide.* Boston: Houghton Mifflin.

Conway, M. A. (1990). *Autobiographical memory: An introduction.* Philadelphia: Open University Press.

Cortazzi, M. (1993). *Narrative analysis.* London: Falmer Press.

Cronbach, L. (1982). *Designing evaluations of educational and social programs.* San Francisco: Jossey-Bass.

Culler, J. (1975). *Structuralist poetics: Structuralism, linguistics, and the study of literature.* Ithaca, NY: Cornell University Press.

Cusick, P. (1973). *Inside high school: The students' world.* New York: Holt, Rinehart & Winston.

Dalton, M. (1995). The Hollywood curriculum: Who is the 'good' teacher? *Curriculum Studies, 3* (1), 23–44.

Dalton, M. (1999). *The Hollywood curriculum: Teachers and teaching in the movies.* New York: Peter Lang.

De Lauretis, T. (1984). *Alice doesn't: Feminism, semiotics, cinema.* Bloomington: Indiana University Press.

Denzin, N. (1989). *Interpretive biography.* Newbury Park, CA: Sage.

Denzin, N. (1997). Performance texts. In W. Tierney & Y. Lincoln (Eds.), *Representation and the text: Re-framing the narrative voice* (pp. 179–218). Albany: State University of New York Press.

Denzin, N., & Lincoln, Y. (1998). Introduction. In N. Denzin & Y. Lincoln (Eds.), *The landscape of qualitative research: Theories and issues* (pp. 1–34). Thousand Oaks, CA: Sage.

Derrida, J. (1978). *Writing and difference.* London: Routledge & Kegan Paul.

Dewey, J. (1916/1966). *Democracy and education: An introduction to the philosophy of education.* New York: Free Press. (Original work published 1916)

Dewey, J. (1933/1960). *How we think.* Lexington, MA: Heath. (Original work published 1933)

Dewey, J. (1934/1958). *Art as experience.* New York: Capricorn Books. (Original work published 1934)

Dewey, J. (1938/1963). *Experience and education.* New York: Collier Books. (Original work published 1938)

Diamond, C. T. P., & Mullen, C. (Eds.). (1999). *The postmodern educator: Arts-based inquiries and teacher development.* New York: Peter Lang.

Diefenbeck, J. A. (1984*). A celebration of subjective thought.* Carbondale: Southern Illinois University Press.

Durkheim, E. (1934/1956). *Education and sociology.* New York: Free Press. (Original work published 1934)

Dykeman, W., & Stokely, J. (1978). *Highland homeland: The people of the Great Smokies.* Washington, DC: Division of Publications, National Park Service, U.S. Department of the Interior.

Eaton, A. J. (1937). *Handicrafts of the Southern Highlands.* New York: Russell Sage Foundation.

Ecker, D. (1966). The artistic process as qualitative problem solving. In E. Eisner & D. Ecker (Eds.), *Readings in art education* (pp. 57–68). Waltham, MA: Blaisdell.

Edelman, R. (1990). Teachers in the movies. *American Educator, 7* (30), 26–31.

Eisner, E. (1991). *The enlightened eye: Qualitative inquiry and the enhancement of educational practice.* New York: Macmillan.

Eisner, E., & Vallance, E. (Eds.). (1974). *Conflicting conceptions of curriculum.* Berkeley, CA: McCutchan.

Ellis, C. (1997). Evocative autoethnography: Writing emotionally about our lives. In W. Tierney & Y. Lincoln (Eds.), *Representation and the text: Reframing the narrative voice* (pp. 179–218). Albany: State University of New York Press.

Ellis, C. (1999). Heartfelt autoethnography. *Qualitative Health Research, 9*(50).

Ellis, C., & Bochner, A. (1996). *Composing ethnography: Alternative forms of qualitative writing.* Walnut Creek, CA: Alta Mira Press.

Fish, S. (1980). *Is there a text in this class? The authority of interpretive communities.* Cambridge, MA: Harvard University Press.

Forrister, D., & McKinney, G. (n. d.). *Art: Arts program booklet.* Bryson City, NC: Swain County High School.

Foucault, M. (1973). *Madness and civilization: A history of madness in an age of reason* (R. Huward, Trans.). New York: Random House.

Foucault, M. (1977). *Discipline and punish: The birth of the prison.* New York: Vintage.

Frye, N. (1967). *Anatomy of criticism.* Princeton, NJ: Princeton University Press.

Geertz, C. (1983). *Local knowledge: Further essays in interpretive anthropology.* New York: Basic Books.

Geertz, C. (1988). *Works and lives: The anthropologist as author.* Stanford, CA: Stanford University Press.

Gergen, K. (1988). *Concepts of self.* New York: Irvington Publishers.

Gergen, K., & Gergen, M. (1986). Narrative form and the construction of psychological science. In T. R. Sarbin (Ed.), *Narrative psychology: The storied nature of human conduct* (pp. 22–44). New York: Praeger.

Goodman, J. (1992). *Elementary schooling for critical democracy.* Albany, NY: State University of New York.

Goodson, I. (1992). Studying teacher's lives: An emergent field of inquiry. In I. Goodson (Ed.), *Studying teacher's lives* (pp. 1–17). London: Routledge.

Goodson, I. (1995). The story so far: Personal knowledge and the political. In J. Hatch & R. Wisniewski (Eds.), *Life history and narrative* (pp. 89–98). London: Falmer Press

Greene, M. (1970). Teaching for aesthetic experience. In *Toward an aesthetic education.* A report of an institute sponsored by CEMREL, Inc. Washington, DC: Music Educators National Conference

Greene, M. (1977). Toward wide-awakeness: An argument for the arts and humanities in education. *Teachers College Record, 19*(1), 119–125.

Grumet, M. (1988). *Bitter milk: Women and teaching.* Amherst: University of Massachusetts Press.

Habermas, J. (1970). *Knowledge and human interest.* Boston: Beacon Press.

Hammond, P. E., & Bellah, R. N. (1964). *Sociologists at work.* New York: Basic Books.

Harvey, D. (1989). *The condition of postmodernity.* Oxford: Basil Blackwell.

Hausman, J. (1970). The plastic arts, history of art and design: Three currents toward identifying content for art education. In G. Pappas (Ed.), *Concepts in art and education: An anthology of current issues.* London: Macmillan.

Hirsch, E. D. (1988). *Cultural literacy: What every American needs to know.* New York: Vintage Books.

Holquist, M. (1990). *Dialogism: Bakhtin and his world.* London: Routledge.

hooks, b. (1991). Narratives of struggle. In P. Mariani (Ed.), *Critical fictions: The politics of imaginative writing* (pp. 53–61). Seattle, WA: Bay Press.

House, E. R. (1980). *Evaluating with validity.* Beverly Hills, CA: Sage.

Iser, W. (1974). *The implied reader.* Baltimore: Johns Hopkins University Press.

Iser, W. (1993). *The fictive and the imaginary: Charting literary anthropology.* Baltimore: Johns Hopkins University Press

James, W. (1890/1960.) Pragmatism's conception of truth. In M. R. Konovitz & G. Kennedy (Eds.), *The American pragmatists.* New York: The New American Library. (Original work published 1890)

Jardine, D. (1992). Reflections on education, hermeneutics, and ambiguity. In W. Pinar & W. Reynolds (Eds.), *Understanding curriculum as phenomenological and deconstructed text* (pp. 116–127). New York: Teachers College Press.

Jipson, A., & Paley, N. (Eds.). (1997). *Daredevil research: Re-creating analytic practice.* New York: Peter Lang.

Johnson, L. (1995). *Dangerous minds.* New York: St. Martin's Press.

Kellner, D. (1989). *Critical theory, Marxism, and modernity.* Baltimore: Johns Hopkins University Press.

Kondo, D. (1990). *Crafting selves: Power, gender, and discourses.* Chicago: University of Chicago Press.

Kozol, J. (1991). *Savage inequalities: Children in America's schools.* New York: Harper Collins.

Krathwohl, D. (1993). *Methods of educational and social science research: An integrated approach.* New York: Longman.

Langer, S. K. (1957). *Problems of art.* New York: Scribner.

Langeveld, M. (1983). The secret place in the life of the child. *Phenomenology and Pedagogy, 1*(2), 181–191.

Lather, P. (1986). Issues of validity in openly ideological research: Between a rock and a soft place. *Interchange: A Quarterly Review of Education, 17,* 62–84.

Lather, P. (1989). *Re-inscribing otherwise: The play of values in the practices of the human sciences.* Paper presented at the International Conference on Alternative Paradigms for Inquiry, San Francisco, CA.

Lather, P. (1997). Creating a multi-layered text: Women, AIDS, and angels. In W. Tierney & Y. Lincoln (Eds.), *Representation and the text: Re-framing the narrative voice* (pp. 233–258). Albany: State University of New York Press.

Latour, B. (1988). *The Pasteurization of France.* Cambridge, MA: Harvard University Press.

Lawrence-Lightfoot, S. (1997). A view of the whole: Origins and purposes. In S. Lawrence-Lightfoot & J. D. Davis, *The art and science of portraiture* (pp. 3–16). San Francisco: Jossey-Bass.

Lesko, N. (1988). *Symbolizing society: Stories, rites, and structures in a Catholic high school.* New York: Falmer.

Lincoln, Y. (1997). Self, subject, audience, text: Living at the edge, writing at the margins. In W. Tierney & Y. Lincoln (Eds.), *Representation and the text: Reframing the narrative voice* (pp. 37–55). Albany: State University of New York Press.

Lincoln, Y., & Guba, E. (1986). But is it rigorous? Trustworthiness and authenticity in naturalistic evaluation. In D. Williams (Ed.), *Naturalistic evaluation* (pp. 73–84). San Francisco: Jossey-Bass.

Lortie, D. C. (1975). *School teacher: A sociological study.* Chicago: University of Chicago Press.

Lyotard, J.-F. (1984). *The postmodern condition: A report on knowledge* (G. Bennington, Trans.). Minneapolis: University of Minnesota Press.

Macdonald, S. (1970). *The history and philosophy of art education.* New York: American Elsevier.

Malinowski, B. (1922). *Argonauts of the Western Pacific.* New York: E. P. Dutton.

Martin, W. (1986). *Recent theories of narrative.* Ithaca, NY: Cornell University Press.

Mattil, E. (1971). *Meaning in crafts.* Englewood Cliffs, NJ: Prentice-Hall.

McLaren, P. (1989). *Life in schools: An introduction to critical pedagogy in the foundations of education.* White Plains, NY: Longman.

Mead, G. H. (1934/1960). The genesis of self and social control. In M. R. Konvitz & G. Kennedy (Eds.), *The American pragmatists*. New York: The New American Library. (Original work published 1934)

Mitchell, C., & Weber, S. (1999). *Reinventing ourselves as teachers: Beyond nostalgia*. London: Falmer Press.

Nelson, J., Megill, A., & McCloskey, D. (Eds.). (1987). *The rhetoric of the human sciences: Language and argument in scholarship and public affairs*. Madison: University of Wisconsin Press.

Nespor, J., & Barber, L. (1995). Audience and the politics of narrative. In J. Hatch & R. Wisniewski (Eds.), *Life history and narrative* (pp. 49–62). London: Falmer Press.

Nietzsche, F. (1887/1968). *The will to power*. New York: Vintage. (Original work published 1887)

Noddings, N. (1984). *Caring*. Berkeley, CA: University of California Press.

Pagano, J. (1990). *Exiles and communities: Teaching in the patriarchical wilderness*. Albany: State University of New York Press.

Pagano, J. (1991). Moral fictions: The dilemma of theory and practice. In C. Witherell & N. Noddings (Eds.), *Stories lives tell: Narrative and dialogue in education* (pp. 193–206). New York: Teachers College Press

Pederson, E., Faucher, T., & Eaton, W. (1978). A new perspective on the effects of first-grade teachers on children's subsequent adult status. *Harvard Educational Review, 48*(1), 1–31.

Phillips, D. C. (1987). Validity in qualitative research. *Education and Urban Society, 20*(1), 9–24.

Phillips, D. C. (1994). Telling it straight: Issues in assessing narrative research. *Educational Psychologist, 29*(1), 13–21.

Pinar, W., & Pautz, A. (1998). Construction scars: Autobiographical voice in biography. In C. Kridel (Ed.), *Writing educational biography* (pp. 61–67). New York: Garland.

Polkinghorne, D. (1988). *Narrative knowing and the human sciences*. Albany: State University of New York Press.

Polkinghorne, D. (1995). Narrative configuration in qualitative analysis. In J. Hatch & R. Wisniewski (Eds.), *Life history and narrative* (pp. 5–24). London: Falmer Press.

Popular Memory Group. (1982). Popular memory: Theory, politics, method. In R. Johnson, G. McLennan, B. Schwartz, & S. Dutton (Eds.), *Making histories* (pp. 174–190). London: Hutchison.

Poulet, G. (1986). Phenomenology of reading. In R. C. Davis (Ed.), *Contemporary literary criticism: Modernism through post-structuralism* (pp. 350–362). New York: Longman.

Richardson, L. (1990). *Writing strategies: Reaching diverse audiences*. London: Sage.

Ricoeur, P. (1976). *Interpretation theory: Discourse and the surplus of meaning*. Fort Worth: Texas Christian University Press.

Ricoeur, P. (1981). *Hermeneutics and the human sciences: Essays on language, action, and interpretation* (J. B. Thompson, Trans.). Cambridge: Cambridge University Press.

Ricoeur, P. (1992). *Oneself as another* (K. Blamey, Trans.). Chicago: The University of Chicago Press.

Rorty, R. (1982). *The consequences of pragmatism.* Minneapolis: University of Minnesota Press.

Rorty, R. (1989). *Contingency, irony, and solidarity.* Cambridge: Cambridge University Press.

Rosenau, P. (1992). *Post-modernism and the social sciences: Insights, inroads, and intrusions.* Princeton, NJ: Princeton University Press.

Ryan, M., & Kellner, D. (1988). *Camera politica: The politics and ideology of contemporary Hollywood film.* Bloomington, IN: Indiana University Press.

Sarbin, T. R. (1986). The narrative as a root metaphor for psychology. In T. R. Sarbin (Ed.), *Narrative psychology: The storied nature of human conduct* (pp. 3–21). New York: Praeger.

Schwandt, T. (1997). Textual gymnastics, ethics, and angst. In W. Tierney & Y. Lincoln (Eds.), *Representation and the text: Re-framing the narrative voice* (pp. 305–311). Albany: State University of New York Press.

Schwarz, N., & Sudman, S. (Eds.). (1994). *Autobiographical memory and the validity of retrospective reports.* New York: Springer-Verlag.

Scriven, M. (1967). The methodology of evaluation. In R. Tyler, R. Gagné, & M. Scriven, *Perspectives of curriculum evaluation* (pp. 39–83). Chicago: Rand McNally.

Silko, L. (1991). Language and literature from a Pueblo Indian perspective. In P. Mariani (Ed.), *The politics of imaginative writing* (pp. 83–93). Seattle: Bay Press.

Smith, D. (1987). *The everyday world as problematic.* Boston: Northeastern University Press.

Smith, S. (1993). Who's talking/who's talking back? The subject of personal narrative. *Signs, 18,* 392–407.

Smoky Mountain Tourist News. (1982, May 21). Bryson City, NC.

Spence, D. P. (1986). Narrative smoothing and clinical wisdom. In T. R. Sarbin (Ed.), *Narrative psychology: The storied nature of human conduct* (pp. 211–232). New York: Praeger.

Taylor, C. (1991). *Sources of the self.* Cambridge, MA: Harvard University Press.

Tierney W., & Lincoln, Y. (Eds.). (1997). *Representation and the text: Re-framing the narrative voice.* Albany: State University of New York Press.

van Manen, M. (1977). Linking ways of knowing with ways of being practical. *Curriculum Inquiry, 6*(30), 205–228.

van Manen, M. (1991). *The tact of teaching: The meaning of pedagogical thoughtfulness.* Albany: State University of New York Press.

Vattimo, G. (1988). *The end of modernity: Nihilism and hermeneutics in postmodern culture.* London: Polity.

Wicomb, Z. (1991). An author's agenda. In P. Mariani (Ed.), *Critical fictions: The politics of imaginative writing* (pp. 13–16). Seattle, WA: Bay Press.

Wieder, A. (1998). Trust and memory: Explorations in oral history and biography. In C. Kridel (Ed.), *Writing educational biography* (pp. 113–120). New York: Garland.

Willinsky, J. (1989). Getting personal and practical with personal practical knowledge. *Curriculum Inquiry, 19*(3), 247–264.

Wittgenstein, L. (1968). *Philosophical investigations* (3rd ed., G. E. M. Anscombe, Trans.). New York: Macmillan. (Original work published 1953)

INDEX

Adams, Henry, 1, 3
Aesthetic experience (Dewey), 139–140
Agenda of writer, 160–162, 163
Agger, B., 172
Allport, Nancy (student pseudonym), 128
Anyon, Jean, 31
Aristotle, 11, 154–155, 161–162, 176
Arts-based texts, 2, 154
Art (school arts booklet), 17–18, 21, 26–27
Asheville Citizen, 15
Associative use of schooling (Broudy),
    128–129
Auden, W. H., 38, 40, 47
Authoritative stance, 160
Authors. *See also* Narrative approach
    notion of author, 162
    persuasive power and, 159
    postmodernism and, 160–161
    writers versus, 160–161, 179
Autobiography, 153. *See also* Narrative approach
Ayers, W., 145

Bakhtin, Michael, 155–157, 162, 166–167,
    171, 179
Baldwin, James, 154, 155
Banks, A., 153
Banks, S., 153
Barber, L., 167–168
Barone, T., 154, 174
Barthes, Roland, 160, 164, 172, 176, 178
Baseline data, 3–4
Bauman, Z., 159
Bellah, R. N., 161
Belsey, C., 156
Bereiter, Carl, 140
Berliner, David C., vii–x
Beyer, B. K., 137–138

Big Questions, 157, 158
Biography, 161. *See also* Narrative approach
Bloom, Harold, 131
Bloom, L., 164
Bochner, A., 153, 162
Brell, C., 138, 140
Briggs, C., 161
Brinthaupt, T. M., 164
Broudy, Harry, 128–129
Bruner, Jerome, 154, 155, 174
Bryant, William Cullen, 15, 16

Caring approach, 28–29, 111, 136–137
Carter, Nathaniel (student pseudonym), 61,
    66, 114
Cartier-Bresson, Henri, 68
Casey, K., 4
Center for Improving Mountain Living, 15
Ceramics, 50–51, 72, 109
Cherryholmes, C., 160, 176
Chrisler, Annie (student pseudonym), 143
Clay cutting, 51
Cole System (Great Britain), 24–25, 31
Conrack (movie), 145–146
Conroy, P., 145
Conway, M. A., 164
Cortazzi, M., 164
Critical perspective, 6, 137–148
    critical utility and, 176–178
    cultural imperatives and, 142–147
    framing life stories and life histories in,
        169–172
    transfer of learning and, 137–142
Crochet, 51
Cronbach, L., 152
Culler, J., 162
Cultural scripts
    critical dispositions versus, 142–147

ABOUT THE AUTHOR

Tom Barone is Professor of Education at Arizona State University, where he teaches courses in curriculum studies and qualitative research methods. He is author of *Aesthetics, Politics, and Educational Inquiry: Essays and Examples,* and co-editor of the online *International Journal of Education and the Arts.*